I0762567

SOUNDS
OF
INFINITY

SOUNDS OF INFINITY

Lee Morgan

The Witches' Almanac
Newport, Rhode Island

First Printing April 2019

Address all inquiries and information to
The Witches' Almanac, Ltd.
P.O. Box 1292
Newport, RI 02840-9998

Softcover:
13-ISBN: 978-1-881098-54-6

EBook
978-1-881098-56-0

On Dalby Mountain, this side of Cronk-yn-Irree-Laa the old Manx people used to put their ears to the earth to hear the Sounds of Infinity (Sheean-ny-Feaynid), which were sounds like murmurs. They thought these sounds came from beings in space; for in their belief all space is filled with invisible beings.

Evan Wentz ,
The Faerie Faith in Celtic Countries

CONTENTS

Sounds of Infinity

PART THREE: The Hands

Sounds of Infinity

PREFACE

Sounds of Infinity

Every real book begins life as a vision. An airy thing that gestates in the eye of the mind and sidles its way down through twisted alleyways to the stews of the heart. If it has power enough to get this far it obsesses the bearer until it must find expression through the hands. The vision becomes a fateful thing, now its owner must find a way to take what they've seen and make it what you've seen. Through Art they must attempt to pierce the wall of the skull and set the memory in the bones to singing and the heart to brewing sanguine epiphanies.

For this reason this book is divided into three parts, the work of the Head, the work of the Heart and the work of the Hands. The first is a dissertation in scholarly tone on the inferences that can be drawn about the Faerie Faith and its relationship with Traditional Witchcraft, after close attention to history.

The second is a work of occult fiction that meditates upon the themes discussed in Part One in the form of a woven narrative which appears sufficient unto itself, but reveals hidden secrets to any paying deep attention. Like all of my fiction it intersects with a larger grand narrative that connects in tangential or direct ways with all of my published novels.

The final part is a practical grimoire that leads the reader through the door to physically manifest the vision they have shared in parts one and two. This is not just a book, but an experience, one which culminates not at the end of reading the volume but in the consummation known in the art of ritual.

This story about faerie began as visions. A cacophony of visions with sharp, bright edges to them that have lain claim to my heart and hands. I trace here the intellectual path I walked in trying to understand, it unpacks the story that scholarship and recorded history can tell us about the denizens of Elphame and their mind-fracturing numinosity. This is the work of the head and skull, in which I show what, with a background in Literary Theory, I can make of the historical records about faeries, if we treat the Faerie Faith and Witchcraft itself as a form of narrative...

In the work of the heart we bypass the rational intellect to experience the touch, scent and feel of the Faerie Faith through symbol and suggestion. What we may have merely understood in the work of the head we come to know in the work of the heart. Older than the magic of the skull we come to the heart later because we have to peel back the cluttered layers of thought to expose deep gnosis. Here is the black, thick heart magic, full of limbic shadows and shifting fluids, for the first time... Here is stone-deep magic of the bone and omens in the guts, the trail of crumbs we follow back into the heart of the primeval forest.

It is truly in the work of the hands that we become as the first tool-wielder, the first man of art... When our hands are reddened with labour only then do we touch them in salute to our forehead where this all began as vision, and magically a still void arises there. Where once we had a head full of facts, now we have a whole body full of knowing. Only the work of the hands can truly reshape the world inside the head, for Witchcraft is a deed. The hands hold the true circumference of our Craft and Art. For this reason the third and final part of this book is a grimoire designed to be read with the heart and hands.

This volume is different to any you have read on the arcane subject of Faerie up until this moment, for it is not merely a list of facts and theories about the condition of Elphame and its denizens, or their interaction with the world of Witchcraft, but a three-part induction into a way of being.

PART I

PART I: INTRODUCTION

INTRODUCTION

> *'I am done with great things and big things, great institutions and big successes, and I am for those tiny, invisible molecular moral forces that work from individual to individual, creeping through the crannies of the world like so many rootlets, or like the capillary oozing of water, yet which if you give them time, will rend the hardest monuments of pride.*
>
> –William James

Every edifice of civilization whether vigorous or in a state of stagnation, originally found its way forth from a story that became myth, ushered quietly forth from the inner eye of sorcerous vision. Every day we are swimming unconsciously in forgotten stories, not forgotten because they are neglected, but because their power is such they've become so familiar we don't even see them anymore. Their invisibility becomes part of their power and it is only by drawing them to the surface of awareness that we can challenge their autocracy over our lives. Until then they remain largely unnoticed and invisible, as water to fish.

Meanwhile we convince ourselves that stories are merely for children, books have no power to alter reality, that the Arts are frivolous, that narrative is now just a form of entertainment. Still we remain enveloped by stories, a smaller and more concentrated set of them as time goes on, and we march towards monoculture. We have the story of capitalism, the story of freedom, the story of scientific rationalism... To the common eyes such things appear to be so much more than tales we tell, they represent unchangeable fixations. To step outside of those dominant stories in some way takes a tremendous amount of will and imagination. It takes a great and powerful story to overwrite pre-existing competing narratives, it takes a mind that yearns to be enchanted.

In today's world power has migrated to fewer and fewer stories and they have great monolithic power, but this makes them intensely beige, lacking all aesthetic appeal. This allows the possibility for other smaller mythologies to edge in at the sides of things.

Those with wildness still left in their minds prowl between the familiar words and repetitive phrases, seeking to see life from a different angle. But such a thing isn't possible without breaking the fourth wall of reality. Because real stories, the kind that have the power to become myths, begin as eruptions of the sacred, as eruptions of the monstrous. There are many ways to make war against a story. You can consciously make war against the mythic integrity of something by actually persecuting it and making it the enemy in your own narrative, as happened to Witchcraft in the past. Or you can make a quieter, insidious war against something by making it ridiculous. By infantising it. You can slowly strangle out its life's blood simply by consistently failing to understand it.

The story of Faerie, at least in the minds of people, has been the target of this unconscious re-writing to an even more profoundly devastating extent than the figure of the Witch. Many will immediately think they know what I mean when I say this, but it would behoove us all to keep our minds open to the idea that we may not already know. We may realize that faeries are not the Tinkerbells of popular fantasies but there is a greater depth dimension to the collective forgetting than just recognizing this fact.

In Iceland today the population remains less affected by this narrative shift. Highways are still sometimes moved to avoid disturbing the homes of elf-kind. There is a little bit of fear evident in these gestures of respect—which seems to be a helpful emotion for humans when it comes to the consideration of whether or not to disrespect something. And yet even retaining a certain degree of awe and terror does not wholly return to our perception of Faerie what has been lost.

Faeries, as experienced by cultures deriving from a British background and saturated in mainstream Western culture, have been so degraded to a creature of whimsy and childish fluff that environmentalists would be laughed at if they evoked the faeries as a reason to not destroy an old growth tree. One must instead evoke a fiscal explanation for why something that stays still, which doesn't scream with a voice that human ears can hear, ought to have value. The result of this change of story, that tells us we don't need to fear something not only causes us to lose respect for it, but robs us of the perhaps uniquely human experience of the sublime. The gorgeous terror, the holy dread.

Yet when it comes to faeries who were once both feared and revered, the cumulative effects of Victorian sentimentalism and commercial New Age vacuity have damaged the world of the fae (and even the word itself) and in many cases led to total misunderstanding. Many seriously-minded Witches try to remedy this by utilizing less popular archaic methods of spelling faerie, such as "fayerie" or "feery." I am not going to take that cumbersome route in this text, for I feel that changing language in response to the trivialization of a word is a form of ceding ground, which then may require the giving of further ground if that spelling too is taken and misused by the chronically unimaginative. I would rather reclaim the word as it stands in modern usage.

Of course there are exceptions to the trivialisation of the word, such as *Viridarium Umbris* by Daniel Schulke, Magister of Cultus Sabbati, a book that balances the luminous numen of Faerie within the green-black heart of Traditional Witchcraft. Schulke uses the form "faerie" and even sometimes "fairy" without any linguistic apologetics, as I will do here. Michael Howard's recent *The Book of Faery* also utilizes a relatively familiar form of the word and strongly expresses the awareness that faeries both have an independent existence to mankind and are not the trivialized creatures of recent fantasy.

This volume is a contribution to that ongoing artistry of returning awe and majesty to the word "faerie" but also teasing out the other ways in which the dominant stories of our era have come between us and their realm. Both a scholarly exploration, a contribution to the growing body of literature produced from within Old Craft folds[1] and practical gramarye, this book is named for the murmurs of infinity only heard by those with the ears to hear and the quiet in their hearts to pay attention.

One of the most fertile and rich aspects of Traditional Witchcraft is the fusion between folk practices and the deep penetration of high culture in the form of ceremonial magic, alchemy, art and literature. To honour this fine tradition and also to work some way toward correcting the degradation of Faerie at the hands of the New Age movement, I will weave grimoire material into my work, but in an earthy, animistic manner. Equally when I approach folk magic, and the belief of the people often known as the Faerie Faith, I will do so by teasing out the deep vein of poetic colour and artistic value that resides under the surface of these narratives. The result itself will be an alchemic act of Conjunctio, which both extrapolates and celebrates the already extant sacred marriage between so-called high culture and folk traditions residing at the heart of traditional witchery.

I have taken this format of the "head, heart and hands" because it echoes the process an idea passes through on its way to physical manifestation. Before a tale can take on mythic power (and to dis-

1 For a deeper understanding of the emergent genre of occult fiction as conceptualized from within Traditional Craft folds please see Richard Gavin's masterful essay "Through the Gate of Horn: Occult Fiction and the Primordial Image" in *CLAVIS: Journal of Occult Art, Letters and Experience*, Vol. III and the upcoming anthology *Penumbrae* from Three Hands Press.

place one myth we must always replace it with another) we need to be capable of conceiving of the need for it. We must then experience its power intuitively, being emotionally and experientially impressed upon by its Otherness. Finally we must act upon it in the physical world. When these three things happen in the correct sequence a birth of sort occurs.

NOT FROM THE SEED OF ADAM AM I

The tales of Faerie and those of Witchcraft are two tangled old thorn trees, one a hawthorn and the other a blackthorn, if you will. They grow hopelessly fused and knotted. After the autumn comes and their leaves fall one is hard pressed to separate them or follow the path of one's evolution without confusing the twigs of the other. Here we will explore that entanglement, trace the path of its growth and attempt to appreciate the variegation of its foliage.

The tales of Faerie are primarily the product of folk wisdom. Stories that come to us from old women who sat rocking in chairs at hearthside, and old men who toked on their pipes, doused the candles and told meandering tales of another world. Children who witnessed strange lights, mothers who looked into the eyes of their infants and saw the Otherwise looking back at them one morning.

Unlike the angels and demons of the ceremonial grimoire, the faerie comes to us almost purely in the words of the common people. But this did not always remain the case, nor were the spheres of literate and illiterate folk always as separate as we've come to imagine. If you observe the table of contents for *The Virid Skull*, you will see that the chapter on "Faeries in the Grimoire Tradition" is left until last. This distinct influx of faerie material into the grimoire tradition (illustrated well in the work of David Rankine) became prevalent in the seventeenth century and is considered to be evidence of cross-fertilisation between ceremonial magic and Witchcraft. I believe this interaction between the grimoire tradition and faerie belief to be crucial to the genesis of Traditional Witchcraft as we know it today. But I don't wish to touch upon it too soon, because there is something about the preserved words arising from folk culture that has the quality of ivy about it, the ability to slowly pull apart the stone and mortar of the calcified stories of modernity.

There can be no complete separation between the stories of the people and the literate folk who took an interest in the topic and sought to record it.[1] There are in fact not two streams of pre-modern magic that run unpolluted side by side, but a cunning craft tradition meandering along beside a literate tradition with both frequently mixing and sharing water, cross-fertilizing each other. This does not make the genesis of Traditional Craft somehow less authentic but is instead the reason for its rich spiritual and intellectual fecundity.

Whilst we cannot always trace the streams and waterways of transmission with total certainty, we can see the later evidence of fusion between animistic folk magic with indigenous roots and literate material stemming from apocryphal Christian material and the grimoires.

As Michael Howard said of a charm bag from Penzance described by Cecil Williamson, *"Such items were typical of the objects used by cunning folk and witches, in charm bags, along with pieces of paper with incantations in Latin or Hebrew lettering" or with "magical symbols."*[2] We can also see the folk influence on the grimoires to illustrate that the influence flowed in both directions.

Traditional Witchcraft today is neither fully folk nor literate in origin, neither fully Pagan nor Christian, it could be said that it exists in an ambiguous, twilight threshold that matches very closely with the body of faerie lore lying beneath it.

Contemporary academics like Emma Wilby[3] and Gustav Henningsen[4] tend to divide cunning folk from Witches, and faeries from demons along basic ideas of good and bad—with many cunning folk keen on this division also. However, when dealing with the faerie substrata of Witchcraft these distinctions become more slippery, and it is less easy to maintain morally-based divisions. Whilst the scholar

1 David Rankine, "Pentacles of Wood," *Hands of Apostasy* (San Francisco: Three Hands Press, 2014), 46-64.

2 Michael Howard, *Witchcraft in the West Country* (San Francisco: Three Hands Press, 2010), 160.

3 Emma Wilby, *Cunning Folk and Familiar Spirits* (East Sussex: Sussex Academic Press, 2010).

4 Gustav Henningsen, "The Ladies From the Outside," *Early Modern European Witchcraft: Centres and Peripheries* (Oxford: Clarendon Press, 1993).

Wilby speaks of Witches who send forth for demons and cunning folk who worked with faeries, we will see as we delve deeper into the realms of Faerie that the entities named demons are often darker types of faerie creatures.

There are no firm and definite dividers of social class that lie between the practitioners of grimoire magic, more inclined to talk about angels and demons and the Crafter (this term is used here to include both Witchcraft and cunning crafts) who was more likely to hold communion with faeries. From the seventeenth century onwards the line has begun to blur evidenced by the incursion of folk material into the grimoires, and magical seals into cunning craft. By the nineteenth century onward the interaction between cunning craft material and secret societies became explicit and organised.[5]

There is certainly not a great deal of obvious class consciousness to be found in the trial records dealing with the persecutions, but to the eye of the educated modern the question of class blares out from the pages. In *Aradia, or the Gospel of the Witches* we do find an explicit reference to Witchcraft as a tool of class warfare and liberation of the poor, the dispossessed and the fringe-dweller. There, Diana Queen of Witches instructs Aradia to go to the outlaws and rebels who have fled to be free of slavery and teach them Witchcraft so that they may throw off oppression:

"And thou shalt be the first of witches known; And thou shalt be the first of all i' the world; And thou shalt teach the art of poisoning, Of poisoning those who are great lords of all; Yea, thou shalt make them die in their palaces; And thou shalt bind the oppressor's soul (with power)..."[6]

This strong statement is quite rare when it comes to written sources, but the link between Witchcraft and the empowerment of those most socially vulnerable (women and the common folk) is far better

5 For more on this historical process please see Andrew Chumbley's essay "The Magic of History: Some Considerations," *Hands of Apostasy* (San Francisco: Three Hands Press), 2014, 9-15.

6 Charles Godfrey Leland, *Aradia or Gospel of the Witches,* (Providence: The Witches' Almanac, 2010), 4–5.

known, even where it is not directly referenced. Whilst not explicit it remained implicit. Witches were frightening because they represented the possibility of underhanded power wielded by those who were kept downtrodden, and the fear of a "return of the repressed" that does not only operate inside one's psyche!

Not only was maleficium often the last and only weapon of a poor person with no physical power, but one reason historically for faerie familiars approaching someone was to offer them a livelihood as a cunning man or woman when they had fallen upon hard times. For these reasons we must begin by listening respectfully to the folk voice, for these are the voices of people who lived much closer to subsistence than we do. Their sorcery was practiced on the razor's edge of existence, an intensely hot furnace of selective pressure. What they worked must have been effective or they could risk death through persecution or starvation. This alone should place an aura of great seriousness around the beliefs and practices of common people from this period.

Pre-industrial common folk were also overwhelmingly engaged in agricultural pursuits that saw them living a life much closer to the land than either their rich contemporaries or us today. Their animistic responses to Place and their knowledge of the land around them is something we should consider with humility. We must work to understand one of the sources of our Art as coming from within the collective wisdom of the people rather than from just the individual who uttered the words that were recorded, as well as being permeated very early on by learned sources. When we approach the genius of the people we should do so as emptied of our assumptions and prejudices as possible.

The illuminated imaginal realm—by which I mean to suggest *imagination that is known to be real* as coined by the Sufi scholar Henry Corbin—of the folk mind is the genius of the people and is to be found nestled deep in the heart of our inherited Cunning. For all the sophistication our Art has acquired over time, Witchcraft still has deep atavistic roots in the soil of this wisdom.

Scholarship has become a part of modern Witchcraft's legacy, especially in the realms of Traditional Craft, and always was in the so-called "grimoire tradition" of ceremonial magic. But we should be wary of ever contrasting the flame of learning with a perceived ignorance of the common folk. When I speak of the "genius of the people" I speak of virtuoso oral performances,[7] incredible mnemonic skills, shrewdness, collective and accumulated wisdom, and most importantly the deep-rooted awareness of another realm. The quick-witted verbal storyteller is just as much a bearer of the "cunning flame" as the scholar, the musician and the craftsperson.

In this book we will therefore tip our hat to the imaginal firebrand of the people, mingled with the flame of scholarship before we let such distinctions fall away, let them in fact be washed away by the power of story and the poetry of ritual. In this way the Work of the Skull is at first the work of a gatekeeper, deciding the worth of what stories can enter therein and which lack sufficient artistry. After this it becomes a weaver, reconfiguring a variety of threads, replacing and carefully matching damaged ones and drawing together a tapestry. Once we can see the picture whole we begin to cannibalize our forebears in the form of their woven stories. Through the cauldron mouth of our eye sockets we imbibe these old tales, inside the skull we seethe and ferment and refine away any dross we discover.

As we seek to understand better what and who faeries actually are, and what they mean to Traditional Witchcraft, we will begin with letting the folk speak for themselves about who and what they believe the faeries to be. I will also draw on what scholars typically term

7 Take for example the rhyming games during the Mari Lwyd ritual of Wales, where poetic rhymes and plays on words were produced off the top of the head in verbal joust with others.

"elite" testimonials. My purpose here is to drop us slowly into the Otherness. At first this will be the traces of historical Otherness of the folk mind of early modern Europe (some of which survived into much later times), to which we owe so much of our Craft. As the thread spools out the story will be increasingly alien. Here, we read fragments of text, ghosts of words, etched with the breath of our forebears. Let us meditate upon them with mindful close reading, even the quotes we may already be familiar with, let us sit with them until the pall of the familiar falls away and we start to notice details and interpretations we may previously have rushed over, until we have read each sentence three different ways. For such is the close attention to detail that Faerie asks of us. Often in close and meditative study new truths emerge from words like a trapped fragrance of history.

"Not from the seed of Adam am I, but of the seed of the proud angel, cast out from heaven."[8](Folk song said to be sung by faeries)

"My father's and grandfather's idea was that the fairies tumbled out of the battlements of heaven, falling earthward for three days and three nights as thick as hail, and that one third of them fell into the sea, one third on land, and one third remained in the air."[9] (Folk)

"The Sidhe, or spirit race, called also the Feadh-Ree, or fairies, are supposed to have been once angels in heaven, who were cast out by Divine command as a punishment for their inordinate pride. Some fell to earth, and dwelt there, long before man was created, as the first gods of the earth. Others fell into the sea, and they built themselves beautiful fairy palaces of crystal and pearl underneath the waves; but on moonlight nights they often come up on the land, riding their white horses, and they hold revels with their fairy kindred of the earth, who live in the clefts of the hills, and they dance together on the greensward under the ancient trees, and drink nectar from the cups

8 W.Y. Evans-Wentz, *The Fairy Faith in Celtic Countries* (Santa Cruz: Evinity Publishing, 2009), 86.

9 Ibid, 85.

of the flowers, which is the fairy wine. Other fairies, however, are demoniacal, and given to evil and malicious deeds; for when cast out of heaven they fell into hell, and there the Devil holds them under his rule, and sends them forth as he wills upon missions of evil to tempt the souls of men downward by the false glitter of sin and pleasure. These spirits dwell under the earth and impart their knowledge only to certain evil persons chosen of the Devil, who gives them power to make incantations, and brew love potions, and to work wicked spells, and they can assume different forms by their knowledge and use of certain magical herbs.

The witch women who have been taught by them, and have thus become tools of the Evil One, are the terror of the neighbourhood; for they have all the power of the fairies and all the malice of the Devil, who reveals to them secrets of times and days, and secrets of herbs, and secrets of evil spells; and by the power of magic they can effect all their purposes, whether for good or ill. The fairies of the earth are small and beautiful. They passionately love music and dancing, and live luxuriously in their palaces under the hills and in the deep mountain caves; and they can obtain all things lovely for their fairy homes, merely by the strength of their magic power. They can also assume all forms…"[10] (Folk)

"On the sea coast of Upper Brittany the popular opinion is that the fees are a fallen race condemned to an earthly exile for a certain period… The old folk say that, after the angels revolted, those left in paradise were divided into two parts: those who fought with God and those who remained neutral. These last, already half fallen, were sent to earth for a time and became the fees."[11] (Folk)

"The Huldu Folk of Iceland were spoken of in folklore in the following way: Other folktales claim that huldufólk originate

10 Ibid.
11 Ibid, 177.

from Lilith, or are fallen angels condemned to live between heaven and hell."[12]

"This leads me to believe that the spirit and body (of a mortal) are somehow mystically combined by fairy enchantment, for the faeries have mighty power of enchanting natural people, and could transform the physical body in some way. It cannot be but that the fairies are spirits. According to my belief they cannot be anything but spirits. My firm belief, however, is that they are not the spirits of dead men, but are fallen angels."[13] (Folk)

"Some of the good people I have thought were fallen angels, though these may be dead people whose time is not up."[14] (Folk)

"The faeries are spirits and ghosts. Faeries and ghosts inhabite darknesse, solitudes, and graves."[15] (Elite)

"There is moreover as hath been above said, a certain kind of spirits not so noxious, but most near to men, so that they are even affected with humane passions, and many of these delight in man's society, and willingly dwell with them.... Hence Plotinus saith, that the souls of men are sometimes made spirits: and of men well deserving are made familiars which the Greeks call eudemons, i.e. blessed spirits: but of ill deserving men, hags, and hobgoblins, which the Greeks call cacodemons, i.e. evil spirits"[16] (Elite)

"First, the fairy-folk—in which are included house and field spirits—may be the traditional remnant of a race of real people, perhaps a prehistoric race, driven into the remote parts of the country by strange immigrant conquerors. Perhaps these primitive folk were elfish, dwarfish, or otherwise peculiar in appearance to the superior new-comers, who would in pride of race scorn the small, swarthy

12 Brian Pilkington, Terry Gunnell, *The Hidden People of Iceland* (Reykjavík: Mál Og Menning, 2008), 4.
13 Evans-Wentz, 112-113.
14 Ibid, 79.
15 Wilby,18.
16 Heinrich Cornelius Agrippa, *Three Books of Occult Philosophy*, (St. Paul: Llewellyn), 567.

aborigines, and refuse all communion with them."17 (Elite)

"Departed souls attending a while in this inferior state."[18] (Folk/Elite)

Two main narratives emerge. One, seemingly very popular story is that the faeries are fallen angels, the second most popular theory seems to be they are souls of the human dead, and later in history still, the remnants of a pigmy race. It is interesting to note that the elite preference is for the two later theories. This may indicate a reluctance to consider that faerie mythology might have in it something so elevated as a theology relating to angels, heaven, and the creation of the world. Also, because the elite testimony is more often the educated Christian perspective it may not so readily embrace a folk interpretation of biblical themes.

Other theories are that faeries are the memory of a Neolithic ancestor people, but this is a comparatively later idea. Though no one specifically says they are nature spirits they say things like "turn your cloaks because faerie spirits live in old oaks." And whilst the early ancestors never say they are the ghosts of our Neolithic selves they continually connect them with Neolithic stone circles and burial mounds.

Despite the disagreement about the origin of faeries we see a hybrid mythology that links fallen angels with faeries so pervasive that it spreads from Scotland, through Ireland, Wales, Brittany and even up as far as Iceland. How does a single story, which has so clearly been overwritten by Christianity, become as widespread and pervasive amongst the relatively unlettered and usually untraveled common people of previous centuries? How early could this shared story have first been disseminated? Or are we encountering an example of shared gnosis?

17 Lewis Spence, *The Legends and Romances of Brittany,* (Gloucester: Dodo Press, 2010), 87.
18 Robert Kirk, *The Secret Commonwealth of Elves, Fauns and Faeries,* (Mineola: Dover Publications, 2008), 53.

Let us imagine we are an animistic Pagan introduced for the first time to the notion of fallen angels, demons and the fall from heaven. We would probably understand instinctually that most faeries are neither all bad nor all good, it is even possible that such a concept doesn't exist in our worldview. So the only way to logically blend this new idea with one's old view of reality would be to add the faerie state as a third to the dual options of angel or demon presented by Christianity.

What it tells us most clearly about how our Pagan ancestors saw faeries is that they weren't human as such. The early Christian—but still animistic—rural imagination was more inclined to associate them with the daimonic or angelic spheres, rather than the sphere of human ghosts. Otherwise it would have been quite easy to write off their existence as ancestors or ghosts without even having to make the more fraught decision between angels and demons.

If the original Pagan inhabitants of Britain had not indeed already possessed a story about faeries amendable to the Christian narrative and the whole story only went back as far as the introduction of Christianity, why bother explaining the faeries at all? Why even have faeries explained at all? The very fact that the Christian story had to be utilized in this manner suggests a nice fit with an older story. We can see from the fact the folk imagination was capable of adding this "third state" and making the Christian narrative conform to it, that Christianity was being interpreted through an animistic faerie-worshipping lens, not the other way around. If early Christianity was anything like later folk interpretations then it's likely that many people's idea of what Christianity actual entailed was fairly fuzzy.[19]

Despite the importance I grant to the fallen angel narrative (especially in regards to how the Faerie Faith touches on Traditional Craft) it's unlikely the other theory of Faerie containing some of the human

19 I think here of William Langland's claim that he knew his ballads of Robin Hood better than his Paternoster and the way reincarnation is accepted as compatible with Christianity among many of Evans-Wentz's informants.

dead is completely without foundation. There are many examples of witches and other faerie seers observing the human dead among the ranks of Faerie, and mounds associated with them are very often Neolithic burial chambers.

Bessie Dunlop, often known as "the faerie witch," said of her faerie familiar that although he was among the faerie he was the ghost of a dead man who died at the battle of Pinkie. Thomas the Rhymer is said to have been taken to join the faeries without having died or left behind a body. I think there is enough diversity within the realm of faerie to wrap around fallen angels and the ancestral dead — in some cases being absorbed into their kingdoms. In fact, most other cultures throughout the world admit the existence of non-human spirits dwelling in natural settings and distinguish them from the souls of the ancestral dead. I think it is possible to find evidence of both beliefs, but the latter option is generally the exception rather than the rule.

One final testimonial may help to clarify matters.

> *"The good people in the mountain, are the people who have died* and *been taken [my emphasis]; the mountain is enchanted."*[20] (Folk)

The very fact that the informant adds "died" *and* "been taken" shows that these are not one and the same thing. One does not have to merely die to end up in Faerie, one has to be taken. Dead bodies were often interpreted as faerie stocks, wooden effigies enchanted with glamour to make the humans believe the individual—who had really been stolen—was actually dead. If death and abduction by faeries was in fact the same thing this belief would seem redundant.

So it might be fair to say that though *some* dead are to be found in Faerie, the ranks of Faerie are not made up only of the human dead, but also of those who do the "taking."

We get another look at the faerie relationship with the human dead in Shakespeare's *A Midsummer Night's Dream* when

20 Evans-Wentz, 76.

Belarius says at the sight of Imogen, as Fidele. Thus Guiderius at the funeral of the above lady—

"With female fairies will his tomb be haunted."

This suggests that the young and beautiful human dead were attractive in some way for faeries, particularly female ones in the case of the male dead and presumably vice versa. Shakespeare also separates the human dead from faeries in *A Midsummer Night's Dream:*

"At whose approach ghosts, wandering here and there,
Troop home to churchyards," etc.

To which Oberon replies—

"But we are spirits of another sort:
I with the morning's love have oft made sport;"

Another folk informant says: *"I've heard and felt the Good People coming on the wind...They are still on earth. Among them are the spirits of our ancestors."*[21] Which suggests one of two things, one is that many of our ancestors are among them as above stated, but it is not the only possible meaning of this statement.

We must also consider the meaning of the word ancestor in relation to families like the Physicians of Myddfai in Wales, who claimed descent from a faerie bride. Changelings, faerie brides and faerie doctors, themselves perceived by the folk as faeries manifest in human form, were believed to walk among mankind on a regular basis, so we can see the question of fallen angel or one of the dead becomes more complex. For if some human families were believed to possess faerie blood, calling faeries "ancestors" comes to mean something entirely different.

When dealing with the slippery Otherworld I prefer to allow more complexity rather than try to reduce diversity into manageable easy answers. So of the faeries, who apparently say of themselves that they are not of the seed of Adam, I say that *some types* of faeries (the Gentry, Sidhe or Tuatha de Dannann)

21 Ibid, 78.

were believed to be fallen angels, not "bad" enough for Hell but fallen from heaven. Sometimes the human dead went with them, sometimes living people that we would obviously identify as human were to our ancestors not considered "human" in the spiritual sense, but faerie-get walking among us.

Faeries were other to us in some way, and yet interpenetrated our human lives at every level including the highly intimate business of mating and reproduction, the ultimate in paradoxical occurrences. There is no hedge dividing their world from that of our forebears, or if there is they are like a wind that blows straight through it. According to Agrippa the souls of bad men could be transformed into goblins, which he separates out from other faeries as a distinct tribe.

Here we have attempted to imagine how faeries could have developed their dual faith aspect of being attached to fallen angels, but let us go deeper now. Given the remarkable similarities of these testimonials over such a wide distance we have already speculated that there must have been broad similarities in the original mythic nature of faeries that allowed such easy and across-the-board grafting of myth to myth.

But there was of course never any single "Paganism" but a variety of polytheistic religions that existed in pre-Christian Europe. Without a single unifying concept of a fall from grace or single, all-powerful god, what would that similarity have looked like? Perhaps what we are actually looking at is an origin story relating to an Upper World, a Middle World and an Underworld, and how faeries originally had their home in the sky or a state of pure consciousness. For some reason now lost to scholarship, perhaps at the beginning of the world, theycame to be drawn into the fabric of matter, under the Earth and below the wave as well?

It will be immediately clear to some people how, if this theory is correct, "homespun Gnosticism"[22] would so easily be drawn into the fabric of the Faerie Faith which underpins Traditional Witchcraft and other forms of Pagan survival and resurgence. The philosophy of Empedocles, which emerges from at least one of those pre-Christian religions of Europe, reflects the idea of a beginning of the world where things were in a pure, unadulterated state and consciousness did not exist in admixture.[23] Empedocles' pre-Christian vision of the cosmos suggests a kind of "fall" where purely intellectual beings become mixed through the interaction of Love and Strife with material from all of the elements.

Theories of a "fall of fire from the heavens" of a Promethean kind may not have been unfamiliar to our Pagan ancestors. Modern Traditional Witchcraft certainly shows signs of the deep impact of such thinking. All Traditional Witchcraft mythos that I have personally received or encountered include a belief that fallen angels, usually the Watchers, gifted the cunning fire to mankind and awakened them. These fallen angels are sometimes identified with faerie, or held to be the "parents" of the faerie folk in some way, identifying faeries with the nephilim.

Another key narrative about faeries is the widespread belief that faeries made the standing stones, menhirs, and dolmens that mark holy sites all over Europe. This association extending from Neolithic, indigenous monuments to faeries and then to an explicit or implicit link to Witches, (some standing stones are apparently Witches turned into stone and some are dancing faerie maidens), strongly links faeries to the deep past of Europe. We cannot ignore this story, as untestable as it is, because the other popular story about faeries is that they represent the memory or continuing ghostly presence of an indigenous culture.

22 Andrew Chumbley's term derived from his essay in *Hands of Apostasy*, 18.

23 Peter Kingsley, *Reality*, (Inverness: The Golden Sufi Centre, 2004).

Although much of the later mythology associated with both Witches and faeries, (fallen angels, Watchers, the Mark of Cain, Lucifer and Lilith), is imported from the Middle East, this tenacious association between faeries and the prehistoric landscape strongly suggests those heretical Christian or Gnostic motifs were grafted over the top of something older.

This strong connection between prehistoric sites and faerie and Witch mythology is crucial not just because it links faeries to a historical people that once raised the stones, but because the stones are also associated with a particular goddess, or series of goddesses with a shared core mythos. These goddesses, which go by different names across the lands, tend to also be the Goddesses of Witches.

In the Basque province, the dolmens are associated both with the Goddess Mari and her attendants the *sorginak*, or *laminak*, who are both Basque "faeries" and sometimes human witches. Faerie cults on the continent, such as those exposed by the Sicilian faerie trials, were almost invariably associated with riding with Diana or another Witch Mother figure. We can see that faeries don't only exist in the Celtic countries but share the same motifs all over Europe (explored directly below) and are usually associated with some of the oldest religious currents in Europe.

The historical anthropologist Eva Pocs[24] makes an important and interesting distinction between "village witches" and "night-witches." Whilst the "village witch" may be a practitioner of magical arts she is more often than not accused of working sorcery through the means of charms, the evil eye or even the intervention of a familiar spirit. A "night-witch" on the other hand is linked to folklore about non-human spirits called variously from country to country mora/mara/mares (nightmares). These crea-

24 Eva Pocs, *Between the Living and the Dead: A Perspective on Witches & Seers in the Early Modern Age* (Budapest: Central European University Press, 1998).

tures were attested as early as the 13th century, but their origin is likely much earlier given that the variation of names in European countries all likely go back to the proto-Indo-European root word *moros* or "death." It is also intriguing that when Agrippa talks about spirits that emerge from the transformed human dead he refers to "hags," another known term for the nightmare.

Whether the figure is Mora (Poland), Mara, Mahr (Germany), Margen (Wales), or Mare the creature is generally similar. They are female, they fly at night, often in the form of something winged, they invade the sleeping chamber either through keyholes or cracks, and they oppress the sleeper through entering the dreams through the breath, pressing the chest and causing sleep paralysis, or bringing about erotic but draining dreams. During the day, however the Mora appeared to be a normal woman. The alp is one example of a male version of the Mora/Mare.

The night-witch is accused of being a monster of some kind, not quite fully human person, who whilst she appears as a person also flies by night and feeds on or sexually harasses the populace. This likelihood (reflected by the shared Indo-European rootword over so many countries for a similar being) that we are dealing with a very early mythic substrata also suggests that the figure of the night-witch is a very old belief figure which perhaps links with a shared Indo-European heritage.

Before the malevolence of the night-witch was explained away by demonology as the predations of Satan, the Mora was likely already a non-human Other existing on the borders of Indo-European human society, yet also penetrating society in their human form. Its darkness and feminine manifestation may reflect key anxieties in the Proto-Indo-European psyche.

Our ancestors seem to have understood that whilst the Otherness might be excluded beyond the hedges and fences of the village, it could never be wholly excluded. Some taint of the outside would always creep in, and attempts to root it out altogether would prove futile. This is perhaps why, though our Pagan ancestors in some nations seem to have still distrusted and even rejected some types of sorcerers even before Christianity, they didn't seek to try to kill all of them or declare "thou shalt not suffer a witch to live."

I am not going to consider at this point the connection between dark elves of the Norse folk genus and the mora-creature, but we should point out that just as a Mora is both human and non-human, the belief figure of the changeling or faerie-witch occupied this same status of being part of the community and yet also someone from outside. These people whose status was one of being both a person and somehow "other-than-person" seems to have acted as a kind of ambassador for that realm in the human community. They might even have been feared and shunned, even prior to Christianity, but they were a necessary eruption of an alien presence.

Let us now look at the notion of faeries in Europe more generally.

Unlike the mora creatures who are immediately recognizable, aspects of Proto-Indo-European culture in Europe are younger by far than most of the standing stones and the Basque language, with their names all deriving from a common root. The other various names for faeries across further European nations don't exhibit this etymological resonance. However, while they are all called different things their attributes bear so much in common it *could* suggest a pre Indo-European origin for Europe's very similar yet differently-named "faerie" beliefs. A thesis we can best explore further by seeing whether Basque faerie mythology is markedly different from those of the Indo-European language countries, or whether it maintains a common pattern.

Vila (southern Slavic spirit):

The Vila is usually perceived as female, dressed in white with long flowing fair hair, they are believed to dwell in meadows, streams, woods, hollow mountains and clouds. Known for their beautiful singing and music any who hears them can lose awareness of the passage of time and be gone for days. They lure young men away to dance with them and after their dances leave downtrodden fairy rings in the grass and are known to braid horse's manes into plaits. The Vila can shape-shift into forms including falcons, swans and snakes. One may only gain control of them by stealing feathers from their wings.

One story tells that every Friday a Vila came from the heavens in order to teach women how to heal. These women had to go with unbraided hair to a grove, and there two of them would climb a tree and while they were listening to the faerie they had to eat yarn in order to better remember what the faerie was teaching them; when they had learned, they became Vilenicas. The two women in the tree and everyone else who was listening beneath were connected by a thread that they held in their hands, and as long as the fairy was speaking, they would have to spin together.[25]

Vila ride on horses or deer and fire "elf darts" from their bows. They are appeased by people with offerings left at the roots of trees. The Vila's power resides in her hair so if she loses some she will die, or if you succeed in plucking some out you will have power to make her reveal her true form. There are also said to be "cloud vile," "water vile"(swans) and "forest vile"(wolves and deer). Mentions of Jesus and Mary send them fleeing. The word "vile" is associated with beauty and used to describe both beautiful young women and beautiful young men. They are able to imbue a hero with strength by allowing him to suckle from their breast. Although most of their actions are benevolent they are capable of desiring bloody sacrifices in return for access to their sacred springs and lakes.[26]

25 Mirjam Mencej, "Connecting Threads," *Folklore* 48 (2010), 61.

26 Dorian Juric, "Treatise on the South Slavic Vila," Open Access Theses and Dissertations, https://oatd.org (accessed December, 2018).

Rusalka (north-western Slavic spirits):

Rusalka are female spirits of the forest or waterways. Their faces are pale like the Moon, and they wear robes of mist or green leaves, or perhaps a white robe without a belt. Their hair is green or brown, decorated with flowers. In the middle of the night, they would walk out to the bank and comb their long hair or dance in meadows. If they saw handsome men, they would fascinate them with songs and try to take them away. Or they would simply come out of the water to comb their hair or climb trees. Their underwater home is a place of vast marbled chambers hung with crystal chandeliers, its walls and floors set with gold and precious stones. When summer approaches and the waters are warmed by the rays of the life-giving light, they have to return to the trees, the so called "houses of the dead."

Like the Vila, which they are sometimes conflated with, they are also known for being great spinners. They hang the results of their labors from the trees and lay it on the banks, where anyone passing should be wary of stepping lest they be caught in it like a net. The Rusalki are also explicitly known for being spinners of fate, who possess a powerful ability to affect the lives of local inhabitants. The Rusalki "decided who died and who would be reborn, who prospered and who perished, who married and who would be barren."

For those who pay their respects to the Rusalki, there can be great rewards. Young women wishing to have a child demonstrate their devotion by decorating the branches of the Rusalki's sacred tree, the birch, with ribbons and specially woven pieces of cloth.[27]

Elfen (Scandinavian, Anglo Saxon spirits):

Elves are either male or female and seem to come in both a light and dark variety, however all are morally ambiguous. They live in mounds, forests or collections of stones much like cairns. Many are

27 Radomir Ristic, *Balkan Traditional Witchcraft*, trans. Michael C. Carter Jr,. (Los Angeles: Pendraig Publications, 2009) 97.

beautiful females and are known for luring humans to join their dance and even forcing men to dance themselves to death with their enchantments.

They are usually fairhaired and white clothed but they carry bows with elf shot that can make people or livestock sick. Their dances leave elf rings, which are circles where mushrooms have come up. They are known for creating "elf locks" in the hair of horses they ride in the night by weaving it together. If a human watches the dance of the elves for too long, he or she would discover that even though only a few hours seemed to have passed, many years had passed in the real world.

They were believed to dispense good or bad luck and could be appeased by offerings at the roots of trees and on rocks known as elf mills—which were Neolithic stones with petroglyphs on them. Elves will sometimes take a baby, leaving behind their own sickly elfin-get as a changeling, but they can be driven away with talismans made of iron.

The Valkyries of Norse origin should also be mentioned here. The Valkyrie was fair of colouring and associated with the colour white. Like many other faerie spirits they are associated with weaving and spinning (albeit with human intestines and body parts which does seem to suggest a slightly darker manifestation of fae power), are all female and sometimes fall in love. A Valkyrie as a bride could occur when surprising them bathing at the lake. The faerie garment motif is repeated in Germanic sources where in "The Swan Maiden," the theft of one of the swan suits by a man while the faerie bathes aresults in marriage. This theft, just like the Irish Selkie when her sealskin is taken, forces the faerie woman to become his bride.[28]

28 Kveldulf Gundarsson, *Elves, Wights and Trolls: Studies Towards the Practice of German Heathenry, Vol.1,* (Bloomington: i Universe, 2007).

Xana (Spain)

The xana is a faerie found in Asturian mythology. Always female, she is a creature of extraordinary beauty believed to live in fountains, rivers, waterfalls or forested regions with pure water. She is usually described as small or slender with long blonde or light brown hair, which she tends to with gold or silver combs woven from sun or moonbeams.

Besides exchanging other women's children for their own, the xanas promise treasures. Some xanas also attack people and steal their food. They live in fountains and caves. A xana can be a beneficial spirit, offering love or water to travelers and rewards of gold or silver to those found worthy. Their hypnotic voices can be heard singing during spring and summer nights. Those who have a pure soul and hear the song will be filled with a sense of peace and love. Those whose souls are not pure will feel they are being suffocated by their very presence and sound, and may be driven insane.

The above facts shed interesting light on the mare or mora creatures, who are also known for suffocation. Here we see ambiguous beings, interpreted as "pressing" by those who are deserving of punishment yet beautiful to those with a pure heart. It begs the question whether the nightmare was also such a figure that could be a pleasurable encounter for the pure of heart and a terrible pressing demon to the impure.

Xanas are usually depicted in one of two ways. In one, they appear as young Nordic girls, very beautiful, with long blonde hair. This image is usually associated with xanas who possess a treasure or those under a spell. In contrast, in tales in which the xanas steal children and enter homes to bite or steal, the xanas are small, thin and dark-colored, suggesting that like the elfen, they come in more than one variety.[29]

29 David A. Wacks, "Some Thoughts on Asturian Mythology." Lecture given at the University of Oregon Osher Centre for lifelong learning, December 10, 2014.

Samovili (Macedonian)

They are presented as pretty girls with golden hair and wings who live far in the mountains, near water or in the clouds. It is believed that they are born from the dew on flowers, when there is rain and the sun is shining on the dew, or when there is a rainbow at the same time.

They serve only those who steal their clothes, and if someone steals their wings they transform into normal women, and also may have hidden hooves. Like many faerie creatures Samovili are known for stealing humans away. Their music is so skillful that human musicians will enter into musical and singing battles with them as the ultimate test in skill, much like the later tradition of challenging the Devil to a fiddling competition at the crossroads.

They arrive at the birth of children to determine their fate and give out good luck or bad luck but can also cause disease and illness. The Zmei are dragon-like and seem to be the males of the species. They are creatures that look like humans but with a snake tail, golden wings, unusual physical strength and are considered extremely intelligent and wise. They live in caves or the untouchably high mountaintops. They are attracted to female beauty and usually grab girls from villages and take them to their homes.[30]

Szepasszony (Hungarian)

The "fair lady" or ladies (the word Szepasszony seems to refer to a Queen of Faeries at times and a collective term at others) are known for their dancing and beautiful singing, for appearing in circular whirlwinds and for carrying mortals away. They are usually blonde and dressed in white and are accompanied by the sound of little bells.

It is considered dangerous to step into a circle of short grass surrounded by taller grass or no grass at all, since it may be the

30 Vesna Petreska, "The Secret Knowledge of Folk Healers in Macedonian Traditional Culture," *FOLKLORICA 13* (2008).

circle where the Fair Lady dances. They can be women above and "horse, goat, deer or cow below" as well as being able to shape shift into a variety of forms such as wild geese, falcons, wolves and snakes. Hungarian fairies also called tündér (or perhaps these are another variety of Hungarian faerie) live in the lakes and rivers, or on the islands where the woods are thick. They look like humans, except a lot more beautiful; sometimes they even come into our world and marry mortal men. They laugh, they dance, they sing, and they have their own queen, who rules over them from her palace shaped like a crystal dome.[31]

Twyleth Teg (Welsh)

The "bright and shining ones" of Wales, the Twyleth Teg are usually described as fair-haired and wearing either white or green and seem to be of both sexes. The Twyleth Teg are only one of the two primarily tribes of faeries in Wales, the others are called the Gwraggedd Annwn, and they emerge from the lakes to spin gold thread or brush their long hair. The Gwragedd Annwn are known for seducing human males but also for being captured while bathing and becoming the wives of human men. If they are ever touched with iron they would immediately return to their original abode forever. When Welsh faeries live with humans for any length of time they often display emotional inversions, such as laughing at funerals and crying at Christenings.

Both faerie tribes enjoy music and singing, being taken away to their underwater, across the water, hollow hill dwellings or even joining in their circle dance will result in loss of time. The places they dance have faerie rings and they are known for riding small white horses. They are known to favour Neolithic stone circles and other megalith sites.

31 Éva Pocs, "Tündéres and the Order of St Ilona or, did the Hungarians have Fairy Magicians?" *Acta Ethnographica Hungarica 54*, no. 2 (2009).

Another Welsh faerie tribe the "Bendith y Mamau" are known to steal children and leaving a changeling in the place of the baby. They keep a strange breed of faerie cattle which when it comes among human cattle provides almost never-ending milk. They are associated with the twilight and other in-between states.

Circular wind patterns such as small whirlwinds are said to be the Twyleth Teg dancing and like faeries in other areas they fire off elf-shot. Professor Rhys, in his *Welsh Fairy Tales*, says, that gossamer, which is generally called in North Wales *edafedd gwawn,* or *gwawn* yarn, used to be called, according to an informant, *Rhaffau'r Tylwyth Têg,* that is to say, the Ropes of the Fair Family, thus associating the fairies with marshy or rushy, places, or with ferns and heather as their dwelling places. It was supposed that if a man lay down to sleep in such places the Fairies would come and bind him with their ropes, and cover him with a gossamer sheet, which would make him invisible and incapable of moving. This is much like the thread that the Vila spin and then turn into nets that capture men.

The Twyleth Teg often require human midwives, or abduct lactating women to feed faerie offspring. These faeries sometimes possess an ointment that can give a mortal faerie sight, but there are other Twyleth Teg who will strike a human blind in one eye if they found out you could see them. They enjoy offerings of milk, cream, butter, and baked goods, and possess great knowledge of herbs and healing arts.[32]

Donas de Fuera

This Sicilian term means "women of the outside" which is a euphemism both for faeries and to refer to the women who work with them. Emerging from caves as beautiful women with hidden horse's hooves or cat's paws the Donas de Fuera are almost always benevolent. The

32 Professor Rhys, "Welsh Fairy Tales," *Y Cymmrodor 5* (January 1882), 75.

male fairies often play the music while the females dance in a circle with their hands linked, processions of light wearing white but others wear black.

They are known to possess "soft flesh" and "sweet blood," which smells sweet, even on the humans who were considered to be Donas de Fuera. They can shapeshift into numerous animals including dogs and cats. Though usually not malevolent could strike humans with a form of cramp or epilepsy if offended and would have to be mollified by offerings. When they came through the houses of the village by night they were inclined to give good luck to any household that was set to rights with offerings left out. The women that work with them are often taught herbal cures and make offerings to the faeries in sick rooms to gain the healing favour of the women of the outside.[33]

Fées or Fadas (Brittany)

Fées are known for abducting human babies in the night and leaving their own changeling child in their place. The fées are associated closely with luck and fate and it is considered unwise to offend them. They are also great shapeshifters and can even turn into megalithic stones either temporarily to avoid notice, or permanently.

Brittany also has another faerie creature known as a Morgan who is fond of coming up out of the water to sing and brush her long hair with a golden comb, luring men into the water with her to drown them. The fées like the Welsh faeries are known for their fecund faerie cattle, which may explain the liking that many faerie races seem to feel for milk.

The legends of Brittany surrounding faerie midwives are similar to Wales. A midwife who delivered a fée carelessly allowed some of the faerie ointment to get on one of her own eyes. The eye at once became clairvoyant, so that she beheld the fées in their true nature. This

33 Henningsen, op cit.

midwife happened to see a fée in the act of stealing, and spoke to her. Thereupon the fée asked the midwife with which eye she beheld her, and when the midwife indicated which one it was, the fée pulled it out.

As a rule, the fées of Upper Brittany are described as young and very beautiful. Some, however, appear to be centuries old, with teeth as long as a human hand, and with backs covered with sea-weeds, mussels or other marine growths, as an indication of their great age. At Saint-Cast they are said to be dressed in toile, a kind of heavy linen cloth.

On the sea-coast of Upper Brittany the fées are said to be a fallen race condemned to an earthly exile for a certain period. After the angels revolted, those left in paradise were divided into two parts: those who fought on the side of God and those who remained neutral. These last, already half-fallen, were sent to the Earth for a time and became the fées.

Fadas or fées are regarded as beings quite different from mankind, not as the ghosts of our dead at all.

> *"This, indeed, we know to be proved every day by men who are beyond all exception; that we have heard of some who were lovers of phantoms of this kind which they call Fadas; and when they married other women, they died before consummating the marriage. We have seen most of them live in great temporal felicity, who when they with-drew themselves from the embraces of these Fadas, or discovered the secret, lost not only their temporal prosperity, but even the comfort of wretched life."*[34]

In the legend of St. Armentaire, composed about 1800 by Raymond, we read of the Fée Esterelle, and of the sacrifices to her, who used to give barren women beverages to drink for fertility and of a stone called La Lauza de la Fuda; that is the Fairy-stone on which they used to sacrifice to her. On the night of the 31st of December the fées enter

34 The Fairy Mythology: illustrative of the romance and superstition of various countries, by Thomas Keightley, (1870), p.468

the dwellings of their worshipers much like the Donas Fuera. They bear good luck in their right hand, ill luck in their left, so it is clear they are neither fully benevolent nor fully malevolent.

Care is taken to prepare a clean empty room and a repast as is suited to them. The doors and windows are left open, a white cloth is laid on a table with a loaf, a knife, a vessel full of water or wine, and a cup. A lighted candle or wax taper is set in the centre of the table. It is believed that those who present them with the best food may expect all kinds of prosperity for their property and their family, while those who do their duty toward the fées grudgingly or neglect them altogether, may expect the greatest of misfortunes.

The fees are small and handsome and they are fond of dancing in the night-time. Their dances are circular and they leave behind the Cercles des Fées, or fairy-rings. If anyone approaches their dance, they are irresistibly impelled to take part in it for as long as they wish you to, much in the way that the elves can force someone to dance until they die.

The visitor is always admitted with great courtesy but as the whirling movement increases and goes faster he falls to the ground exhausted. Instead of dancing him until he dies the fées amuse themselves by flinging him up to a great height in the air and if he's not killed by the fall he is found next morning very bruised. These little beings haunt solitary springs where they wash their linen, which they then dry on the megalith stones.

They sleep in the hollows of rocks or the barrows but at night make use of horses. They arc fond of mounting and galloping the horses, their seat is on the neck, and they tie together locks of the mane into elflocks to form stirrups. Their presence, however, always brings luck. The cattle thrive where they are, and if any tack or utensils are used and broken, they are mended and made as good as new.

The fée of Normandy are, like others, guilty of child-theft.

Corrigans are another tribe of faerie found in the area and they are associated with the time of twilight and milk is offered to them.[35]

Iele (Romanian)

The Iele are said to live in the sky, in forests, caves, isolated mountain cliffs and marshes, and are reported to have been seen bathing in springs or at crossroads. They mostly appear at night by moonlight dancing in secluded areas such as glades, the tops of certain trees (maples, walnut trees), ponds, riversides or abandoned fireplaces, dancing naked, with their breasts almost covered by their disheveled hair, with bells on their ankles and carrying candles.

The places where they have danced will remain carbonized, with the grass incapable of growing on the trodden ground, and with the leaves of the surrounding trees scorched. Later, when grass finally grows back, it will have a red or dark green color. The animals will not eat it but instead mushrooms will grow in a circle.

The names of the Iele must not be used randomly, as they may be the basis for dangerous enchantments. It is believed that every Witch knows nine of these faerie names, from which she makes combinations which are the basis for spells. The Iele are said not to be solitary creatures, but gather in groups in the air, where they can fly with or without wings. They can travel with incredible speeds, either on their own or with chariots of fire. The Iele appear sometimes with bodies, at other times only as immaterial spirits. They are young and beautiful, voluptuous immortals, their frenzied music and dance causing delirium in onlookers. They come in groups of three or seven.

Iele are not generally considered evil, resorting to revenge only when they are provoked, spied on while dancing unaware of your presence, when people step on the trodden ground left behind by their dance, or sleep under a tree which the Iele consider their property, or drink from

35 Spence, op cit.

the springs or wells used by them. In fact it is quite easy to anger them!

Terrible punishments are inflicted upon those who refuse their invitation to dance or who mimic them. Anyone who randomly hears their songs becomes instantly mute. They have beautiful voices that are used to enchant their listeners. Invisible to humans, there are however certain moments when they can be seen by mortals, such as when they dance at night. When this happens, they abduct the victim, punishing the guilty one, after they previously caused him to fall into sleep with the sounds and the vertigo of the frenetic Hora, which they dance around their victim, who is abducted, to disappear forever without a trace. They are also capable of making people dance themselves to death.[36]

Sidhe (Irish and Scottish)

Whirlwinds appear when they descend from the sky with a sound like the humming of thousands of bees. The sidhe are said to be descended from the Tuatha De Danann, an early race of Gods who came down from the sky into Ireland. The sidhe are known for their enchanting music and their ability to cast glamours simply through speaking. When Oisin was being spoken to by a sidhe woman no dog barked, no birds sang, and everything went eerily silent.

They are known for their dances and music and are deeply associated with the old raths and stone circles.Their land, sometimes known as Tir Nan Og, lies to the West and is responsible for the West that Tolkien's elves retreat to. In the land to the West no one ever grew old, and all things were abundant at every time of year, but the place also possesses the power that nothing you enjoy whilst there is ever able to tire or cloy you. If the sidhe took you away to the land beyond the West the time would seem to pass quickly but a great deal of time would pass in the human world.

36 Eva Pocs, *Fairies and Witches at the Boundary of South-Eastern and Central Europe*, (Helsinki: Suomalainen Tiedeakatemia, 1989).

The sidhe are known for their abundantly rich clothing and beauty and their circle dances. In Scotland they are called "siths" which is pronounced "shee" the same as in Ireland, and enjoy of gifts of milk, cream, butter and baked goods. They also are able to destroy the goodness of the milk if angered. It is interesting to note that this ability to make milk curdle, or to skim off the cream or goodness from the milk was also an ability ascribed to Witches in Scotland and elsewhere.

The Sidhe woman Aine was bathing and combing her hair on the bank of the river and had her cloak snatched by the Earl of Desmond, thus making her his wife.

Both Ireland and Scotland associate the hag stone, or holy stone (a stone with a natural hole worn through it) with allowing people the gift of seeing the sidhe. Greener patches in grass that came up in a circle, or circles of mushrooms known as faerie rings as they are elsewhere are sacred to them. These circles will also appear as rings made up of twelve flowers growing where no flower should appear.

Households that wished to gain the good opinion of the sidhe would offer milk to them and they like to find a good fire burning when they come in at night. If this is done some types of faeries will finish work left out for them. Mortals will also find themselves called on as a midwife for the sidhe, or lactating women might be taken to breastfeed their babies, just as is experienced in the other Celtic speaking countries.

Ireland had professional sorcerers, sometimes accused of being Witches, known as Faerie Doctors that dealt with healing afflictions brought on by the faeries such as the Stroke and the Dart. Bessie Dunlop is an example of a Faerie Witch in Scotland who received her gifts from the faeries and healed the sick but was later accused of Witchcraft on account of it.[37]

37 Evans-Wentz, op cit.

Laminak (Basque Province)
Finally we find our way to the primordial caves of the laminak. They are the only type of "faerie" from a non-Indo-European language group that we have explored here. If the laminak are an entirely different type of entity with different characteristics we might safely guess that faeries are a shared Indo-European belief-figure like the mora/mare.

The Basque laminak is said to be very beautiful and more of their females make an appearance than males. They are known for spending a lot of time combing their long hair, often with golden combs. It is the laminak who built the Dolmens and all standing stones, according to the Basque tales. Their women are excellent spinners with a spindle and distaff. Some tales recount them going to the river for nocturnal laundry and spinning sessions which would often involve special songs, as they were very fond of singing.

Householders make offerings to them and they may come down the chimney to finish work left out if bread and milk is prepared for them. If they came to visit in the night they would often give good luck to people with clean houses. But the laminak also abandon areas where churches are built and no longer frequent them once this symbol of the new religion is installed. They mostly congregate at crossroads, caves, bridges and of course dolmen stones. They enjoy coming to human dances, but when they appear disguised as a mortals they will always have their feet covered. Laminak often have some kind of abnormality about their feet, such as webbed feet, a cloven foot or paws.

Generally speaking the laminak only come out at night and will disappear around cock's crow. Some Basque legends tell about the people being stolen into their world as brides or grooms but other stories tell of the capture of a laminak maiden as a wife by a human man. The laminak have a preoccupation with honesty and in fact are said to be incapable of lying, much like True Thomas in Scotland

and his tongue that cannot lie. Consequently they will punish liars severely, even for a white lie.

Despite their problem with falsehoods they still take children and replace them with their own offspring. It is not known how laminak reproduce but when they do they seem to require human midwives to deliver their children just as in other Celtic areas. In fact it is difficult for laminak to complete their life cycle without some form of human intervention as humans are also sometimes asked to say a "mass" for the dead so a laminak could die at last. Whether in the process of being born, suckling with milk or passing on, it seems that human participation in the laminak's lives is as necessary as laminak participation in human lives.

If you want to see the laminak the best was to do this is with one foot inside the threshold of the house and one foot out. But when you make an offering to them or leave their company you should never look back after you do. Although they don't create faerie rings when they dance they do leave "fairies holes" (Lamiñaziloak), spoken of in the Heren-Suge tale; they take the form of bare spaces in hedges, which become covered by the web of the gossamer spider. This is very reminiscent of the "faerie ropes" of gossamer made by the Twyleth Teg.[38]

So it is quite clear that the Basque region does not only exhibit the basic format of the European faerie belief system, but almost exemplifies it. The only major discernable difference between the laminak and the sidhe, for instance, is that they don't seem to have quite such strong divisions between gentry and other less high-ranking forms of faerie life. The images of beauty and gold combs and dancing are to be found in the same place as the strange misshapen feet and the finishing of household chores—something usually left to the brownie in Britain.

38 William A. Douglas, *Essays in Basque Social Anthropology And History,* (Reno: University of Nevada Press, 1989).

The similarities between the Basque laminak and the other faerie creatures of Europe, along with the link to megalith sites and burial mounds, tentatively suggests a pre-Indo-European substrata to the faerie belief figure that was later overwritten by the fallen angel narrative due to internal similarities in story. The explanation for how such beliefs endured so long is answered easily for the occultist rather than the pure scholar, in that constant new eyewitness accounts have reinvigorated the material over time.

Shared Characteristics:

Here is a list of the shared characteristics that faeries of European nations almost always possess.

- Spinning and weavings
- Associated with megaliths
- Beauty, hair flowing freely if female and more likely to be fair
- Combing the hair with golden comb
- Changeling children
- Taking mortals away
- Being taken away by mortals, sometimes by the theft of a skin or feathered garment
- The circle dance—often with fairy ring, sometimes mushrooms. This feature is less discernable in the English-speaking material available from the Basque province where they are instead associated with "faerie holes" that are doorways in hedges. Though a closer analysis by a Basque speaker may yield different results.

- Wearing white or green. If not in these colours they may be naked
- Associated with forests, bodies of water hollow hills or mountains
- Shapeshifting particularly into birds or possessing bird feet or wings. If not this then some oddity like a hollow back or other abnormality will be found somewhere on their body
- The liking for milk and clean houses
- Usually nocturnal or associated with threshold times like twilight and dawn, in-between states
- Closely associated with Fate and the ability to control the fortune of worthy humans
- Honesty is valued, they may like True Thomas possess the "tongue that cannot lie"
- Time is skewed and back to front once you enter Faerie
- If you eat or speak there you must stay forever
- Singing and Music
- Elf-shot
- Ambivalent moral character.
- Sleeping near one of their trees, mounds or rivers is potentially dangerous
- More females than males, female-appearing creatures often in charge

Sometimes:

Here are some shared narrative features that come up frequently but are not quite so prevalent:

- Importance of the faerie's true name
- Small or changeable stature
- Inverse emotional behaviour laughing/crying
- A need of mortals for certain services involving birth, sex and death, especially in the Celtic and Basque regions[39]
- Things other than emotions held in reverse, such as gifts of gold are ashes, ashes can be gold.
- Bells and processions of light such as carrying candles
- Having an ointment that can make mortals see them but may blind those to whom they haven't given permission
- Dislike of iron
- Respond badly to being mimicked, mocked or watched without their knowledge
- May own fairy cattle which are never dry of milk
- May tell you not to look back when you leave their presence
- May cause elf locks in horse's manes
- May be associated with crossroads
- A faerie garment may give you control over them

Given that we can see the Basque province as almost an exemplar

39 This may be of interest given recent genetic evidence that much of the older population of the British Isles, particularly in Wales, share close connections with the Basque area. For more information see Stephen Oppenheimer's *The Origins of the British*.

of the features of faerie lore it is intriguing to note that the sorginak, Basque Witches, are of the "night witch" variety rather than the village-witch type posited by Eva Pocs. That is, there is little distinction given between the mythical attendants of Lady Mari who fly through the sky and are often blurred with the laminak, and human Witches.

Exactly the same word is used in the Basque province for these disincarnate faerie-like night-witches as for the human Witch. It seems this is a very old way of viewing Witches, and that faeries are intimately bound up with them. The figure of Lady Mari in Basque folklore is perhaps a partial key to deepening our understanding of this link between faeries and Witchcraft.

Mari is seen as leader of both the sorginak and the laminak who both live with her or visit her in her great cave. Mari is considered to be at the top of the Basque pantheon, and whilst she flies through the air and is seen at times as a 'woman of fire' she is primarily to be discovered below ground in certain caves, which is significant because it makes the Basque pantheon the only remnant European pantheon to be headed by a female spirit who is said to have her dwelling underground rather than in the sky.

She is known for possessing a golden comb with which she is want to comb her beautiful hair. Significantly the Basque pantheon is the closest thing we have that is suggestive of a pre-Indo-European belief system, so it makes sense that this chthonic aspect should be unique among European polytheisms and lends further credibility to the Basque claim. It is also hard to ignore how those distinctive characteristics tie into faerie lore.

Mari is not only a Goddess but a laminak herself which makes her very much a prototypical Faerie Queen. If the head of a pantheon is a faerie this gives new meaning to the term "Faerie Faith." Just as happens to other faerie women there is a legend where Mari becomes the wife of a human man, in this case a Lord of Biscay. As with all such marriages there is a condition placed upon the mortal party. Whilst the husband may keep his Christian faith he must keep it outside the house and away from Mari. Further indication that Mari is a figure whose mythos reaches back into antiquity is found here in that she will have nothing to do with the Christianity.

But when the husband discovers that Mari has one leg that resembles that of a black goat he immediately makes the sign of the cross and Mari and her daughter both vanish. This mixture between being a beautiful woman made of fire, combing her hair with a golden comb but also possessing the black he-goat leg, is a feature that appears to be a primordial ambiguity of texture that emerges in all the oldest-seeming faerie material.

Mari's goat, sometimes she is riding it, other times it is integrated into her person as in the story above, is explicitly a he-goat. This he-goat is an enigmatic, almost multi-gendered symbolism in the Mari legend, something we will return to puzzle over again later when we address the Sabbatic Goat.

Mari's consort is Sugaar, whose name means male serpent, another cave-dwelling entity capable of flying across the sky as a ball or sickle of fire, who helps Mari generate storms. This serpent God storm creation is a motif that will take on greater resonance later as we explore the deep nature of faeries and other spirits with their origins in the sky, as we make further attempts to unravel what might have been the original mythos behind the fallen angel gloss.

The night that Mari and Sugaar come together is Friday night, the traditional night of the Akelarre, or Basque Witches' Sabbat. Friday is a Witchcraft day all over Europe and is sacred to various Goddesses associated with sorcery. The faeries inside the Sibylline Mountains transform into serpents on this day, and it is connected with Venus of the Venusburg.

As Mother of both laminak and sorginak, Mari tightly links together faeries and Witches along with goat-horned Gods, serpents, hollow mountains, Sabbats, thunderstorms and sorcery. We find in this Basque tale a possible source myth from which to understand faeries in relation to Witchcraft. Whilst Indo-European sky Gods largely dominate the pantheons of most other cultures in Europe the realm of faerie has remained exempt and usually has more in common with the Basque pantheon, in that Faerie Queens outnumber kings and hollow hills and mountains are usually filled with light-bearing faeries.

In Sicily the Faerie Witches were told that because mankind was ruled by Christ, who is male, that Faerie, either in balance or reversal, was ruled over by the Faerie Queen. In Ireland and Wales respectively, where the progenitors of the sidhe were the Tuatha De Danann and the Plant Don, or the people of the Goddess Danu and the people of the Goddess Don, we can also see this Queen of Faeries figure being remembered.

Whether Old Europe was religiously matrifocal (as opposed to actually matriarchal which is another matter entirely) or whether this faerie quality has always been a matter of inversion, Faerie itself certainly appears to be a world with strongly feminine features.

Types of Faeries:

As we have seen, folk wisdom from numerous European countries tells us that faeries are also "fallen angels." We have suggested the idea that in some way this pre-existed the coming of Christianity and simply had the word "angel" grafted on over a different term for these Upperworld beings. If this is the case the fall of the angels begins to hint at a creation story, where fire from heaven penetrates every order of creation, illuminating not just the marked brow of witch-kind, but much earlier, the very interior of the Earth, allowing it to spring forth with a myriad of consciousness bearing life-forms. Given that we have established there are strong chthonic features in the Faerie Faith of Old Europe we now need to explore the meaning of all this sky-derived imagery.

Many stories of the fall of the faerie races speak of more than two types of faeries. The faerie worldview cannot be divided into angels and demons, up and down, black and white. There is always at least three ways of being, which most likely reflects an old three-tiered cosmos (which itself may be divided into further zones), traces of which survived both Celtic and Norse mythology.

John Walsh, a Witch of Dorset, claimed in his trial to have much of his knowledge of Witchcraft from the faeries that he visited at their mounds. These burial mounds link faeries, Neolithic mounds, and Witches during the persecutions and therefore at a much earlier time period than most folklore was collected. He also encountered faeries that he describes as coming in three "colours," white, black and green.[40] This testimony from the West Country reflects the same three-tiered reality found in the folk origin story of faeries falling from heaven and caught in air, water, or under Earth, which was collected during the nineteenth century and shows a basic mythic consistency over two to three hundred years.

Agreeing with the Manx account of the angelic fall, Walsh says the black faeries are "the worst." You will note he doesn't say the white and green faeries are good. In fact his statement seems to imply that all of them are quite dangerous, and the black ones are only the *most* to be feared. Let us examine some more testimonials to see if we can tease out where certain faerie beings belong in this three-tiered world.

> *"As aerial beings the Tylwth Teg could fly and move about in the air at will."*[41]

40 Wilby, *Cunning Folk*, 79.
41 Evans-Wentz, 138.

From this and other reports we can connect the Twyleth Teg or Shining Ones with aerial flight. But just because they are capable of flight doesn't necessarily give them a dwelling place in the air. Given their association with twilight, mist, and wearing white this might also suggest the Twyleth Teg, along with other names for the "Shining Court" occupy that midway space between Earth and sky, that twilight place betwixt and between the edges so often associated with all of Faerie in general.

Searching through records relating to the faerie familiars of Witches will also expose us to further use of colours to define different faerie types, though here they are called "devils." The very fact that there are white ones exposes a faerie substrata, as does the mention of Robin Goodfellow and brownies.

> *"A type of fairy familiar that the vulgar call white deviles, which possibly have neither so much power or malice as the black ones have, which served our great grandfathers under the names Brouny and Robin Goodfellow."*[42]

This testimony is particularly valuable because it gives us a working example of the way the word "devil" was taken on board by the people and made to fit around a pre-existent faerie faith, rather than the other way around. If devil could be used so flexibly, it seems easy to believe that angel could also.

Shakespeare also expresses the knowledge of faeries coming in different colours, and hints he has some understanding of their origins in the following quote:

> *"Fairies, black, grey, green, and white, You moonshine revellers, and shades of night, You orphan heirs of fixed destiny, Attend your office and your quality."*

The phrase "orphan heirs of a fixed destiny" is revealing as it suggests Shakespeare was aware of the fallen angel legend. Why would

42 Wilby, 18.

he refer to them as "orphans" unless he knew the story of them being fallen from heaven? The "fixed destiny" is redolent of the folkloric belief that faeries cannot alter their destiny as man can, nor can they be saved on Judgment Day, yet nor are they damned—they are simply fated to cease to exist when the world ends. Perhaps this was a way of finding a place in the middle during the ultimate Biblical act of separating everything into two categories? If only Heaven or Hell were the options on Judgment Day then anything whose nature is "third" must surely cease to exist. Either way the quote suggests Shakespeare knew these legends as early as the 1500s which places the use of colours to define courts of faeries back another hundred years from Walsh's confession.

It's crucial that we address this question because contemporary scholarship (especially Henningsen and Wilby) tends to separate Witchcraft testimonials into black and white Sabbats, or Witches and cunning folk, based on whether the familiars of the magical practitioner are seen as being demons or faeries. Pointing out that faeries may also be referred to as black or white devils it is highly likely that demons and "black faeries" were one and the same thing. Which begs the question whether we can really make this distinction between Witches and cunning folk based on whether their familiars are faerie? It might be a useful distinction for the professional scholar, but what use does it serve for the practitioner looking for viable clues to help us better unpack our own history?

If all the familiar spirits of Witches are in fact faerie, some being black, white, green, or whatever colour folklore might ascribe to them, then we have found an archaic layer, lying under the imposed black and white worldview that guided the persecution of Witchcraft. Of course, if we do we risk losing some of the usefulness of the term "faerie" when it comes to describing certain phenomena, with the term disappearing into a vague mist meaning nothing more specific than "spirit."

To accept all these creatures as faerie or elven without losing preciseness I will decide on some terminology so we can be clear about what we are naming. Scholars like Gustav Henningsen have written whole tables defining the differences between faerie magicians and black Witches and Emma Wilby has gone to some trouble to define the difference between Witches and cunning folk. Most of these differences are drawn along moral lines that separate things into black and white, bad and good, or at least bad and ambivalent.

When it comes to the familiar of a Witch who appears with all the black Sabbatic imagery to go with it, we will apply the term "dark elf." This seems appropriate as the Manx story of the fall recounted above describes exactly this relationship. To repeat the relevant part of the testimonial already quote above:

> *"Other fairies, however, are demoniacal, and given to evil and malicious deeds; for when cast out of heaven they fell into hell, and there the Devil holds them under his rule, and sends them forth as he wills upon missions of evil to tempt the souls of men downward by the false glitter of sin and pleasure. These spirits dwell under the earth and impart their knowledge only to certain evil persons chosen of the Devil, who gives them power to make incantations, and brew love potions, and to work wicked spells, and they can assume different forms by their knowledge and use of certain magical herbs. The witch women who have been taught by them, and have thus become tools of the Evil One, are the terror of the neighbourhood; for they have all the power of the fairies and all the malice of the Devil, who reveals to them secrets of times and days, and secrets of herbs, and secrets of evil spells; and by the power of magic they can effect all their purposes, whether for good or ill."*

Here we see that these dark elves are entirely connected in the folk imaginal with Witches. But within that description of secret knowledge we find much to question a charge of pure evil, including love spells, herbal secrets, and a deep understanding of natural rhythms needed for sorcery. The dark elf of Scandinavian tradition seems perfect to describe some of these faeries of the deep underworld because the term is often connected in folklore with the Mare or Mara, the succubus/incubus, nightmare-bringing entities that had such a large impact on the formation of the figure of the night-witch.

The widespread versions of the word mora/mara/mare with their root in the Proto-Indo European word "moros," or death, suggest a very old origin for this dark elf. It suggests neither the dark elf nor the Witch working with one is purely the creation of a hostile Christian world, but something with a far older origin.

Unlike the general and ambivalent word for faerie, which is idiosyncratic in most European languages, this sameness suggests a specifically Indo-European origin. Would it be too much to suggest that this is why we find no term for a division between light and dark in the Basque laminak? Was the original archaic European faerie creature purely ambivalent? Did the change come later than the introduction of Indo European languages? Was it part of the grafting process of Christian to Pagan worldviews?

The Germanic "alp" or incubus is a word that derives from the same root as elf, thus the word for nightmare, *alptraum*, means "elf dream." The archaic form *alpdruck* means "elf pressure" because it was believed that nightmares were a result of an elf sitting on the dreamer's chest. This aspect of German elf-belief largely corresponds to the Scandinavian belief in the Mara, "presser" or nightmare. Originally it suggests no separation into elf and dark elf, but merely implies that cleaning your house and pressing your chest were both possible behaviours for faerie spirits.

We do not know much about the dark elf can be used to confirm this idea, but he does seem to derive from later sources. We know they lived below ground and were often dark of colouring or even had black faces. Here we can see a connection between the black faeries described in folklore as living below ground, and also in the numerous black-faced devils and spirits that appear in Witchcraft testimonials both in Britain and the Continent. It is also difficult to draw a strong divide between the dark elf appearance and that of some demons in grimoires and testimonials.

When referring to spirits usually designated faerie by writers who create a contrast between Witches and faerie magicians I will use the term "Shining Court Faerie," an Anglicisation of the Welsh Twyleth Teg or Shining Ones, who we have already associated with the airy regions. Although these Shining Court faeries are connected with images of light and white clothing *"passionately love music and dancing, and live luxuriously in their palaces and can obtain all things lovely for their fairy homes, merely by the strength of their magic power,"* they are still wholly ambivalent and not "good."

These are the beings of Alfheim in Norse mythology, the maidens of Avalon in English myth and the youths of Tir Nan Og in Gaelic myth. Their dwelling is always separated from mankind by water or a bridge over a precipice or beyond a mist. This term will refer to what the Scandinavians termed "light elves." These would also be the faeries referred to as "white devils."

"Faerie" I will continue to use very broadly to describe all spirit beings that have an other-than-human origin, yet have a strong connection with the faith-echoes of our Neolithic ancestors. I will not use the term to describe the human dead, except in cases where the human was considered faerie stock whilst alive, or were abducted and thus changed after death.

Faeries that relate to Middle Earth and dwell inside particular mounds, mountains, forests or bowers of the sort called "green" I will call "forest elves," and those who live in the sea or in rivers, "water fae," might be considered "grey." These terms do not have moral connotations but relate to the greyness of sea mist and the greenness of the Earth. Whilst I consider there to be a race of faeries that might be termed green due to their tendency to live in the natural world of forests, grassy mounds or mountains, I separate these from some other nature spirits, using the term forest elf only to refer to members of the Gentry who are believed to be either fallen angels or somehow derived from the spawn of fallen angels.

The same distinction is used to separate water fae from other mythical creatures that might dwell in the sea. As can be seen from examples like the rusalka and the Iele, many faeries associated with water liked to come out of the water. They were not strictly an expression of elemental power, but may have presented a liminal space between Nature and the human dead. They resided in water but could also emerge to comb their hair, spin, climb trees or dance. In fact the water seemed to have served as a portal to their realm of crystal castles and beautiful cities as well as to the land of the dead. So there could be quite a bit of crossover between faeries green and grey, especially among the ruskalia who were said to migrate between rivers and trees depending on the time of year.

Rusalka were said to be present in the waters up until the peak of the summer heat when life-giving rays began to penetrate the waters. Then they would move to the trees, which were called the "houses of the dead." We can see from this that the spirits of water might specifically possess a connection to the dead, which like vampires makes them sensitive to direct sunlight. This term, houses of the dead, might also reach back to old practices of planting a tree over a human burial. This clue linking water fae with death might help us to better understand the dynamics of faerie beings and water and shed some light on the Traditional Witchcraft practices relating to the element.

We will notice when we go back over the country-by-country break down of faeries, that some nations' faeries are almost entirely associated with water, and the common motif of combing the hair next to their lake is found across Europe. However, this characteristic is part of the archaic substrata of the faerie. It exists even in countries that still retain the multi-faceted faerie. The anthropologist Eva Pocs explores this "archaically ambivalent" faerie and Witch as interlocking figures in her monograph *Between the Living and the Dead.*

Pocs remarks on the prevalence of Witches with fairy characteristics in the trial records throughout central and Southeastern Europe.[43] It seems she believes the "white sabbat" to have been the original before the "black sabbat" was invented by the inquisitor and demonologist. But by white she really means ambivalent, because despite the bells and music, faeries everywhere are associated with elf darts and blasts of disease as much as they are with helping with the spinning.

When you find those shreds of archaic material where faeries are neither black nor white, deathly nor heavenly, angelic or fully animal, but a mixture of both it is easier to see how Witchcraft emerged out of the faerie narratives. One example of this in action is how faeries are known for granting prosperity. This didn't make it into the typical narrative, yet the elf dart, the faerie person's ability to send illness in the form of shot, on the other hand made its way straight into Witchcraft and we find in *Malleus Malificarum* the concept of the "archer-witch."

In the picture on page sixty-six a Witch is shooting a man in the foot with an enchanted arrow from *De Lamiis et phitonicis mulieribus* by Ulrich Molitor, 1489.

The testimony of Isobel Gowdie is also well known for reporting the firing of darts from her fingertips whilst in flight, darts that were supplied to her by "elf boys."[44] So whilst the famous faerie Witch of the British Isles, Bessie Dunlop, was famed for her be-

42 Wilby, 18.

44 Emma Wilby, *The Visions of Isobel Gowdie: Magic, Witchcraft and Dark Shamanism in Seventeenth Century Scotland,* (East Sussex: Sussex Academy Press, 2011), 39-40.

nevolent healing with the help of faeries, only a few counties over Isobel Gowdie was being instructed by the denizens of faerie in making darts to shoot down human beings as well as cows. These stories of an airborne faerie host (described in Scotland as the Sluagh) shooting elf darts at humans for breaking certain taboos like working outside after dark continue up until Evans-Wentz's testimonials were taken in the late 1800s–1900s.

It is fair to say that moral ambivalence is indeed the archaic condition of faeries across many nations. But does the idea that faeries are not divided into a good court (with faerie magicians and healers working for them) and a bad court (with malefic Witches working for them) necessarily mean that faeries have one single nature of which the appearance of courts is just a post-Christian invention?

One faerie believer interviewed by Evans-Wentz said the following:

> *"I have heard it said that the faeries live in knolls on a higher level than that of the ground in general, and that faerie songs are heard from the faces of the higher rocks. The faeries of the air (the fairy or spirit host) are different from those in the rocks."*

The testimonial goes on to say that people who are awake at midnight, especially if they are outside, are risking being taken by the host or shot with elf darts.[45] Whatever difference there is between faeries of the air and the holes in the ground it clearly isn't a heavenly benevolence coming from above!

On the other hand, both the faery boy of Leith and Webster's North-country cunning man claim to have entered through the gates in hollow hills, essentially below ground and there feasted and had music and dance amid beautiful glowing lights, with healing skills and powders given to them.[46]

45 Evans-Wentz, 98

46 Wilby, *The Visions*, 86-87.

So whilst the post-Christian story of the angelic fall relegates bad faeries to the darkest pits of hell and the more benevolent ones to higher up, there is plenty of folklore and confessions confusing and muddying the standard Christian picture of down/bad, up/good. The host of aerial faeries being associated with elf shot attacks and blighting blasts of wind are spread too far and wide to be a local peculiarity.

What we find is a vision of faeries who indeed seem to come in differing types, some dwelling below ground, some in the air and others in both water and land. The confusion comes in when we try to inflict human notions of good and evil upon these creatures. Like the primordial-seeming laminak the faerie of antiquity probably had some among them who preferred the water and some the woodland, but there was no moral difference between the faeries from below ground and those from above. Not until the faerie framework had to be fitted to a Christian worldview.

THE NATURE OF FAERIES

One of the prime opportunities for observing the personalities of faeries is in relation to changeling lore, or whenever faeries are said to move among humans. It is interesting, following from our above discussion of grey faeries of the water that it is the Gwragedd of Annwn in Wales (literally women of the Underworld) who we find as faerie brides whose personal characteristics are best reported on.

The Gwragedd of Annwn are somewhere between being grey faeries who follow the pattern of emerging from water to comb their hair or remove a garment, and the more archaic faeries who unite the characteristics of many realms. It is often in the outposts of Europe where you find this, around its edges. One begins to wonder if this itself is "the fall" that later became Christianised into an angelic story? The loss of the archaic faerie who could be almost everything, beautiful woman and beast, and who fell into differentiation, into black, white, green, and grey, becoming linked with separate parts of nature. Could the story of the fall into the realms described in the Celtic stories be a folk memory of this division of the once integral nature of the fae?

The Gwragedd Annwn when won in marriage continued to experience emotional inversion. This is precious and important material because it is one of the few times we get an insight into faerie psychology. We are told the faerie woman "weeps at births and laughs at funerals."[1] Not out of any malice but because her perception of the value of these events is entirely reversed to ours, she sees the birth of the child in our world as a tragedy and the death as a release. As a grey faerie her essence mingles

1 Wirt Sykes, "Lake Faeries," in *British Goblins: Welsh Folk-lore, Fairy Mythology, Legends and Traditions*, (Gloucester: Dodo Press, 2008).

closely with that of the human dead. We find this in all countries where faeries are associated with rivers and ponds. We hear it told that they are dead girls, drowned men, that they must return to the houses of the dead when the bright light of the Sun hits their water too sharply, which may predispose them to this inverted vision of things.

An Irish faerie seer when asked by Evans-Wentz whether any of the sidhe were inimical to humanity replied:

> *"Certain kinds of the shining beings, whom I call wood beings, have never affected me with any evil influence I could recognize. But the water beings... I always dread, because I felt whenever I came into contact with them a great drowsiness of mind and I often thought a draining away of vitality."*

So if the faerie woman of the underworld is closely associated with the submerged world of the dead then birth implies a death in her world, and death a release from this backward condition. When changelings were discovered in Wales, it was considered proper to return them to their people by throwing them into the lake, so deeply were the class of faeries known as changelings associated with the great lakes. In changeling tales we hear a little more of the faerie personality coming through.

The following advice was given for dealing with a changeling:

> *"When you are getting dinner for the reapers, clear out the shell of a hen's egg and boil some potage in it, and then take it to the door as if you meant it as a dinner for the reapers. Then listen if the twins say anything. If you hear them speaking of things beyond the understanding of children, go back and take them up and throw them into the waters of Lake Elvyn. But if you don't hear anything remarkable, do them no injury."*

So when the day of the reap came the woman did all that the Wise Man ordered, and put the eggshell on the fire and took it off and carried it to the door, and there she stood and listened. Then she heard one of the children say to the other:

"Acorn before oak I knew,
An egg before a hen,
But I never heard of an eggshell brew
A dinner for harvest men."[2]

There is a chillingly knowing, ancient and altogether alien quality to the children's discourse. We can see that faeries live long enough to watch a grown oak come from an acorn and are intrigued by new and novel things, enough to blow their cover to remark on it. Their perception of life and death and therefore their ability to relate to human emotional responses would be entirely skewed by these simple differences we have uncovered so far.

It wouldn't be at all difficult to pick out examples from folklore and trial records of different types of faeries behaving in ways that can only be described as sociopathic. However, we do have to allow that some ways of thinking may differ between courts. In the tale of True Thomas, for instance, we discover that faeries give to their favoured ones a "tongue that cannot lie," laminaks are also incapable of lies. In fact it appears that at least one faction of the faerie world has not time for liars at all, and will punish them severely. Yet on the other hand we find, from Isobel Gowdie's testimony, a Witch flicking elf-darts from her thumb into people and their cattle.

Are these examples of two different courts and their differing ways of thinking? Or are we simply looking at incredibly complex and unpredictable beings who disapprove of lying but are okay with immediate murder?

This is what one seer of faeries had to say on the topic of the faerie good/evil complex:

2 Joseph Jacobs, "Chapter XXV," *Celtic Faerie Tales,* (Alcester: Pook Press, 2013).

"I think the spirits about us are the fallen angels, for when old Doctor Harris died his books on witchcraft had to be burned in order to free the place where he lived from evil spirits. The faeries too, are sometimes called the fallen angels. They will do good to those who befriend them, and harm to others. I think there must be an intermediate state between life on earth and I think it must be in that state that the faeries live."[3]

So what we can gather from this is that there are no good and bad courts of faerie, regardless of how high they dwell in the upper atmosphere or how deep in the Earth. In fact the biggest throwers of elf darts seem to be from the aerial host who have warrior connotations and are usually male. But if faeries of all kinds are morally ambivalent, with different courts having their own particular rules and modes of operation, why does at least one type have a preoccupation with honesty? This insistence on honesty and the dealing out of harsh justice on the other hand, might tell us more about the realm or realms of Faerie than we might realize at first glance.

It is commonly repeated as fairytale logic that what is beautiful in the realm of Faerie is beautiful on the inside as well, and what appears ugly or terrifying is so also. You can see this at work in virtually all fairytales. In fact, there is no inside and outside in the way there is here. Things appear as what they are. True Thomas was not just given a *conscience* when it came to lying, he was given a tongue that *cannot* lie, an awesome and potentially terrible gift. It may just be possible that this gift allows us to see into the internal logic of their world rather than simply a system of morals.

Just as exterior appearance perfectly reflects one's nature in the world of the fairy tale, speech and expression perfectly express thought and feelings without the possibility for dissembling. If this is the case then faeries (certainly of some sorts, maybe excluding goblins

3 Evans-Wentz, 140.

who are known for their trickery) might not be so much ethically opposed to lying, as *unable to understand the possibility for it.*

If some types of faeries are literally unable to lie it would explain why they traditionally react with such excessive vengeance to confusing displays of human duplicity. If the relation between sign and signified is actually almost collapsed in Faerie, then it would also explain why the possession of the name, or the word for a thing, also gives you power over the thing or person themselves.

Humans live in a multilayered reality with inner and outer components, a true "middle world." A close analysis of faerie behavior and lore suggests they do not. They can trick a human into seeing gold when they are holding a lump of coal, but only if that human is dishonest with them first or has broken one of their rules. A human who has a pure heart and isn't driven by greed will see a lump of coal where the greedy man sees faerie gold. If a faerie wants to make something appear other than it is to humans they must affect the mind of a human with what is usually called a "glamour," because otherwise the truth will be immediately self-evident.

Is this the inner truth behind why faeries who deal with mortals tend to specialize in glamours? Could they be said to be the only mode of defense when interacting with a creature that can hide motivations and tell untruths? Are glamours actually a form of untruth or are they instead the use of magic to highlight and underline truths, bringing those truths to human eyes through the use of enchantment? If this is the case then a glamour would temporarily initiate a human being into a faerie way of seeing the world. Such as when Robert Kirk tells us of the Faerie Seers placing one hand upon the head and one on the foot of another to share the Sight with them. A skill like this could be used either to befuddle a human or induct them into a new world. To paraphrase Dali, like art, glamours are lies that help us see the truth.

Pause for a moment to consider this idea, and the truly alien perspective on life you would have if you existed in such a world. Remember when you do that time passes differently in Faerie, that you no longer have the burden of time weighing on you, waiting to age you, the spectre of human death before you. That you possess, perhaps, a tongue that not only cannot lie but a mind with no proper understanding of being able to conceal truth. When you encounter a creature that does lie and cheat your only defense in the face of it is to mirror their own nature back at them with an enchantment, dazzle them with their own greed. Rather than actually needing to glamour them your ambiguity becomes a blank space, a mirror for their own projections.

And yet in this imagined scenario you are countlessly old and everything about the lives of the humans you occasionally interact with seems reversed and upside down. You are capable of emotion, strong, passionate emotion but your emotional responses have never carried the heavy consequences that human emotions do. You can flick an elf dart into someone or claim them as your lover in their dreams without waiting for consent. You can glamour them into seeing you as their lost teenage love. You will never get in trouble for executing swift vengeance on those who confused you by breaking your trust. Your cognitive dissonance in the face of dishonesty and greed is so complete—never having wanted for anything seriously in your life or felt the kind of pain that humans can. You may dislike the ugliness and unfairness of human suffering and seek to doctor it, you may take a liking to a human, even appearing to grant them wishes if the whim moves you, but you could remove that support for what a human might see as a mere slight. Because from your perspective the life cycle of that human is no longer than that of an insect.

This is important to contemplate before attempting to encounter these creatures. It frequently surprises me when anyone undertakes work of this sort without first conducting a careful analysis of the nature of the beast with whom they plan to dally.

THE EMBODIED LIFE OF ELVES

Our pre-modern ancestors seem to have had room in their collective imaginal life for humans walking among them who were deemed ontologically different in some way—enough to be considered faeries or nightmares (mara or mora). This is not to say, of course, that such people were physically inhuman, (though it's debatable whether Witches or werewolves were considered human by persecutors of the Craft in the past) but that they were believed to carry a mysterious taint of otherness.

The idea that spirits themselves possessed a body of kinds was also entirely natural to people in the past. The church's philosophical positions tended to decorporealize the spirit[1] and it wasn't until the Spiritualist movement and the concept of ectoplasm that the Western World seemed to start thinking about whether ghosts and spirits had substance of some kind. In searching for a pseudo-scientific rationale for the Otherworld we had come full circle back to something close to what our ancestors believed.

Modern writers on faeries, even gifted ones like the Frouds tend to position faeries as existing in the imaginative, or perhaps "imaginal" dimension of the human psyche. To our forebears the Otherworld was a far more embodied place and testimonials given by people who saw and interacted with faerie beings in the past stress that they possessed a kind of substance, though less substantial than our own forms. How else could folk beliefs about faerie marriages have begun?

In pre-modern Europe humans possessed a shadow in which they could walk at night, sometimes it appeared as an animal, sometimes

1 For more on this topic see Claude Lecouteux's *The Return of the Dead: Ghosts, Ancestors and the Transparent Veil of the Pagan Mind*, (Rochester, VT: Inner Traditions, 2009)

as a human double or a partly human form.[2] There was no such thing as something that was not "body," which is one of the reasons the mainstream insistence on a strong body-spirit dichotomy sits awkwardly with the spirit of some Old Craft traditions.

Consequently, if we are to understand Faerie from the perspective of the folk genius then we will need to soften the edges of this body-spirit binary and try to imaginatively descend into an older way of seeing. If we can achieve this we will find ourselves immersed in an exuberantly sensuous way of being, and rediscover our senses anew as portals to the Otherworld. What begins as a historical curiosity becomes a stretching of our own imaginative faculties and eventually yields to mystical ecstasies.

Anthropologists and historians often take a patronizing view of the idea of spirits leading embodied lives much like our own. The general explanation being that people in the past were literally unable to imagine anything much different to their own way of life. Or, that being unable to visualise something made of nothing they dressed their airy imaginings in a kind of subtle form or body.

The other option presented to us as practitioners is to simply have the humility to take the folk at their word and accept that these observations of the lives of faeries, made over countless generations, might reflect real experiences of another world. We do not need to intellectually commit to that perspective if it is too uncomfortable, but let us explore it with openness. Let us allow for a moment that the conglomerated wisdom of generations, the collective imaginal experience of an entire people or peoples, may in fact know better than we do.

Yorkshire biographer Durant Hotham described the faerie body in the following way. He said they were "lodged in Vehicles of a

2 Once again, this topic has been beautifully covered by Claude Lecouteux, in this case in his book *Witches, Werewolves and Fairies: Shapeshifters and Astral Doubles in the Middle Ages* ((Rochester, VT: Inner Traditions, 2003))

thinner-spun thread than is (otherwise than by condensation) visible to our dim sight."[3]

So whilst they are made of something thinner spun they are certainly made of something other than just the substance of our imagination. This notion of bodies made of a lighter stuff was agreed on by Robert Kirk earlier who said faeries possessed: *"light changeable bodies like those called astral somewhat of the nature of condes'd cloud."*

So far we find images of finely-spun thread and clouds or mist being used to describe the faerie form. Both of these images are taken from the widespread faerie mythos we have traced across Europe, as faeries are intimately associated with spinning and appearing out of mists or as condensed clouds. The suggestion here is that they are able to condense or expand their form, weaving it in tightly or loosely so as to be perceived or otherwise invisible to humans. What their bodies are woven *from* is only ever hinted at, but vapor and mist seem to be strong candidates, which would suggest there is some degree of air-born moisture in their form.

Somerset surgeon John Beaumont touched a fairy's hand in a chillingly tactile encounter, he describes how it: "yielded to my touch, that I could not find any sensible resistancy in it."[4] Though it did not resist him this does not sound like something that felt like simple air, the words "yielded to his touch" suggests something fragile but nonetheless of substance. Another testimony confirms this description: *"I have often seen that way while in my bed. Many women are among them. I once touched a boy of their's, and he was just like feathers in my hand; there was no substance in him, and I knew he wasn't a living being."*[5]

Feathers in one's hand could not in fact be a more perfect physically evocative image to describe something of substance that is very fragile

3 Wilby, *The Visions*, 19.
4 *Ibid.*
5 Evans-Wentz, 80.

but still provokes a sensation on your skin. Kirk tells us they have "bodies of congealed air" and "chameleon-like bodies swim in the air."[6]

In his poem "The Witch of Fife," written in the early Romantic era, Thomas Hogg describes the elf man's form as "having no blood in him and pale like cauliflower."[7] He also describes faeries and Witches both travelling some distance to attend Sabbats in other lands. This is significant because Hogg's father is rumored to have been the last man in his area to possess the faerie sight. So any knowledge about the faeries that found its way into Hogg's work would likely have been influenced by the input of a genuine Scottish faerie seer of the eighteenth century.

One of the best ways to pursue a deeper understanding of how the faerie body works is to study occurrences where faeries have appeared as corpse candles or faerie lights, only to condense before the viewers' eyes into a humanoid form. Here are some examples of such sightings. Let us use them to compare faeries manifesting out of pure light with the so-called corpse candle observed to leave the body of humans when in sleep or near death.

> *"At first it seemed no more than a light in some house; but as we came nearer to it and it was passing out of our direct line of vision we saw that it was moving up and down, to and fro, diminishing to a spark, then expanding into a yellow luminous flame. Before we came to Listowel we noticed two lights, about one hundred yards to our right… Suddenly each of these lights expanded into the same sort of yellow luminous flame, about six feet high by four feet broad. In the midst of each flame we saw a radiant being having human form. Presently the lights moved towards one another and made contact whereupon the two beings in them were seen to be walking side by side. The beings' bodies were formed of a pure dazzling radiance,*

6 Kirk, 48.

7 This is my Anglicization of the original Scots English.

white like the radiance of the sun, and much brighter than the yellow that surrounded them."[8]

Now of course humans have a corpse candle that can leave the body also, as Elias Owen describes in his *Welsh Folklore: A Collection of the Folk-tales and Legends of North Wales:*

"It was believed that it was possible for the spirit to leave the body, and then, after an absence of some time, to return again and re-enter it. The form the spirit assumed when it quitted the body was a bluish light like that of a candle, but somewhat longer. This light left the body through the mouth, and re-entered the same way. The writer was informed by a certain female friend at Llandegla that she had seen a bluish light leave the mouth of a person who was sick, light which she thought was the life, or spirit of that person, but the person did not immediately die."

How do faerie lights differ from the corpse candles that emerge from human beings? Well it seems like the phenomenon is the same but in reverse. Faeries can body forth a human-looking form by condensing a very fine mist-like body until it becomes a bright spark of light, whereas humans belong in a dense body that nonetheless conceals a body of light.

Romani lore compiled by Patrick Jasper Lee suggests that the faerie body is ethereal but very real and that it can become denser through the consumption of life force. The ghostly dead and ethereal fay both shared one great trick, they could become *tsochano*, or vampires, and drink the blood of the living and in this way gain an "ectoplasmic body." Over time they might be mistaken for a living person.

The status of the body may often be an ontological difference, rather than one of solidity. A study of faerie lore overturns numerous insistences of abduction, which would look like simple death to one outside the Faerie Faith. But for those with the

8 Evans-Wentz, 83.

eyes to see the corpse was interpreted as a *stock*, a fake, a piece of wood glamoured into taking the appearance of the dead while the fae made off with their real body.

So whilst we may have trouble believing in a faerie creature becoming more tangible through consuming life force, or of humans being bodily taken away, the lore is so copious that we should retain an open mind around the topic of exactly what "body" and "real" meant when our ancestors used them. What is clear is that faeries were firmly believed and experienced by many people as existing in some tangible way that was not merely within the world of shared imagination but was sensual and actual.

Here we press up, almost uncomfortably close, to the knowledge of our foreparents' quite literal belief in the physical existence of faeries. Because this journey into the folk imaginal realm of the past is about leaning into discomfort rather than fleeing from it, let us look closely at a faerie narrative that falls somewhere in the uneasy middle place between mythic story and recent folk legend.

The Green Children of Woolpit

There are many tales of faerie brides coming who emerge from lakes and marry men, but most of them happened "back then," before anyone can rightly say. Even the fabled Myddfai family of healers, descended from a faerie woman of the lakes, can't date the emergence of, or give multiple witnesses for the presence of the Myddfai foremother. But Agnes Barre, the likely name of one of the green children, can be dated and was witnessed by multiple sober individuals. If anything brings us into proximity with faerie bodies and our ancestors' firm belief in them, it is this story.

During the reign of King Stephen (1135–54 CE), Woolpit village was named for the deep surrounding trenches that protected the inhabitants from falling victim to the prowling wolves of the deep, dark surrounding forest. One day during this time, two small children crawled out of these trenches: a boy and girl, malnourished, frightened and speaking a language none could comprehend. Two contemporary scholars recorded the story, a Benedictine abbot, Ralph of Coggeshall, contributor to *Chronicon Anglicanum*, and William of Newburgh, author of *Historia rerum Anglicarum*. Abbot Coggeshall named Sir Richard de Calne as his source, noting he had frequently heard the story from him, while the historian from Newburgh noted he believed the story because of the weight of so many and such competent witnesses.

Like Thomas the Rhymer's faerie narrative the land the green children come from has no sun or moon, yet is in possession of a rarified kind of light. As Katherine Briggs points out this narrative is full of traditional faerie lore like the presence of a twilight world with no sun and the strong association with the green realm of nature via their eating habits and skin colour.

The testimony of these expert witnesses allows us to observe a kind of transformation from faerie body into mortal woman's body in the surviving child. Originally her body is marked out as different to those of others and found in a wolf pit—a deep hole with stakes in it dug out to catch wolves. In this place, meant to kill the ultimate outsider in the British world, they caught something else from beyond the hedge. Her eyes were light sensitive, her skin faintly green and she was only able to eat beans and peas. Unlike her brother who did not survive, Agnes' skin slowly normalized away from its green colour. She learned the language and began to eat normal human food. In this way her body, previously marked out by these signs of faerie otherness, was able to cross from the liminal space of the wolf pit into the world of man. Just as eating faerie food is notorious for transforming humans in such a way as they can no longer return to their world, so it appears that food in our world has the same power in reverse. For the little brother who died would not make the transition to earthly victuals.

From this story, even if we wish to consider it as narrative rather than fact, we can see that to our ancestors the faerie body was differently positioned somehow. Other, wild, of the outside like the wolves were, but perhaps in some way closer to the green world of plants, and alike enough to our own to be capable of change or perhaps a kind of skin-turning mimicry of human form and functions.

DEATH, SEXUALITY AND GENDER OF FAERIES

Declared one Scotsman, "There is no growth nor increase, no death nor withering upon the faeries."[1] Others simply say that they have no idea of the precise life cycle of faeries: "I never heard that they grew old, and whether they multiplied or not I cannot tell."[2] Yet despite this uncertainty one very common motif regarding faeries, especially in Celtic speaking areas, the faerie midwife, rests on the idea that some form of reproductive activity is occurring between humans and faeries.

Throughout both folklore and encounter narratives we hear stories of human and faerie inter-marriage. The Romani view that when faeries do manifest in our world, such as was claimed by the numerous stories of lake brides, selkies and swan maidens who married mortal men, they must do so by drawing off the vitality of a human victim, fits perfectly to the sexual love model. Faeries such as the Leannan Sidhe are already known to use sexuality as a method to draw vitality off from artists, whom they gift in return with inspiration. These stories, which we may choose to hold somewhere in the misty space between truth and metaphor if we prefer, suggest to us that faeries may breed, but only with the agency of humans.

The changeling mythos also provides us with the notion of faeries in the form of babies. However, the rest of the traditional narrative seems to point to them not really being babies, as the changeling test is to get them to reveal their hidden age and knowledge of the world. An acorn before an oak I saw, says the changeling watching beer about to be brewed in an eggshell.

The midwife narrative is mirrored by other stories telling of lactating women spirited away to Faerie Land and compelled to deliver babies or

1 *Ibid*, 109.
2 *Ibid*, 138.

be wet-nurses because faeries are presumably unable to do these things. The fact they require our midwives suggests that reproduction in the way we perform it is not a natural state of affairs in Faerie.

There are more than enough tales of faeries drawing the life out of people, even without the very succinct Romani explanation, for us to see that faerie engagement in sexuality and the appearance of reproduction may actually be the only way the human mind can interpret what humans contribute to faerie bodies. A woman who is taken away whilst lactating may experience a glamour that she was suckled by a faerie changeling when perhaps she is simply being drained of her abundant life force.

The children of the *vila* are said to create thunder and lightning with their play so it is presumable that there are males of the species and that reproduction occurs in some way, though like the changeling it may be quite difficult to tell which ones are really children on first inspection, as some faerie tribes are short and appear to play in the carefree manner of children.

The most immediately significant thing we observe about gender among faeries is that females usually outnumber males and that there are more faerie queens than faerie kings. But as reproduction may not mean to them what it does to us, we may be led to ask: are they actually "female" in the way we understand the word at all? Or do we humans merely interpret all delicate things as female?

One faerie seer, interviewed by Evans-Wentz, said that he saw faeries as: "Some male, some female, some do not suggest gender at all." Coming from a world that is non-mammalian they may not require two genders for the sake of reproduction, so there is no reason why faeries would require a gender that mirrors our own precisely. Given the importance of the number three in faerie lore one wonders if this male, female, and not suggestive of a sex observation, might suggest the existence of three genders.

It seems that we know more about death in Faerie than we do gender or sexuality, though there are a few suggestive testimonies that might advance our understanding somewhat. The story of Grace from Cornwall tells us:

> *"They don't always live together like Christians and turtle-doves; considering their long existence such constancy would be tiresome for them, anyhow the small tribe seem to think so."*[3]

That they find constancy tiresome politely suggests that monogamous marriage was not part of faerie culture. She makes her point more clearly on the monogamy question still when asked if there are children among the fae:

> *"'Very few indeed,' she replied, 'though they are fond of babies, and make great rejoicing when one happens to be born amongst them; and then every little man, however old, is proud to be thought the father. For you must remember they are not of our religion,' said she, in answer to his surprised look."*[4]

She also mentions these old man faeries as becoming more and more worn but not dying. This is interesting because it suggests a wearing away to a less substantial state over time, becoming see-through and of finer stuff. Robert Kirk also seemed convinced that eventual death would come for the faerie folk. In *The Secret Commonwealth* he tells us: *"They live much longer than we yet die at last, or least vanish from that state."*

Of course whether the relative normality (from a human perspective) of faeries presenting themselves as old people or children is legitimate or the result of faerie glamours is difficult to say. The very fact that faeries have always been believed to possess a body makes it likely that some kind of life process exists though it may be radically different to our own, or even vary between types of faeries.

3 William Bottrell, "The Fairy Dwelling on Selena Moor," *Traditions and Hearthside Stories of West Cornwall, vol. 2,* (London: Forgotten Books, 2018), 100.

4 Ibid.

THE FAITH—RELIGION OF FAERIES

In the Sicilian Faerie Trials we hear that the Witches who were taken away by the faeries to be taught their Craft were forbidden, whilst in the presence of the faeries, to utter the name of Jesus Christ or Virgin Mary. Church bells are also widely deemed to be offensive to the fae and the Basque laminak will pack up and move if a church is built. Even Robert Kirk asserted that whilst it wasn't known if they had religion they certainly weren't Christians! It has also been stated by an eyewitness that among them "religion is not known of."

The following is more from the tale of Grace where a man is reunited with his supposed-dead fiancé who is actually trapped in Faerie. During his encounter with her she explains the lifestyle, beliefs, and manners of the faerie folk.

> *" 'For you must remember they are not of our religion,' said she, in answer to his surprised look, 'but star-worshippers.' "*[1]

More detail about their beliefs is offered by Robert Kirk:

> *"For 'tis one of their tenets that nothing perisheth, but (as the sun and year) everything goes in a circle, lesser or greater, and is renewed and refreshed in its revolutions, as 'tis another that every body in the creation moves (which is a sort of life), and that nothing moves, but has another animal moving on it, and so on, to the utmost minutest corpuscule that's capable to be a receptacle of life."*[2]

Between these two fragments of information we can perceive a clear description of animism. The worship of stars as seraphic beings of wonder, bringers of the Cunning Fire

1 *Ibid.*
2 Kirk, 52.

to mankind in the form of angels, the knowledge (as opposed to the belief) that nothing perishes but instead moves in cycles. By the very virtue of it having movement, every body in the cosmos, every chunk of stone is alive because everything is moving, even if it's just through space. It is clear this is knowledge rather than belief in the way we understand it, as Kirk's account of the religion of faeries presupposes our modern understanding of microscopic and bacterial life forms by hundreds of years.

It is in fact true to say of them also then that "religion is not known among them," for the faith of the faeries is far more a matter of direct experience much more akin to the direct gnosis of the mystic than blind belief.

There is enough depth in these small fragments to make us ask if the term "Fairy Faith," meaning the faith humans place in faeries, should instead be taken to mean the faith *shared with* faeries.

THE CROOKED PATH AND ITS CROOKED FRUIT

"O see not ye yon narrow road,
So thick beset wi thorns and briers?
That is the path of righteousness,
Tho after it but few enquires.
And see not ye that braid braid road,
That lies across yon lillie leven?
That is the path of wickedness,
Tho some call it the road to heaven.
And see not ye that bonnie road,
Which winds about the fernie brae?
That is the road to fair Elfland,
Whe[re] you and I this night maun gae."

Thus says the fair Queen of Elphame to True Thomas when he is presented with the three paths. The choice offered here is rich and deep in layers of metaphysics. It positions the realm of Faerie or Elphame, just as the old stories about the genesis of faeries did, as an in-between realm that is neither Hell nor Heaven, neither rejection and transcendence of the material world nor materialistic immersion in it, a third option, a thing that human thinking seems to struggle with.

Although the fallen angel origin story may seem a concession to a Christian worldview, this thirdness actually subversively deconstructs it from the inside. The moment the story presents a third alternative between angel and demon, heaven and hell, it changes the discourse to suit itself, as well as participates in it. Such is the power of the faerie mythos and faith, which I contend is the deepest origin point of Traditional Witchcraft.

Contemplate for a moment the importance of this as if you have never heard the story before... Empty your mind and reencounter the narrative afresh. This tale of Elphame offers up another option between the thorny and impenetrable path of virtue and the wide road of Hell. In this they offer a possibility of mystical revelation and salvation outside the confines of church stricture, and yet manage to absorb many useful Christian terms and motifs. I believe it was this third path to mystical revelation, this faerie road that nourishes the taproot of the nameless deed we came to know as Witchcraft.

But how do you get a chance to view this third road?

True Thomas has to wade through gore up to the knee where all the blood that's spilled by mankind above seeps down into the country below, where Elphame is situated. For a moment let us return to the Cornish story of Grace the lost fiancé by way of comparison between abduction narratives:

> *"No, no! My dearest William, you must not touch me, nor the fruit in this orchard, nor any flower or blade of grass, for all this is enchanted. A plum from one of these trees was my own undoing three years ago.... This is how it came about. I was looking for one of our goats lost upon Selena Moor at the edge of dusk. Hearing your voice call to the dogs not far away, I struck over the moor to reach you, my beloved William, but I became confused and lost, buried in bracken that was head high, and surrounded by bogs and streams. At last, very tired, I came upon this orchard. Beyond lay a garden filled with roses and the sound of music, surrounded by trees. I know now that I was piskey-led, for once in the garden I could find no way out."*

The abducted woman Grace went on to explain how she had eaten a plum, the sweetness of which turned bitter in her mouth and she swooned. Just as the green children of Woolpit must eat the human food to become of our world, the faerie food changes Grace's status to someone Otherwise. On awakening, she finds herself surrounded by hundreds of Small People, rejoicing that they now had someone to care for them, as well as tend to their numerous changelings.

The two methods of coming into Faerie presented by Grace and True Thomas have parallels but they also exhibit an important and instructive difference. True Thomas speaks of a sense of flying "like the wind" as if the wind were raised whenever bells on the faerie woman's reins ring, but soon finds himself wading through blood up to the knee for a staggering forty days and nights.

This should be understood as an extreme initiatory ordeal that is far too often glossed over in commentary on the poem. This is a true harrowing, an initiatory death and dismemberment tale which lasts for the full period of Christ's temptation in the desert and thus for the number of days that Lent endures. Thomas is being treated like an initiate into the lower world.

The Cornish girl Grace is also engulfed by the land when the bracken ferns come up somehow above her head to swallow and digest her. She also finds herself in a wet place of bogs and streams where she wanders until she is very tired. There seems to be a passing of a water membrane involved in both experiences, though one is described as a bog and one as human blood.

Thomas sees neither Sun nor Moon but hears the rushing of the sea. This poetic description of the waters of the Underworld strongly evokes the rushing sounds of the mother's circulation and heartbeat a baby hears in-utero, as well as the white noise many people hear when entering a deep trance.

Finally after passing through the dark, chthonic world (shortly after riding away with a woman on a white horse with bells on, associating her with the "white sabbat" in current academic perspective) and a long harrowing he finds himself in a garden with fruit just like Grace did. There is clearly fruit in the garden because he wishes to eat from the apples there, but the Queen of Elphame acts towards him like a benevolent fetch mate or faerie lover and prevents him. Explaining the food there has all the plagues in Hell upon it and that she brought some human food with her for him. After he eats and "lays in her lap" she proceeds to present him with three options. Some commentators have suggested a sexual interpretation for this lap-laying.

Grace in Cornwall doesn't have a faerie benefactor looking after her, so hers is an abduction story rather than an initiatory narrative. She wanders at the end of her weary experience in the bogs and hostile bracken, into a garden full of sweet music and an orchard of fruits, but there's no doorway back out again for Grace. She is left alone long enough that she eats one of the plums, but it turns bitter in her mouth and she passes out.

When she wakes the pixies that have taken her captive rejoice at being able to use her as a drudge to feed (feed to?) their numerous changelings. This narrative follows the same process of a swallowing and digestive story where the abductee must pass through a wet, challenging environment to emerge in a beautiful orchard full of sweet music and tempting fruit, but the outcome is determined by whether or not one possesses a faerie ally.

The Green Children of Woolpit said that they became lost when they followed cattle into a cave, and after being guided by the sound of bells. Eventually they emerged into our land to be startled by the bright light and find themselves at the bottom of a wolf-catching pit. As you can see the transition between the worlds includes bells and light changes in both directions.

The green visitors find our food as initially inedible as their food is to us, and discover that beans grow in pods rather than inside the stalks, as they had in their realm. Things are reversed, and yet the sounds of bells and bright lights were alerting them to our land, not to a paradisiacal world of Faerie, which contrasts somehow with gloomy subterranean narratives.

The visitors still pass through a cave after hearing a strange sound to arrive in a pit they get pulled out of by strange beings. This journey through a dimly lit cramped space does not seem to be indicative of the faerie realm only but instead of *the experience felt when passing between in both directions*. In this green children story we see faeries were deemed just as vulnerable in our world as we can be in theirs.

Here we find some of the inner experience of passing through the veil that separates the world of faerie from that of humans. Whether fruit is a bitter poison or a source of knowledge and whether you are lost or found by your experience with faeries all depends on whether you have their patronage or not. Without the patronage of the Queen of Elphame Thomas would have shared the same fate as Grace. What is death to the uninitiated is transmuted into a source of power for the initiate.

For Thomas we see the shades of initiation happening in the Queen's apple bower. She feeds Thomas a sacramental meal of bread and wine under the tree of Hell. And it seems that faerie food in its processed form, such as bread and wine, passed through the hands of the Queen of Elphame, is safer than eating directly of the fruit. Then he lies in her lap. Whether or not we interpret this as code for sexual congress it still signifies an intimacy and suggests a bond has been formed or ratified between them in some way. After they break bread he sleeps, presumably his first comfortable moment for forty days and forty nights.

Thus Thomas is given the vision of the Three Roads, and he is not just asked to choose but the Queen helps him make the decision by explaining the nature of the other two. One is thought to be the path to Heaven but is actually the broad well-worn path to Hell. This is a potentially radical statement in the extreme. It is broad not because it is easy or good, but because it is used by more people.

What you expect to hear is that the other road leads to Heaven, but that is not revealed in all forms of the ballad. It is only said that the other road is the road of righteousness but after it few enquire. It is covered with thorns from disuse but also indicates that the path is very hard. Is this meant to be the path to Heaven? Or is the path of righteousness actually leading you back to Earth? Just calling something righteousness doesn't tell us whether Heaven is reached in this way. Robert Burton suggested in his 1621 *The Anatomy of Melancholy* that the green children fell from Heaven, which is an interesting conflation of Faerie Land with the Christian heaven, considering how closely the story links the green children with Faerie.

This idea that Faerie Land might be Heaven, the thorny path life on our Earth, and the broad well-worn path to Hell the direction of the Christian faith is taking its adherents would certainly be a heretical interpretation of the three roads.

By this interpretation one road will take you back to your world, which is the virtuous path of learning but probably also hardship. That more popular road over there will take you away from life and into the Underworld, but this third road will lead you to something that lies beyond the Underworld which we have already passed through during initiation.

Elphame then is the occultist's promise of immortality, the result of the great work, the philosopher's stone. This all being said, other versions of the poem do identify the thorny path explicitly with Heaven, which fits better with faerie being a state between Heaven and Hell in their traditionally Christian senses. But the close connection between Faerie and Heaven and a difficulty separating out a native sense of the heavenly, as produced by such places as Avalon and Tir Nan Og from the Christian vision leads to this narrative ambiguity around the roads.

The third road is "bonny" and ferny and winds, serpentine, through a land of small hills and dales. This is the road to Faerie, and Thomas is not allowed to make a mistake in his choice. He is guided by his faerie co-walker and told where they will go. But he is given one caution, he mustn't speak human words whilst he is in Faerie, or he will never get back to his own country.

The fact that he spends some time in that land and presumably keeps this arrangement suggests there is another form of more direct communication possible. This assumption supports the idea of faerie transparency and the *apparentness* of emotion and motivation as discussed above in relation to the tongue that cannot lie and the faerie response to deceit.

If everything is *apparent* and nothing is hidden in Elphame then it would seem that somehow human words, which immediately narrow and solidify the things they name, may have the power of making your presence in Faerie a solid reality. If he does not speak, like a newborn babe doesn't yet speak, he is still in a liminal space, as an unannounced guest. Or maybe human words, like human food and human love, have the power to break and re-make faerie enchantment.

Note the Queen doesn't tell him you will be sent home if you speak, she tells him that if he speaks human words in Faerie "he will never get home again." Like eating faerie food, speaking words has the effect of naturalizing the human into the world of Elphame.

But there is a missing piece of information here. Grace in Cornwall has assumed herself to have been stolen away by faeries after being "pixie led," but the True Thomas narrative tells us that after wading through blood up to your knee for forty days in a subterranean environment you are not yet in Elphame. That place is only reached via selecting one of the three roads and walking down it. This gives further weight to the idea of a descent and harrowing experience as a bridge between our world and experiencing Faerie.

If you have to pass through terrifying experiences like flora that wants to swallow you, dangerous bogs, blood and gore dripping down from the Earth above you, and the feeling of being in a tight cave to get to Faerie, but meanwhile such experiences are often interspersed by the sound of bells and flashing lights. Whether you are coming or going, we need to stop associating bells and music with some shining realm of Faerie that is separate entirely from the chthonic Underworld you must pass through to access it. By recognizing this we get closer to the animistic heart of the Faerie Faith, with its Neolithic stone chamber echoes and its atavistic traces, and closer to sensing the deep roots of Witchcraft.

Like the Faerie Faith, Witchcraft is full of chthonic and subterranean themes, but if one must actually pass through this initiatory darkness to reach the realm of Faerie you cannot actually separate Witches and their infernal imagery out from Faerie and its bells and music in the way contemporary scholars are want to do.

Perhaps the greatest clue to the connection between Witchcraft and Faerie is the existence of this third winding road that leads to Elphame. This is our very own Crooked Path, found in the middle. The winding, mysterious way — both beautiful and challenging — full of perilous hooks and crooks in the road and littered with fascinating fungi and temptations to stray off the path. The point is not simply to arrive at Elphame but it's the path one walks to get there that we experience as *Witchcraft.*

We know Thomas arrives at a degree of Mastery of the Art in fair Elphame because we hear he is given a green doublet and velvet green shoes. This theme of re-dressing the mortal in the clothing of the Otherworld is an important theme that signals Thomas's translation to a new higher/deeper state.

Considering that the modern Western Occultism mindset immediately connects left and right hand roads with the Left and Right Hand Path we must take a moment to position the road to Faerie, and thus Witchcraft, within this wider structure of Western Occultism.

The Right Hand Path as understood in mainstream occultism ultimately involves re-absorption into the godhead via the complete union of the ego with the divine. The Left Hand Path is in some ways opposite, the refusal to merge with the demiurge and the deification of the self. The Middle Road to Faerie manages to be both and neither—an eternally unfolding paradox, a continual dance, an in and out breath, or a love making with the Beloved that never collapses into ultimate union, yet never entirely rejects it either.

WHAT DO YOU WANT WITH ME?

Centuries ago faeries were well and truly associated with dying and danger. Judging by the bulk of the stories there was far more chance of ending up like Grace than like Thomas. In this way faerie lore is very much like Witchcraft lore, in that both are associated with the death mysteries. In *The Merry Wives of Windsor* Shakespeare puts it starkly: "They are fairies. He that speaks to them shall die."

Just like Thomas who was not allowed to speak to the faeries when in their land, to even so much as talk to faeries is death in our world, and a birth of a kind in theirs. Eating their food results in the same thing. Those who are fey, or faerie-touched are not long for this world; faerie darts are omens of impending death. Faerie Doctors were required to treat many forms and symptoms of disease that were caused by the malignancy of faerie. Faeries liked to steal milk or sour it, taking the goodness out. Like faeries, Witches were blamed for stealing the cream off milk at a distance through spinning it backwards into their own churn. Faeries were also good at spinning but sometimes they used this skill to spin nets or webs to catch people in. We have seen all of this in the testimonies above, including that drowned girls were sometimes made into faeries.

Witches like Isobel Gowdie who were involved in firing elf darts often had their own kind of arrow they threw. The causes of diseases were often ascribed to Witches and speaking aloud of them was a perilous business. As we have said before, Basque mythology links the laminak (faeries) with the sorginak (witches) without seeming to present one as more evil than the other, and placing both in the service of the Goddess Mari.

What then is the working relationship between the Witch and the faerie? Emma Wilby goes into this topic in her book from the perspective of a scholar in *Cunning Folk and Familiar Spirits: Shamanistic Visionary Traditions in Early Modern British Witchcraft and Magic*, but her accounts of magic practitioners interacting with faeries divide magical experiences along the cunning folk/white magic/faerie familiar versus Witches/black magic/demon familiars.

Although this wonderful book and its author make it explicit the moral dimension isn't always so clear-cut and highlights the ambiguity between the two categories, the categories are drawn nonetheless. An angle that ends up suggesting there are some pure faerie narratives to be found among the Witch Trials, and some other "black" ones that reflect demonological contamination. But what exactly is a demonological contamination of Witchcraft and where does this apparent thing begin? Before we can better understand the interaction of Witches with their faerie familiars we must be able to distinguish them from demon familiars as introduced in demonology texts — if such a division is indeed as straightforward and important as we have been led to believe.

In relation to demonology the waters are muddy from the start because the very word demon originally meant the same as daemon or spirit. Certainly, a great deal of spirits were listed as demons by the early church that were originally Gods of other nations, with Astarte (Astaroth) and Bael being some famous examples. So certainly, from the beginning Pagan and animistic material already lay behind demonology and was not somehow invented out of thin air by the church.

This notion of animistic faerie beliefs being overwritten by this entirely foreign and Christian demonolatry-infused witch-figure is a little over-simplified. In fact Paul Carus argued that it's possible to trace the influence of European fairytales and local magical thinking on the

Christianity that emerged in Europe specifically, rather than just the other way around. As he puts the beginning of his argument:

> *"Teutonic legends and fairy tales frequently mention the Devil, and there he possesses many features that remind us of Loki. In addition, the ice giants of the Norsemen, the Nifelheim of the Saxons, the Nether-world of the Irish, all contributed their share to the popular notions of the Christian demonology of the Middle Ages. The very name 'hell' is a Teutonic word."*[1]

Which casts an interesting light on the "anxiety of influence" so often experienced by practitioners of Witchcraft in relation to trial records and the projections of inquisitors.

With the so-called demons taking on many qualities previously ascribed to giants and trolls, who were not strictly evil but regularly required some sort of "tithe to Hel" be paid them, we see more of a distortion than an invention. We will return to this notion of a tithe to Hell below.

With demons we have a word that means spirit, a history of appropriated Gods and wind spirits from the Middle East who were demonized, mixed with a good deal of British and European folklore. By the time the churchmen came to ascribe demonic characteristics to the Witch the very concept of a demon had been deeply reverse-colonized by folk animistic thinking from both the Middle East and Europe. You might say that when you build your church over a stone circle, it isn't just the Pagan site that is infiltrated with Christianity, but your church has animistic roots.

The early genealogy of Christian demons reaches back into Babylonian and Sumerian entities that caused diseases, as well as dethroned Gods. But for Witches to work with spirits that cause disease is little different to the shamans of Siberia who had to appease and learn from the Small Pox Spirit. It doesn't mean one is worshipping

1 Paul Carus, *The History of the Devil and the Idea of Evil,* (Whitefish: Kessinger Publishing, 2004), 246-252.

the disease, the shaman or sorcerer is instead learning its ways and hoping to defeat or placate it.

Of course demons began to really change shape when Judeo-Christian concepts of total evil were brought into play. Lilith herself is one of the most interesting figures in demonology. She has been seen as a fertility Goddess, the first wife of Adam, the original old hag/succubus, mother of demons, and the Queen of Hell. Originally, in Jewish lore, she was known for sitting upon her victims in the night and choking the life out of them just like a nightmare.

Here we find an early example of a demon who is identified acting in the same way as a mara/mora and engaged in the witch-work of hagging. Was this concept that far spread or ancient, or are we looking at another kind of European/Jewish cross-fertilization here? Clearly given the spread of the mora figure in Europe the concept could not have come originally from the Jewish side and still have a root name recognizable in many European tongues, but European influence on the early idea of Lilith is equally unlikely.

The developing of the demonological narrative is complex and partially shrouded in mystery, as much of it occurred during the poorly recorded Dark Ages. It's also mysterious because the part of the story that scholars don't normally address is the possibility, from an occultist's perspective probably, that these similarities exist simply because there *are* spirits of this nature who do these things! Considering spirits themselves as actors within human history requires not just a scholar of the occult but occultist scholars. How can one properly explain the deep penetration of European animistic themes into Christian demonology if not via the fact that ancient spirits keep reminding us of their presence in the land, long after history would otherwise have forgotten about them and relegated them to oblivion?

As textbooks on the subject were circulated around Christendom, and even more so later in history via the writings of Thomas Aquinas and St Augustine, there was a possibility for admixture between European cultures with Latin, as European creatures like the mara could now be included as a "succubus" across the board with the attributes of local deities and spirits included in the mix. We see this quite actively in Reginald Scot's *Discovery of Witchcraft* where the spirits are both familiar demons found in other books on demonology and local spirits like the faeries Sibylla, Oberon and Luridan. The significance of this for researchers of Witchcraft is that whilst the persecutions and witch-hunting manuals certainly ascribed all kinds of evil to Witches, the tropes that lay behind them were to be found as much in those of Apuleius's *Golden Ass*, prior to Christianization, as in imported Judaic demonic qualities.

When the church demonized things they tended to keep their original characteristics and just said they were bad, that way they could be recognized by their former worshippers and hopefully reviled. The demonology that informed the Witchcraft narrative of Europe was much like this, mixed with native faerie lore and the original practices of "witches" but simply had total evil ascribed to it.

The rest wasn't necessarily fabricated just misunderstood. The darkness, the descent into the ground, the harrowing, the images of death, grave robbing for body parts, and the appearance of actuality of ritual cannibalism, sex acts with spirits, atavistic transformations into terrifying bestial forms, all of that is part of the process of getting to the point where you can start walking the Crooked Path, the road to Faerie or Mastery of the Art. All of it has a hidden meaning. Once again a scholar can only get so far with this topic because he or she is forced not to consider the possible truth of the existence of spirits.

We find ourselves at a place where the question of whether the myth of Witchcraft is native animistic material and how much is imported via demonology becomes a much more complex one, as there is

European native material on both sides of this imagined divide. The things we hold in caution when considering the Witchcraft of the past are often the wrong things. It is not all the images of darkness, bones, milk-skimming, elf-darting and cannibalism but the great black versus white moral divide which has been inflicted on this material. If we can just remove that question, something that current scholarly research doesn't fully do, we can see the matter more clearly.

Even the darkest familiar spirits of Witches in Britain may be faeries or elves of one kind of another. The image of the Witch predates Christian demonology as can be seen in Roman sources like Apuleius, and they were linked to Underworld faeries much like dark elves in Celtic lore. But by this stage the word "witch" itself had been well and truly linked only to dark magic in most areas. The shared roots of the concept of the Witch as dangerous and associated with darkness precede that propaganda however, and much of truth has found its way into demonology.

When the beautiful and benevolent Queen of Elphame still has to take True Thomas through a dimly-lit ordeal full of an ocean of gore before he can reach Elphame, it is clear the Faerie Faith that gave birth to Witchcraft was originally linked both to the chthonic realm and to a shining one. Christianity[2] had no place for such ambiguity in its moral universe yet it still crept in through the third path that the Faerie Faith held firm to. Witches, or whatever the humans who worked with faeries were called in each country, were associated with darkness and death because they were the liminal guardians of the threshold of harrowing and initiatory Underworld descent, a required experience before a human could enter Faerie.

An illuminating question is to ask ourselves how the experience of Witches with faeries differs from the ordinary folk experiences of

2 Neither Catholic nor Protestant.

faeries. Emma Wilby[3] draws a very convincing parallel between the request for blood from the Tungus shaman's spirits and the feeding of blood to the familiars of British Witches. In the Tungus tradition the body and blood of the shaman is even fed to explicitly evil spirits during his initiation ordeal. These experiences of shamans with evil spirits of disease, involve being eaten by the forces of destruction and then peeled back to their bones, a horrifying experience which nonetheless gives them special insight into the nature of curing things caused by these same spirits.

In Britain blood was dropped into vessels or given directly to familiars for jobs well done. Even if one of those imps *was* imagined to be a demon how would this be any different to the way shamans in other cultures would feed, appease and learn to eventually trick or control the spirits of disease and death?

As Wilby put it:

> *"Just as the English witch believed that allowing the animal familiar to consume her blood gave her access to the spirit's magical powers, many North American and Siberian shamans believe that in order to gain access to the supernatural power they must allow themselves to be bodily consumed or 'spirit hardened'."*[4]

Were these demons that might bodily consume the Witch and also grant her power different in any fundamental way from faeries? We have heard above that some types of faeries were well capable of consuming people or drawing off their vitality and about illnesses simply known as "the fairy." The answer seemed to depend on whether or not you were a Witch (or an initiate, someone with a faerie patron, but who may not have identified as one for obvious reasons) or whether you were normal lay folk. One of Evans-Wentz's faerie informants touches on the matter of being consumed by faeries:

3 Wilby, *Cunning Folk*, 144.
4 *Ibid.*

"My father lived two mile from here, where there were plenty of the gentle folk. In olden times they used to take young folks and keep them and draw all the life out of their bodies." [5]

Like poor Grace in the Cornish abduction story these unaware young folks were stolen and used to feed faeries in some way. With Witches or faerie magicians this concept of an energy exchange takes on a different manifestation, one that empowers the human partner. Here you start to see the results of human pacts, marriages or agreements with faeries. Like True Thomas who had a powerful faerie patron, the returns on engaging with faeries are only there for the initiate, everyone else is potentially damaged by the experience, or even lost. This fact remains exactly the same whether the spirit is called a demon and worked with in a Goetic circle, or a faerie worked with at crossroads or standing stones, except for the fact the Church wanted people to believe that all spirits were demons, and that such pacts were always a bad deal for the human.

The deeper strata of the belief system give away a very different story, one that Wilby picks up on quite clearly in the following quote. Talking about the comparison between English Witches feeding blood to familiars and being eaten by disease spirits in shamanic traditions she says:

"Taken together as a whole, these aspects of shamanism strongly suggest that early modern beliefs concerning the giving of blood as part of compact with demon familiars or faeries were rooted in this bedrock of ancient belief concerning the process of interchange between the physical body of the human and the supernatural power of the spirits." [6]

The folklore of the Leannan Sidhe and even to some extent the Gancanagh or Love Talker, both from Ireland, preserve what this

5 *Ibid*, 76.
6 *Ibid*, 145.

process of interchange was all about. In the above case life force was exchanged, often during the sexual act in return for inspiration. Of course this idea that a pact with the (or a) devil can result in inspiration, artistry or skill has found its way all the way down to modern times where some musical greats are still rumoured to have sold their soul at the crossroads for their skill.

In earlier times soul wasn't a singular finite entity, it was possible to speak about giving soul to something in return for spirit. Soul is vitality, spirit is consciousness. The human sells, or more properly exchanges, their soul essence to the demon, who gives them heightened enhanced consciousness and skill in return.

FAERIE DOCTORS AND MAGICIANS

"You, your eyes, your ears are elsewhere; you are a seer and a hearer of the lower regions; you perceive the floating images and discern the hollow sounds of the people of the manes; or live, literally, among them. What am I saying? Under the form and appearance of a man of today you are in reality one of them, ascended to the day and reincarnated."[1]

—Professor Anat`ole Le Braz

The above is not a modern declaration made by some adherent of the so-called Otherkin community, as you can probably tell by its advanced literacy, but a quote from a Breton scholar from 1909 expressing a sentiment about a gifted friend Evan-Wentz believed embodied Breton lore regarding rebirth and the interaction of human seers with the fae.

Despite the hefty contemporary misuse, misappropriation and misunderstanding of this concept Professor Le Braz's quote very distinctly outlines the beliefs of people in Celtic-speaking countries, but also elsewhere in Europe, held until quite recently in regards to Faerie Doctors and magicians.

As much as modern takes on the concept may make many of us cringe, the truth remains that Faerie Doctors weren't always called Faerie Doctors or Faerie Magicians, they were sometimes just called faeries. The *Donas de Fuera* (meaning: ladies of the outside) was the Sicilian name for faeries, but also for the ladies who went with them to Benevento. These human *Donas de Fuera* were originally attractive to their less corporeal cousins because of their sweet blood, suggesting both

1 Evans-Wentz, 313.

a kind of Mark that is visible to spirits and a furthering of the narrative of consumption of human fluids by spirits, as suggested by tasting the human's blood.

This concept of people who were later tried as Witches with sweet blood making them a kind of manifest "woman of the outside" can also be connected with witchblood, the notion that they carry the blood of certain individuals who were Otherwise. This genealogy of witchblood is in some way, whether believed mythically or actually, the bloodline of Faerie and the house of fallen angels.

In the case of Faerie Doctors and women of the outside, unlike maras who were such a part of the European and Jewish imaginal life that they virtually created the frightening attributes of the Witch, human faeries seemed to have been allowed to flourish in society despite their Otherness and to have offered something valuable to their community. Unlike today where characteristics once deemed fae and special would doubtlessly see you heavily medicated, there was a tangible place for such individuals as recently as the late nineteenth century.

Lady Wilde's source material on Faerie Doctors is some of our best evidence for this, and whilst its sometimes considered a doubtful source by scholars, if one cross-culturally compares it to Greek, Serbian and Albanian data, accounts from Brittany and even the grimoire material we can see a number of suggestive parallels. In Eva Pocs's work we hear of faerie magicians that:

> *"...during their curing practice, make contact with their fairy patronesses, can conjure them up in 'fairy time', in fairy places or by symbolically setting up the fairy otherworld at a crossroads, under fairy trees, by drawing reverse circles, etc... An Albanian woman healer takes her patient to a deserted place, makes him or her dress in white, kneels down in the middle of a previously drawn circle, and welcomes the fairies.*

They will then wait in perfect silence, while the woman watches for secret signs." [2]

Lady Wilde describes the Faerie Doctor's practice thus:

"After prayer he takes a dish of pure water and sets it by the fire, then kneeling down he puts the three hazel rods he had marked into the fire, and leaves them there till they are burned black as charcoal... After this he draws a circle on the floor with the end of one of the burned sticks, within which circle he stands, the dish of pure water beside him. He looks for signs in the water using the hazel sticks." [3]

There are also further parallels with Lady Wilde's report we will discuss more when we cover "Faeries and the Grimoire Tradition." Additionally we can observe a kind of faerie logic attached to this report of Doctoring, such as that you aren't to pay for the actual Faerie Doctoring itself, as the faeries hate being paid in coin and will leave in offense. Eva Pocs' material on faerie healing reports that offenses are often linked to locations where wrong doing was done by accident, Lady Wilde also often notes the harms healed by a Faerie Doctor are usually done by faeries, either from their darts or getting in the way of the blast when the Host is on the move. Both some aspects of the form of the ritual, the interest in putting faeries inside a circle, a practice also mirrored in Reginald Scot's invocation of the faerie Sibylla which we will explore later, but most importantly the internal logic of the procedure stands up to scrutiny.

There are other figures that stand out as Faerie Doctors even if they might not have used that name for themselves. Anne Jefferies, a Cornish woman whose connection with the faeries is well known.

"Anne said that she had been in the arbour knitting when she heard a noise in the bushes, then six tiny men appeared, all dressed completely

2 Pocs, *Fairies and Witches*, 49.

3 Lady Wilde, *Legends, Charms and Superstitions of Ireland*, (Morrisville: Samhain Song Press, 2008), 225.

in green, with unusually bright eyes. The leader of the fairy group, who had a red feather in his cap, spoke to her lovingly and then jumped onto her palm, which she placed on her lap. The little man then climbed up her body and began kissing her neck, which she apparently enjoyed. He then called his five companions who swarmed all over her body kissing her until one of them put his hands over her eyes and she felt a sharp pricking sensation, and everything went dark.

Anne was then lifted up into the air and carried off. When she was set down again she heard someone say 'Tear! tear!' and her eyes were opened. The girl found herself in a paradisiacal land of temples, palaces, gardens, lakes and brightly-coloured singing birds. The richly adorned people who lived in this magical land were human-sized and spent their time dancing and playing, and Anne herself was treated like royalty. She again met her fairy friend with the red feather in his cap, but whilst they were alone together his five companions arrived accompanied by an angry mob. In the ensuing struggle her fairy lover was wounded trying to protect her and the same individual who had blinded her before did so again. Anne was once more taken up into the air, this time with a great humming noise, and finally found herself back on the ground in the arbour." [4]

Anne's abduction and likely erotic connection with the fae left her with healing abilities so strong that she was able to cure simply via the laying on of hands or stroking the afflicted space. Just like the Irish Faerie Doctor she was believed to know the identity of those she would heal before they even arrived to consult her. Like the famous mystics of many other schools of spirituality Anne was believed to no longer require human food.

She never allowed a moonlight night to pass without going down into the valley, and walking against the stream, singing "Moon shines bright, waters run clear, I am here, but where's my fairy dear?" But in contra-

4 Robert Hunt, "Anne Jefferies and the Fairies," in *Popular Romances of the West of England*, (London: Forgotten Books, 2008).

diction to the false dichotomy between Faerie Doctors and Witches her familiars were well capable of doing harm. Despite Anne's reputation as a healer she was also capable of sending a faerie to hurt the leg of someone who had angered her. It's not recorded whether Anne Jeffries used her faerie-given magic to heal problems caused by faeries but Margaret Stothold was certainly an "unwitcher" who removed supernatural problems in a way greatly redolent of spiritual healers who might be called shamans elsewhere in the world.

The figure of the sucking doctor is very well known in numerous shamanic cultures but Margaret Stothard was practicing an almost identical faerie related practice in Northumbria England in the 1600s. Stothard was alleged to have put her mouth over the sick child's mouth and making such "chirping" and "sucking" noises "that the mother of the said child thought that she had sucked the heart out of it and was sore affrighted." The child however recovered. This sucking out of the malignancy is also suggestive of a partial transformation into an animal familiar during the operation, judging from the report of chirping noises.[5]

Although this sucking doctor procedure is not often reported in the British Isles the process of transferring illness from one body to another is quite common. A cunning woman named Mistress Pepper used suckling infants to draw out a malignancy.[6] Joan Guppy was an expert in treating the condition that she called the "black fairy," which was a particular type of bewitchment, that once again links back to the idea of faeries that come in different colours and cause illness. This example shows a cunning woman who was popularly interpreted as a Witch and even had blood drawn above the breath in an attempt to take her sorcerous virtue, treating an ailment believed to originate with some kind of faerie-bewitchment.

5 Wilby, 36.
6 Diane Purkiss, *The Witch in History: Early Modern and Twentieth-Century Representations*, (Abington: Routledge, 1996) 123.

Guppy was not the only practicing healer called a Witch who dealt with faerie-related illness.

Another magical practitioner Jenkyn Pereson was also known to have been called in to treat "the fairy." Her doctoring ran as such: The mother of the sick child was to send two people to fetch some south running water from a stream or river, these two could not speak on the way (again we encounter the faerie magic prohibition on speaking). The child would be washed in the south-running water and its shirt also. The shirt needed to be hung on a hedge (a traditional boundary between our world and that of the wild forest where the faeries rule) and in the morning it would be gone and the child cured.[7]

Purkiss notes that the disease of "the fairy" is meant to come from wild nature and the ritual with the running water sends it back again. This is much like how Lady Wilde reports the blast water being poured over the head of the afflicted and them being made to drink the ashes from the very hazel wood staves that predicted their fairy ailment in the first place, and Eva Pocs testimony about returning to the place the faerie illness happened among the eastern European contingency. Lady Wilde also says the healers themselves lived for a while in Faerie before they came back and then were considered Faerie Doctors. We find a similar prohibition on speaking in Lady Wilde's material, and of not allowing the crystal ball used to make the water to be out after dark.

Things Put in, Things Taken Out

> *"The transitory death of those abducted into an alternative existence was, in one sense, an initiation. Being there meant belonging there... These initiations had a common negative variant whereby the victims returned from the Otherworld devastated or sick, and bringing illness instead of knowledge. In such cases, initiation was incomplete in that symbolic death had not been followed by rebirth."*

7 *Ibid*, 124.

Says Eva Pocs in *Between the Living and the Dead.* The idea that associating faeries and Witches with the dead related to an initiatory phase of the faerie encounter makes sense of why faeries are often confused with the dead, and why Witches are relentlessly associated with death. The Witch as poisoner of the well and bringer of disease is much like the apples of the Underworld upon which the Queen of Elphame claims "all the plagues of hell are upon," which could even be taken literally as diseases.

There is a risk in passing through the realm of the dead to get to the Crooked Path, there is a risk of an incomplete initiation that brings back demons of madness and disease instead of healing powers. For this reason many of the motifs of Witchcraft have to do with initiatory death and the Underworld, even though it is as much about the realm of Faerie as it is about the world of the dead. What we see in Witchcraft are images of blackness, skulls, bones, poisons and narcotic ointments, curses, animalistic transformations, cannibalism, perverse sex, and sorcerous tortures. This is all the uninitiated or partly initiated ever get to see. Our faerie light, the cunning fire, is hidden from view, but hidden in plain sight.

Initiation in other shamanic cultures involves things like dismemberment, eating of the flesh and blood by demonic entities and heating and forging symbolism. Eva Pocs talks about the way something was often removed or put in during a Witch's initiation in the Balkans.[8] She says the removal of a bone or even the little finger was required in some parts of Europe. Just as Witches sucked illnesses or fairy darts out in the British Isles so did other Witches remove a bone from the body of an initiate, scratch them and take their blood for a pact or take something else from them that would serve as a relic of their personal power. The procedures of healing and the processes of induction into the cult resonate profoundly, and initiation can be seen as a form of drastic healing.

8 Pocs, *Between the Living*, 83.

Things may also be inserted into people's bodies, both by faeries and Witches. You can see in the following charm that way back since the dark ages both faeries and Witches have been linked together in the practice of throwing elf shot or "witch shot" as it was also called.

The tenth century metrical charm "Against A Sudden Stitch" (*Wið færstice*) offers remedy against sudden pain (such as rheumatism) caused by projectiles of either *ése*, *ylfe* or Witches (*gif hit wære esa gescot oððe hit wære ylfa gescot oððe hit wære hægtessan gescot* "be it Ése-shot or elf-shot or witch-shot."[9]

This brings to mind the physical ways in which Witches are renowned for putting things in people, such as pins of blackthorn into the heart of a poppet doll. The bewitched were sometimes seen to vomit up pins, and the tangled hair of the one who had hexed them. In this way both for good or ill, Witches and faeries were united in being held responsible for either removing strange body parts like an extra unnoticed bone, or instead inserting magical objects into the body of either a victim or potential initiate. As we have seen, when it comes to the realm of Faerie and humans the only difference between victim and initiate is a strong familiar spirit who acts as a kind of bridge and guide between the worlds.

Eva Pocs[10] gives an account of how death and resurrection experiences were part of becoming known as a woman or man of Faerie. Lady Wilde also spoke how Irish Faerie Doctors often acquired their trade through having spent time in Faerie following abduction. Pocs tells us in her *Fairies and Witches at the Boundary of South-Eastern and Central Europe* that the living ones, as in people who had not passed through the initiation trauma, were not permitted to gaze upon the Otherworld in Balkan traditions. But the light-shadowed people who were either faerie already, or who had been taken away and "changed"

9 Albert C. Bough and Kemp Malone, *The Literary History of England: Vol 1: The Middle Ages* (to 1500), (Abington: Routledge, 2003), 38.
10 Pocs, *Between the Living*, 48.

were allowed to know it. The light-shadow was perceived as an aura around the person's head like a halo.

"As far as 'transitory death' and temporary soul journeys are concerned, they, according to several beliefs, mean initiation; if someone has ever looked into that other world,—eg. Has seen the fairies who must not be seen by a living person,—from that time on he/she is considered initiated."[11] Or as another account from the area puts it: *"The faeries killed him but revived him, giving him power."*

During these abductions the *iele* takes out a piece of bone and replaces it with a stake or wheel spoke. One year later in the same location they put back the removed bone. This trope of something being removed or inserted into the body of the initiate is found in many shamanic cultures throughout the world. In some cases the shaman is believe to be in possession of an extra bone that must be counted by the spirits.

These faerie motifs of abduction, initiatory death and repatriation into the community with altered status, and the insertion or removal of body parts and blood are all clues to better understanding how Witchcraft flows forth from the Faerie Faith. Eva Pocs points out the following similarities. Just like faeries:

> *"The witch, for instance, flies in the form of a crow or a whirlwind, sits in a swallows nest, where she seems to sometimes be little, sometimes big, and sometimes disappears, she walks on the top of trees as quickly as the wind; or the whole witch company 'transforms into crows and alights on willows'. They travel in green coaches on the top of the trees..."*[12]

Of course this close connection between the Faerie Faith and Witches was muddied by persecution of the Craft. The faerie practices were increasingly assimilated into the household and moved away

11 Pocs, *Fairies and Witches*, 42.
12 Ibid, 36.

from the wilderness, with Sicilian Fairie Witches going from house to house, rather than out into the forest. Meanwhile Witchcraft was given all of the dangerous Otherwise characteristics, the ones so crucial to initiation that were slowly being stripped from the faerie narrative. In the process the realm of Faerie was losing its teeth and claws, and Witchcraft was being vilified almost out of existence.

All of the negative or dark attributes of the faeries, which were originally part of their primordial ambivalence, were gradually settled on Witches. Cunning practices became strongly associated with Faerie, and Witchcraft with demons, even though originally it is almost impossible to make this distinction in a meaningful way. In this way most forgot that Witches serve with the right hand as surely as they blight with the left, a characteristic shared with the fées of Brittany. Faeries throw darts and blast crops as surely as they bestow blessings and cure the diseases they cause.

Once faeries, and the human practitioners of magic who had faeries for familiars, both shared in those characteristics, including the ones that do mankind good, and those that do mankind ill. Faeries, and the Witchcraft that grows forth from it into the human side of the hedge, carry with them all the plagues and poisons of the Earth, and also the potential inoculation and medicine that affects every cure.

Only those who have passed through the world of the dead are offered access to the Third Path. Only he who has walked that path and come back wearing the virid doublet of Faerie and learned to keep silent, can now come back and eat of the fruit upon which all of the plagues of Hell alight to find the secret of their cure. In the Underworld, the Tree of Knowledge and the Tree of Life and Death are the same tree.

Even in Britain where we don't find the bone taking motif and only occasionally see an explicit spiritual death followed by resurrection, we do find the passing of the breath, where a Witch's shadow is able to enter someone else, giving them soul, through the breath and mouth, or illnesses is sucked away with the mouth. Witch teats also allow something to be sucked away as a form of nourishment to the familiar, who also sometimes drank the Witch's blood drops. Familiars were sometimes put in another person by blowing them into someone's mouth and we may conjecture during sexual encounters with faerie beings where vital force was being taken out and inspiration put in.

The relationship between faeries and Witches is as much peppered in the language of consumption and assimilation through eating as it is in sexual expression. Witches and their familiars *live off each other*, eat of one another. Here do we perhaps find the origins of the "eat of me" theme behind the Housel or Red Meal. Where some Witches consume the body and blood of their Devil and his Dame, just as the Christians consume Jesus Christ.

In this natural religiosity of consumption and mutual nourishment we see the foreshadowing of all such edible sacraments. The spirit world is understood to enjoy blood. As early as the 13th century in Ireland Alice Kyteler sacrificed a black cock at the crossroads to the spirit Robin Artisson, her spirit lover and familiar—himself a man of Faerie, a dweller at crossroads.

Jeffrey Burton Russell says of Robin Artisson: *"As much like a faerie as a witch's familiar, Robin appeared in a number of shapes, a cat, a shaggy dog or an Ethiopian."*[13]

Alice was also said to gamble about on a salve-covered broom (no talk of flying on it only of putting ointment on it mounting it and moving around) so perhaps something was introduced into her body via the salve. Even if the straddling of the broom does not suggest intimate applications of the unguent, flying ointments, regardless of how they are administered are always an herbal formula given to them from outside the hedge, which is put into the body via the pores of the skin.

13 Jeffrey Burton Russell, *Witchcraft in the Middle Ages*, (Ithaca: Cornell University Press, 1984) 191.

Another Witchcraft tradition, prominent mainly in Britain that involves taking something out, is the practice of taking blood above the breath. This procedure, where one suspected of bewitching someone was attacked and scratched badly enough to make blood flow, usually above the nose and mouth, was believed to neutralize their power for a time.

We can conjecture that the reason has to do with the way power or Virtue is considered to be stored in blood and breath and is connected via an invisible thread to the power of the familiar spirit nourished by these two things. The Witch's power and virtue is expected to leak out in great glut in blood above the breath because so much power lives in the skull. Drawing the blood above the breath can be seen as an attack on the Witchs familiar as well as herself. It is quite illuminating to look closely at the scratching attack on Joan Guppy, whom we have mentioned earlier in relation to Faerie Doctoring.

"They scratched her face with overgrown brambles, saying that Guppy 'was a witch and they came for the blood … and they would have it and her life also before they left her."[14] Not just blood but *"the blood"* —witchblood. This statement is reminiscent of the sweet blood faerie Witches were believed to have in Sicily. We can conjecture that when they say they came for the blood and would have "her life" before they left, what they actually meant was her soul force or magical virtue, as they didn't actually kill her. Witchblood, sweet blood, the power that holds a tenuous thread, like a bridge made of one hair, between this world and the paradise of Elphame—a thread that must cross the abyss of Hell and is likewise just as capable of unleashing it.

14 G.J Davies, Tochying *Witchcrafte and Sorcerye*, (Dorset: Dorset Records Society, 1985) 27.

THE FAERIE AS WITCH'S FAMILIAR

Under the earth there exists a delicious place, the dwelling of witches, where all things abound, especially milk and honey, which run in abundant rivers."

—Basque tradition from Ataún

The Witch, like the faerie, was a feared bringer of contamination, and a divine healer bringing salve from a land flowing with milk and honey. It is this very ambiguity that originally made faeries and Witches both so unpredictable and fearful to the average hedge-bound mind. The process of removing this ambiguity, infantizing faeries and making Witches into kind herb wives, has been the process of defanging and declawing the Otherness, a breaking up of a whole. It does nothing to readdress the imbalance created when Witchcraft was made the black repository of all undesirable faerie characteristics, but instead damages both sides of the divide it creates. Of course it is not actually possible to declaw the Otherworld, we only ever neuter our own awareness of it.

In Italy the mistress of the magic witch mountain, flowing with milk and honey, was called "wise Sibillia." It was said the ancient sibyl of mount Cumae had taken refuge in a cave at the crest of the Appenines. In *Reductorium Morale* (c. 1360) Pietro Bersuire wrote about her Underworld paradise entered through a grotto in the mountains of Norcia, a region famed for its Witches. Nearby was a magical lake fed by water from a cavern. Whoever stayed longer than a year could no longer leave, but remained deathless and ageless, feasting in abundance, revelry, and voluptuous delights.

Sibillia was regarded as Goddess of the Witches. In Ferrara people said "wise Sibillia" led the cavalcade of Witches in their flight. At the end of their feasts, she would touch all the bottles and baskets with her wand, and they would quickly refill with wine and bread. They would then gather the animal bones into their skins, and at the faerie wand's touch, the animals recovered their flesh and returned to life.

This archaic-sounding tradition of a faerie woman inside a mountain hitting dead animal bones and reanimating them is suggestive of the themes of initiation. Just as the faerie Witch's bones are taken or counted and put back in, and the Witch is resurrected from a death-like sleep where they have journeyed beyond the grave, so the animal's bones recover from death due to faerie magic.

But true to the archaic ambivalence we've discussed above, Sibylla is not only associated with golden wands and beautiful paradises, but with a half-serpent body and ordeals that involve being covered in snakes and even having to have sexual intercourse with them. No matter what country the narratives of faerie come from there is never any making it to the land of milk and honey without a harrowing of hellish proportions first, but in some areas the faerie creatures contain more obviously archaic mixed natures. Sibillia is one of these beings.

We will encounter Sibillian traditions of the Craft later in this book, as she appears both in the English Robin Goodfellow faerie traditions as Sib, and as the faerie Sibylla in Reginald Scot's grimoire of faerie magic. From the Sibillian mountain and the Witchcraft associated with it we can see that in Italy Witches and faeries were very closely connected, just as they were elsewhere. The fairy mountain was the place you went to learn your magical arts.

One of the most striking ritual connections between the faerie seer and the Witch in Britain, as opposed to the continental examples, is the "all that lies between these two hands practice," which we find originally in faerie material and later as a British Witchcraft initiation posed in the trial records. As early as Robert Kirk we hear of the faerie seer putting one foot under the foot of the one to be admitted to the secrets of faerie seership and the other on the head whilst looking over the wizard's right shoulder, thus sponsoring them with their own power.[1]

We see a similar ritual repeated in trial records of the Wincanton Coven who supposedly adopted a kneeling version of this posture at their initiations. The woodcut of a Witch in this position is drawn from Joseph Glanvill's *Saducismus Triumphatus*. But the traditions of Witchcraft and faerie were often quite chronologically parallel rather than one developing off another, as Kirk admits to the fact that the posture has an "ill appearance" which implies the surrender of what is between the hands, suggesting that he already knows that such postures might be used in relation to the Devil.

We have already said that Robin Artisson, whom Alice Kyteler was devoted to, was a demon by the estimations of the times but most likely also a kind of faerie. In many cases the true "religion" of Witches, if they could be said to have religious feelings that come through to us from the records, is toward their familiar spirit, who was sometimes but not always associated with *the* Devil when they were probably often *a* devil.

The Witch's faerie familiars present us with a scene of great variety. The faerie Witch Bessie Dunlop seems to have maintained a business-like platonic relationship with her faerie familiar Tom.[2] John Walsh of Dorset mentions working with faeries as though going out to the faerie mounds were a natural part of Witchcraft, but he never mentions a deep bond with any of them.[3]

But there are many other than Alice and her Robin who do, such as Isobel Gowdie's sexual passion with her "devil" and Andro Man's ongoing relationship with his Faerie Queen and almost worship for

1 Kirk, 57.

2 When asked in item 16 of her trial if she had carnal relations with Tom she replied indignantly to the contrary. Transcription Wilby, *Cunning Folk*, xiv.

3 *Ibid*, 79.

Christsonday who sounds angel-like. Ann Jeffries not only experienced romantic love with her faerie man but was bravely defended by him when she was threatened and Thomas the Rhymer was treated with affection by his Faerie Queen at the very least.

Alison Peirson, also a faerie Witch, had an almost religious devotion to a deceased cunning man who now lived among the faeries, one William Simpson, who she said protected her from the worst intensities of the coming and going of her faerie visions by warning her when they were afoot.[4] And Isobel Haldane, a Scottish Witch, acquired her powers after she was saved from an unwanted faerie abduction by "he that protected me from the faerie folk,"[5] who was himself a faerie.

In this way a traditional abduction and blighting narrative was transformed through the agency of "he who protected me" into an initiatory ordeal from which the person emerged a Witch of power. Her devotion to "he who protected me" was no doubt almost religious in its intensity. Yet despite the obvious correlation between Witches and faerie familiars those intent on painting Witches as pure evil were loath to associate them with faerie seers. Even King James with his almost pathological fear of Witches claimed in his *Demonologie* that "those people whom spirits (faeries) have carried away and informed they were thought by the common folk to be the soniest [wisest] and best of life."

Emma Wilby has taken note of this religiosity that Witches often felt towards their faerie familiars:

> *"[The witch] Alice Nokes (1579) claimed, when reprimanded before a church congregation, that 'she cared for none of them all as long as Tom (her familiar) held by her side.'; … an unnamed Cambridgeshire witch (1653), being 'on the point of execution… declined to renounce the faithful friend of threescore years (that is, her demon familiar) and 'died in her obstinacy.'"*[6]

4 *Ibid*, 237.
5 *Ibid*, 115.
6 *Ibid*, 242.

If there could be said to be an observable religious impulse behind historical Witchcraft it is not the Pagan fertility religion of early Wiccan and Neopagan projections, it is the animistic faith *shared* with faeries, and sometimes the worship of particular powerful faeries. It is a religious faith both *in* faeries and the knowledge, shared with faeries and perhaps *given* by them, that the stars and all things in life have spirits in them from the largest to the smallest and many microcosms are in each with everything moving forever in cycles. The Faith that there is an inalienable sanctity in the relationships between those that mutually nourish each other, including the relationship between a Witch and familiar spirit.

Other examples of the theme of mutual nourishment can be found in relation to the powerful hobman and witch-devil, Robin. We have already mentioned a "Robin" familiar in relation to Alice Kyteler and her Robin Artisson but this name for the witch-devil reoccurs elsewhere, including in the Robin Goodfellow story and in Somerset during the trial of the Wincanton Coven.[7]

The "Robin" of the Wincanton Coven appeared to the principle Witch ten years before the trial as a handsome man, and later as a black dog. He promised her money and pleasure in this life if she would provide him with some of her blood that he might suck it, thus giving her soul (as in virtue rather than spirit) to him and observe his laws. This she did, pricking the fourth finger of her right hand, between the middle and upper joints. He gave her a magical sixpence in return and vanished.

Although the Wincanton trial[8] involves plenty of *maleficium* and they don't directly make references to faeries, interpreting their "Robin" as a faerie man, much like Robin Artisson, has other support within the evidence. The Wincanton Coven were those who claimed

7 This will be a familiar fact to anyone who has read Margaret Murray's work, which though it went far beyond the reaches of evidence on many points certainly picked up on the importance of the name Robin.

8 Please see Joseph Glanvill's earlier mentioned *Saducismus Triumphatus* for more information on the Wincanton Witches.

their initiation involved placing everything between their two hands and thus mimicking the logic, if not the exact posture, of the faerie seer position. After her pact with this mysterious man Elizabeth Styles was fed "bread and wine," much like the sacrament Thomas the Rhymer engages in.

This simple act might seem common enough but this repast that we've previously called the host also carries echoes of the "faerie food." The provision of food by faeries is given as a sign of great love from a faerie man to a woman he has impregnated. One very potent story to this effect is that of the birth of Robin Goodfellow, fathered by the Faerie King Oberon (or Obreon in older sources) upon a mortal woman. As a sign of his love for the human mother of his child he continuously feeds her. Mutton, lamb, pheasant, woodcock, partridge, quail, a never-ending supply of food is laid before Robin Goodfellow's mother by her faerie lover. He also provided her with fine wines of many types.

The Wincanton Coven received very similar faerie food from their Robin, including a wide variety of meats and fine wine they discuss frequently, presumably because such high quality victuals would usually have been far out of their price range. At their Sabbats the Coven's "devil" Robin, "the man in black," would "play on a pipe or cittern" and they danced. This image of Witches dancing with a man called Robin whilst music plays is very evocative of the famous image of Robin Goodfellow, a book poster from the 1600s called "Robin Goodfellow and his mad japes" and further suggests we consider these "Robins" to be the same powerful faerie patron.

This pattern of a faerie man piping for dancing Witches is also seen quite vividly in James Hogg's poem *The Witch of Fife*, where Hogg writes this particularly evocative piece of poetry about the experience of a Witch (1835) which I have transcribed out of Scots English and into standard English for ease of reading.

"And then we came to Lommond Height
So lightly we touched down;
And we drank from the horns that never grew,
The beer that was never brewed.

Then up there rose a wee wee man
From beneath the moss-grey stone;
His face was wan like cauliflower
For he had neither blood nor bone.

He set a reed-pipe up to his mouth
And played it bonnily
Till the grey curlew and the black cock flew
To listen to his melody."

He then speaks of how all the animals answered the faerie man's piping and faerie, Witch and animal dance until dawn[9]. Later in the story (which she is relating to her husband) they fly on their hemlock as far as Lapland, were they find the local faeries all in array, for the "geni of the north" were keeping their holiday. Hogg then writes:

"The warlock men and the weird women
And the fays of the wood and steep,
And the phantom hunters all were there,
And the mermaids of the deep."

Here we see faeries, Witches/Warlocks, the phantom hunters of the Wild Hunt and mermaids linked together in a Sabbat narrative, which

9 . It is worth noting that animals also sit up to attention in relation to the dancing and piping on the Robin Goodfellow poster. This suggests the figure of the Devil's piper is associated with animal charming in a way that brings to mind such figures as the Pied Piper of Hamlin. Hogg mentions the response of the animals and also the Word, a reference to the Horseman's Word which further links to animal charming.

is so explicitly a Sabbat narrative that it involves the Witches ending up in the arms of the Warlock men, but like many faerie Sabbats no diabolism occurs. Although they do learn how to "throw the faerie stroke," but here it is unequivocal that Witches are learning their skills from faeries who are not labeled demons.

If we consider these links between the "Devil's piper" or the "Devil as piper" as a faerie man, then the figure of Robin Goodfellow is strongly suggested by Style's "Robin." What we have in the form of Robin Goodfellow, or Puck, is a particular faerie figure who is connected over a wide area with teaching, piping or having an off-sider who pipes for Witches, and even possibly animal charming.

Just as there was a Puck (the other name for Robin Goodfellow), there was a Poucca of Wales, a Puca of Ireland and a Bucca of Cornwall, the alternative "Robin" as the name of a prominent faerie man might have been equally widespread in Britain and Ireland. Even the Welsh prophet and conjure man Black Robin (Robin Dhu) exhibits some Puck-like qualities suggesting he may be connected with this figure. As of course does the English Robin Hood with his leveling trickster qualities and his almost exclusive Mary worship. If Robin is indeed the name for one well-known tutelary faerie who teaches Witches—not just the "white" ones—then the link between faerie familiars and the genesis of Witchcraft is quite explicit.

Given how clearly we can see British and Irish Witches learning their skills from faeries, it must have been very familiar to our forebears when they heard the "Watchers" had been the ones to teach Witchcraft to mankind. It seems increasingly obvious why the connection between faeries and fallen angels would have been forged and remained strong in Old Craft traditions, long after the threat of church persecution diminished. Dual faith observance, it seems, may have been about more than hiding the Craft in plain sight, but also to do with intrinsic intersections between certain aspects of the two stories, particularly between the Faerie Faith and some of the apocryphal material.

Given that the earliest testimony about a deep committed relationship with a familiar is Alice Kyteler's "demon worship" of Robin Artisson, it might behoove us to more deeply explore demonology and whether we find any faerie-like characteristics in prominent demons. We have already noted earlier that Reginald Scot's work draws together both faerie beings and demons without really specifying too much difference between the two. Like the powerful hobman Robin/Puck, the faerie woman Sibylla mentioned by Scot or as Sib by Shakespeare, lives inside a mountain teaching Witches all the way over in Italy and yet also emerges in England and Scotland. Some faerie entities were so powerful that they had numerous Witch familiars and were linked to more than one location. Here the line between "faerie" and "God" or "Goddess" becomes very blurred. But in the Faerie Faith, which seems to display a continuous sliding scale of power, rather than clear distinctions between human, faerie and God, this is not to be thought unusual.

The Testament of St Cyprian the Mage by Jake Stratton-Kent discusses how the Goetic tradition and its demon-teeming grimoires are influenced by Witchcraft and folkore relating to the Wild Hunt. His reference to the Hunt is particularly interesting after Hogg's poem and his phantom riders participating in the Witch's Sabbat.

There are also many famous witching animals like toads, owls and black dogs among the forms the grimoire demons take and plenty of references to objects from European folklore, such as the hazel wand. So whilst demonology certainly overwrote the witchcraft narrative in certain ways, the realm of faerie and folk sorcery also colonised demonology in return, as Paul Carus explored in his *History of the Devil*, quoted above. Many of the darker faerie attributes—those connected with the Underworld, dark elf, Wild Hunt, nightmare or winter hag figures—became attached to demons and then back into Witchcraft.

The picture that begins to emerge for the intuitive observer is not a history with a universal "white sabbat," associated with faeries and full of goodness and light, overcome later by a "black sabbat" imposed from above via demonology and persecution. What we see instead is the suggestion, the smallest echo, of an early Faerie Faith replete with all the characteristics of both, layered on by emerging demonology that was itself already colonized by folkloric sources. It seems as if the so-called "white sabbat" of faerie magicians that Henningsen postulates is actually just a different layer of Otherworldly experience, the "black demonic sabbat" having its place in relation to initiatory ordeals in particular and the dark elf beings who preside over such powers.

FAERIE CULTS

In many parts of Europe it is quite possible to talk about entire "faerie cults." I believe looking more closely at their highly extant formats will help illuminate our understanding of our Witchcraft legacy, especially in relation to the Sabbat.

> *"...the otherworldly soul battles of the groups of initiated shamanistic wizards who were 'taken away' by animal guardian spirits... who fought against werewolf demons and against the magicians of the neighbouring community as well as the fairy groups and those whom they 'carried away' to their other world, were important antecedents of the images of witch feasts and witch companies."*[1]

In other words (because Pocs is capable of very long sentences) she believes the benandanti, taltos, and faerie magicians fighting for their community are important ancestors of the Witch's Sabbat. However, we need not assume all the material we class as benevolent is pre-Inquisition coming from faerie folklore, and that everything dark was brought in by the persecution.

Faeries come in forms quite dreadful such as pressers/mares, red cap goblins bathing their hats in fresh human blood, and the life-draining vampiric half-animal creatures of the highlands. If Witches were taught their craft by faeries (who are linked with dual-faith observance by an interpretation of faeries as Watchers), it would seem to follow that Witchcraft would be just as many-shaded concerning moral ambivalence as faeries. It might also follow that the Witchcraft of an area would be deeply shaded by the character of the faerie courts or tribes that have residence there. This would mean specific traditional craft systems would be by nature an outgrowth of their immediate environment, possessing diverse characteristics that reflect the land they came from.

1 Pocs, *Fairies and Witches*, 61-62.

Despite this it is no surprise that the benevolent side of faerie is given more airtime after Witchcraft became a hunted practice, because sanitizing the realm of faerie was the only way to preserve its practices. Nor should this focus be seen as *entirely* a post-persecution touch, done to become more acceptable. Humans of Europe would have always wanted to emphasize warmth and longer summers for harvests and entered into pacts with faeries of darkness and winter with far more trepidation than those of the Shining Courts for this reason.

Most Europeans even in temperate zones were far more likely to die of cold than heat exhaustion, not to mention the dangers of famine that could follow inclement weather before harvest was complete. But before we return to this idea that both the faerie secret societies of Europe and the diabolized Sabbat of those styled "witches" BOTH have their origin in indigenous European faerie beliefs, we cannot ignore the Sicilian Witch trials.

The Sicilian example is the most immediately relevant to our subject matter, as they are often thought of as "The Sicilian Faerie Witches" and thus there are enough of them for their behavior to be considered cultish.

> *"Quaestio de Strigibus (Venice 1525) describes a witches Sabbath in the province of Ferrara that is presided over by Domina Cursus, whom the witches also call 'The Wise Sybil. During the nightly meetings that are held twice a week on the bank of the River Jordan. The Wise Sybil tries again and again to fly down to touch the river... for if she can only get her finger in the water she will have power over the whole world. But she never manages it! Here again we find the resemblance to the Madonna Oriente cult from Milan and the fairy cult of Sicily, but a new element has appeared: Domina Cursus demands of her Ferrara witches that they must kill a child once every fortnight, so they run around in the shape of*

cats... where they suck the blood from small children who die a few days later."[2]

This idea of benevolent magic workers gradually "diabolized" is of course a familiar theory to anyone who has read Ginzberg's famous *Ecstasies* or *Night Battles*, a thesis he developed primarily in regard to Benandanti confessions. Matters become complicated though when we consider the folkloric origins of demon narratives. It isn't entirely a replacement of a Pagan narrative with a Christian one, but an overreliance on interpretations that make all spirits into "winter demons" like the mara, the incubi and the red-cap goblin. By attaching demonology to the winter spirits and dark elf creatures the churchmen implicitly associated themselves with everything that European people would find most life-giving. If the Devil was winter and cold, then Christ was clearly summer and life and warmth.

Even in the above quote we can see the evidence of this. Yes, they've got an evil-sounding confession that involves child murder, just what the persecutors are looking for, but in what form do they do this work? As vampiric, cat-changing creatures who leap upon children. The folkloric belief that cats can "suck a child's breath" while they sleep is brought into service, as images of death and darkness already familiar to the population would have been far more accessible and effective. Even when the persecutors were putting on pressure to get negative confessions the accused would have had to answer based on their own idea of evil, their local stories of darkness and winter demons.

The Sicilian faerie trials, despite this gradual change towards diabolism, did not actually turn up any convictions. The Witches told of a beautiful world, full of music and wonder, presided over by a Queen and tolerant of copious sexual intercourse between humans and faeries, but they never suggested maleficium or mentioned a devil figure. For this reason, at that time period and location, they were not convicted of ma-

2 Henningsen, 205.

leficium. Nonetheless, the Sicilian faerie trials did discover evidence of a cult of faerie practice significant in size enough that many faerie Witches would recognize others from their town during the flight to the Faerie.

The mythic images we now associate with Witchcraft, including the Sabbat, owe a lot both to the faerie cults we will speak more of below, and to many of the other types or sides of the faeries, that people might have wished to placate rather than worship and dance for. As we have seen when we spoke of Faerie Doctors, the very faeries that bring the disease heal the disease. This is the essence of the primordial ambivalence of the faerie realm that appears to predate the hard separation of faeries and cunning folk from demons and Witches. If there was separation at all originally it seems to have been one of season or element with a small European prejudice towards the rare warmth and light.

Let us take for example the Rusalia and Calusari festivals of Bulgaria and Romania, as a prominent example of rituals deriving from a faerie cult. In a way these rituals bring together all the dimensions of "Faerie Faith" that we have thus far looked at spread across Europe. What is most evident is the ambivalence of the faeries named rusulka, vile, wili, etc, depending on the region. Throughout the rituals there is confusion or seeming confusion, about whether the intention is to placate and drive away faeries that bring disease, or to encourage faeries because faeries bring fertility.

An example of this is the use of the horse's head on the pole that the calusari dance around. In this part of the world the horse's skull is known to frighten away faeries, as is wormwood and garlic, which are also attached to the pole. The dancers wear white trousers and white tunics, with brightly-coloured ribbons streaming from their hats. Bells are attached to their ankles, and dances include the use of ornate sticks held upright whilst dancing, or pointing at the ground as a prop. The dance itself is highly acrobatic, emphasizing extension and high jumps. Speed, strength and dexterity are all required of the men for this ritual to be successful.[3] This emphasis on male athleticism, virility and weapon-wielding places the calusari dancers in the more spiritually militant, male-focused traditions like that of the Benandanti and Taltos.

It is interesting from a British Witchcraft perspective that "calusari," the name for this particular male mystery translates as "horse men," which is evocative of another all-male order. Like the Horse-men of Britain the calusari were highly secretive. The herbal knowledge and animal charming skills of British horsemen, as well as the single removed toad bone which will flow against the current of a river if cast in the moonlight also suggests faerie features in the Society of the Horseman's Word.

In the Banat region in the nineteenth century the calusari dance was performed by eight *căluceni*, a *ceiuş*, two pipers and a *bloj*, they would begin rehearsals ten days before Whitsuntide. On the eve of the holiday, they went to an isolated spot near a mound separating several properties where they became blood brothers and said the Our Father prayer after the *voivod* had reminded them of what a great sin it was to disobey the custom's commandments.[4] The sharing of blood emerges here as a motif again, similar to the exchange with the Devil that occurs in the Witchcraft initiation or the nourishing of the familiar. The emphasis on secrecy and/or not speaking is also a feature absorbed into Witchcraft from the Faerie Faith. The Moldavian *căluşari* would wear female attire, and wreaths of wormwood and flowers in their hair, speak with a female voice and hide their faces under pieces of white linen, to conceal their identity. This kind of inversion of standard behaviour are strongly suggestive of the "world turned back to front," a feature of faerie lore from all over Europe.

Strict rules had to be obeyed for as long as the dancers were under oath: not to sleep anywhere but under the church eaves, because of the

3 Pocs, *Fairies and Witches*, 61-66.
4 Carmelia Firica, *The Romanian Calus: Symbol of National Identity*, (Bucharest: Spiru Haret University, 2010), 3-5.

belief that they might have been crippled by ghosts if they rested in other places; those who joined the group had to stay for at least nine years and if anyone absconded, they were believed to be tormented by evil spirits and wicked fairies; no living creature was allowed to reveal a dancer's identity, so anyone who ventured to uncover their faces might have been killed under a right granted to the *călușari* by an old rule; when two groups of dancers met they fought and the defeated were to be subjects to the winners for nine years.[5]

The *căluș* performance coincides with the time when the *iele* are most dangerous to humans, when they arm themselves with all sorts of cutting weapons to punish those who do not observe the holiday. In order to overcome their human condition and gain power over the *iele*, power to heal the sickness caused by them, the *călușari* must venture beyond their normal human space. They must face the liminal space by going to the boundaries that separate human habitation from non-human, a trip that differentiates the dancers from other members of the village community, defining them as an esoteric group and in the same ritual category as the "light-shadowed ones" discussed earlier.

The dancer's attitude towards uninhabited places such as mounds, which they surround three times firing a gun and running away, or waters, near which they suddenly turn around to see if they are being chased indicates these are the places where the *iele* are believed to dwell and that the relationship with them is one of both fear and respect.

The custom fulfils several functions:

- The magical transfer of fertility that the *călusări* achieve by casting a spell upon large lumps of salt, which the country people then give to cattle to lick, or upon seeds meant to be sown in the fields, garlic and wormwood later used for healing purposes, a pot with water and coins inside, a horse

5 *Ibid*, 5.

halter, raw wool, all meant to bring prosperity when they are brought back and distributed in the town afterwards.

- Encouraging the marriage of young girls and the symbolic fertilisation of wives performed by their joining in the dance and touching the wooden phallus carried by the Mute, one of the group members.
- Healing people, particularly those "taken" by the iele, achieved through the magical transfer to the sick person of a) the sound soul of a clay pot broken with a stick by the leader of the group, b) a chicken violently killed, or c) a *călusăr* that undergoes a ritual death. Healing is accomplished by virtue of the ground rule that in order to function properly, the community has to recover the one who has been blighted. You can't just let them go, the whole community will suffer if one is left "taken" and not reclaimed. Yet once reclaimed the faerie-touched individual returns with power.
- Preventing children, held in arms by the *călusări* during the performance, from being taken ill, a ritual believed to drive away diseases, especially fever. There is also a general belief that these children will be vigorous and protected against evil spirits.
- Banishing the more aggressive iele through the instrumentality of clubs, wooden swords, bows and arrows and apotropaic plants, as well as the noises produced by bells and spurs, and the shouts of the *călusări* during the performance.

From this we can see the rituals are complex. They are not simply to drive faeries away or to bless them and absorb their healing virtue and knowledge. They are an entire ritual configuration for dealing with every aspect of human and faerie interaction.

"Given certain common elements… the point of view that the călusări men who do the dances are in fact the very personification of the iele. Firstly the appearance of the dancers who, according to Cantemir, used to wear female clothes and cover their faces with white veils, reminiscent

> *of the fairies' white appearance; The structure of the group—both for iele and their ritual dancers their groups are always made up of odd numbers in both cases. The călusări's performance coincides with the period when the power of the fairies reaches paroxysm; their frenetic dance, when they seem not to touch the ground, imitates the fairies' dance. There is also the belief that one who steps on the spot where the iele danced falls sick."* [6]

They are very watchful not to follow in one another's footsteps or to keep the outsiders away from the flag or from themselves during the performance so as not to go insane. Both the *călușari* and the *iele* hold the secret of the healing plants. Although their performance is public they go to liminal places like mounds and rivers where the *iele* live to get their leaping skills and practice in secret so they can bring those powers into the town safely mediated. A witchlike figure also offers them protection and help at the beginning of the ritual by offering them the kerchief of a wicked woman who had it on her at her death. This is clearly a "pass" of sorts from the dangerous world of faerie wildness, mediated by the faerie's representative—the Witch.

Within this faerie cult the members are unconditionally obedient to their leader. The most skilled of the dancers chooses those who form the group, decides upon the type, duration and location of the dances, states who will be cured and leads the dance, for it is he who first shows how the figures should be performed. As master of the sacred ceremony, the *vătaf* performs the ritual acts and magical practices related to the binding and breaking of the flag, oath taking and healing of the sick. He must be an outstanding character, familiar with all the secrets of the *călusă*, knowledgeable of incantation, charms and spells that must not be disclosed to anyone, except for his successor, who he chooses when he retires. This position, highly esteemed by village society, is held for several years and transmitted from one generation to another. Once invested, the *vătaf* be-

6 *Ibid*, 8.

comes a sacred, respected and feared character considered to have magical power over the dancers, which he shares with the Mute.

Firica also goes on to explain how an equally interesting and highly respected member of the group, (a substitute for the protective God of horses, defender of the secrets of the initiated ones), is called the Dirty One, the Masked or the Mute. He faces a prohibition against speaking for the whole period of Whitsuntide. He dresses in patched clothes like a beggar or outcast, he wears a leather mask, a goat beard, or, in some cases, he soots his face and carries a primitive weapon such as a painted wooden broadsword, bow and arrows, hatchet or a whip, which he lashes to chase away evil spirits.[7]

The mask and his state of dumbness help him conceal his identity, while the weapons he carries make him invulnerable to the *iele*. A pouch full of healing plants and a red wooden phallus tied to his front, with which, it is believed, he can make girls marry or women get pregnant by a mere touch, are elements that complete his costume. Except for the prohibition against speaking, the Mute can do whatever he pleases: freely join or leave the performance, disobey the group leader, make dancers err and then beat or lash them with his sword or whip, and kiss girls and married women. But his role ensures safety while injecting the appearance of chaos, for he ensures the dancers should not be approached by any bystander who might go insane or fall sick. By being outside of all boundaries he is somehow gifted the ability to safely navigate boundaries, just as by fraternising with faeries and becoming like them other faery magicians become able to safely do things that are prohibited to others. The Mute must be a very good dancer, an athlete, and a performer of some skill as his responsibilities are not easy: he performs particularly difficult stunts, climbs tall trees, and dances on his hands.

The Mute has much in common with the Witch role of summoner, who is often seen as not quite a member of the Coven and able to move

7 *Ibid*, 9.

between Covens, offering both news and messages, whilst sometimes also serving a protective function. The flag bearer, called *arătătorul* is entrusted the special care of the flag. Dressed in ordinary clothes, he does not, as a rule, dance but is ready to replace any of the performers in case of ailment or weariness. During the performance, the flag bearer must hold the flag in upright position in the middle of the group, which is why he has to be strong. If the flag falls down, which is bad omen, reparation can only be made by disassembling the group, making a new flag and repeating the vows all over again. Thus it is clear that the pole erected in the middle of the dance is somehow pivotal to the magic that is occurring within the circular space.

The dancers very vitality, virility and virtuosity are presented to them by supernatural forces that guide and protect them. The fact that the *călușari* must take an oath of allegiance and secrecy when they join the group, has been seen by some as evidence that the dance is "devilish." In fact they are to keep away from churches during the time they are connected with the dance, just as faeries in Sicily forbid the mentioning of Jesus and Mary.

After taking the oath, the dancers were considered sacred,[8] their behaviour was much like war. They would sleep and eat together to avoid being under the influence of evil spirits. The state of purity obtained by sexual abstinence was the best and safest way to avoid exposure to the supernatural and its related hazards. Witholding of sexual force and accumulation of virility and a certain type of magical power are in close interrelation when it comes to *călușar*. They follow the sunrise and sunset in their performances, the time of the living as opposed to night and dark, the time of the *iele*—they would never dance before or after these times of day. In Dolj County, the *călușari* used to ask for the help and protection of a

8 Mircea Eliade, "Notes on the Călușari," *Journal of the Ancient Near Eastern Society* 5 (1973), 115–122.

Witch.[9] Every family would welcome the dancers, who could chase away the wicked fairies and spirits and encourage the helpful. The households and villages in which the *căluşari* danced were blessed and fortunate, protected from evil forces and would supposedly become prosperous.

Here is a sample of the oath taken at admission:

> *"In the name of God we commit ourselves to dance rightly, without feeling offended or complaining. I swear that I will fully obey the vataf's orders, comply with the regulations, act honestly and not keep anything secret from my companions. We commit ourselves to be united, to help one another, not to disunite the group, hide money and touch women as long as we dance, so help us God! I swear to serve the căluşari with faith, honesty, obedience and fear of God… I swear by God, by the soul of my ancestors, by my horses and cattle, to abide by the law of căluş until the flag is undone."*

In some places in Wallachia, the *vătaf* used to measure the height of the dancers on a red thread, a process known in some Witchcraft traditions as "taking the measure." They would then bind the measure together with the apotropaic plants on the flag, or he would make a sign on the very pole of the flag, kept in vertical position, indicating the height of each *căluşar*. This was considered as a surety of their pledge of secrecy and obedience given to their patron the Queen of Faeries, much like handing over an object link such as hair or blood.

The healing treatments offered by the cult take place in one of the three days of Whitsuntide, in a liminal space or at the patient's dwelling place, in complete silence like many other rituals associated with faerie. The *vătaf* or the Mute traces the circle—the barrier between the sacred and the profane, inside which the *căluşari* always perform their dances and rituals—thus ensuring the necessary conditions for the treatment to have the expected effect. The

9 Firica, 10.

patient is laid down in the middle of the circle, head eastwards—East symbolises life and the Sun—and covered with a white cloth.

Here we can see a very similar procedure to the Faerie Doctoring reported by Lady Wilde, a circle drawn a white cloth laid out and the facing east and the use of special helper herbs and the whispered words or songs known only to them. Beside the patient's head the flag is placed as well as the necessary ritual props prepared by relatives beforehand: garlic, wormwood, vinegar, a new earthen pot, a black chicken, water taken from a well or spring (at dawn, lest anyone else take water first). The *călușari* dance anticlockwise around the patient, who is meanwhile rubbed all over with garlic, wormwood and vinegar, then jump over him touching him with their feet or clubs.

While they perform the dance associated with the patient's disease, some acts, different from village to village, meant to achieve the transfer of health from the ritual objects, or from one of the *călușari* to the patient, are carried out. The *vătaf* either induces a state of trance to one of the dancers, who undergoes a ritual death, and then breaks the clay pot and kills the chicken, or he breaks the pot and kills the chicken and when the drops of water and pot shards touch a dancer, that dancer symbolically dies, transferring his life force to the sick person.

The *călușari* also lie the sick person down, jump over him, and at the leader's order all tread on his body from head to foot. This echoes the motif of the *donas de fuera* dancing on the bodies of sleeping patients with their feet. After this symbolic trampling of the illness the dancers of the calus whisper secret words into patient's ears words known only by them and command the disease to leave that body. When someone "falls" or symbolically dies with faerie possession during the dance or at other times it can have either positive or negative connotations depending on how it is ritually processed. This fact is at the heart of the seeming ambivalence of faerie ritual in all European countries, but is perhaps at its most explicit in Romanian custom. This sense of "both/and" rather than "either/or" in faerie relations is emphasized further by the fact that in Romania there are other festivals in honour of the faeries that focus on a different but complimentary approach.[10]

Under the plural form *Sânziene*, there is another annual Romanian festival in the fairies' honor which takes a more feminine vent. Etymologically, the name stands for *sân* (common abbreviation of *sfânt*—"saint" or "holy") and *zână* (a word used for fairies in general). In other words "saint-fairy," which tells us a great deal about the way new concepts of holiness mixed easily with folk beliefs around faeries. Because the *zână* are described as a "gentle type of faerie" this aspect of faerie mythology has been less threatening to the Church. In Romania the *Sânziene* holiday annually is celebrated on June 24. This is similar to the Swedish Midsummer holiday date and seems to suggest the faeries being honoured are of the "Shining Court" summer variety.

The folk practices of *Sânziene* involve the most beautiful maidens in the village dressing in white and spending all day searching for and picking bedstraw (*Galium verum*) flowers. In Romania this flower seems to act as a faerie gateway much like the hawthorn and its heavily tabooed blossom does in Britain. They are instructed to remain alone and unseen, especially not to be seen by any males. Like the Calus practice which seems aimed to enhance the viril, masculine energy via continence and keeping the company of other men, so the women here are engaged in a similar form of exclusiveness. In this case they are not meant to be gazed upon by anyone during the taboo period of isolation.

10 Pocs, *Fairies and Witches*, 60-61.

Using the flowers they picked during the day, the girls create wreaths as floral crowns they wear upon returning to the village at nightfall. The girls are then believed to have turned into *sânziene* via possession, and dance in a circle around a bonfire, into which all remains of the previous harvest are thrown. People are prevented from speaking to the girls during this ceremony. As we see again this faerie taboo on speaking. Sometimes the degree of benevolence of local faeries has more to do with the landscape than it does necessarily with mankind's ideas, or even the progression of the seasons. The spirits of dangerous treacherous mountains are often dangerous faeries, such as the Welsh *gwyllion* known for leading the unwary astray into the mist or off the edges of treacherous mountain passes. The spirits of plush cow pastures are often soft and beautiful. The type of faeries in a place relate to the temperament of the place not just of season.

Another country where we can see remnants of faerie practice in a regular ceremony is in the Italian Deer Man. In this archaic-seeming practice a ritual drama is enacted around "deer man" and "deer woman," who are represented by people wearing animal hides. The *martino*, or faerie man, comes from the woods, along with "the witches" who show up with sooty faces and skins, accompanying deer man and deer woman. The faerie man acts as mediator between the two sexes of the deers who are inclined to fight, and his wand has calming abilities. Here we see a faerie man presented almost as an androgyne, or one of the faeries who, "did not suggest a sex at all," or the motif of cross-dressing found in some misrule folk festivals.

Here the faerie man is given the job of mediator and matchmaker of the animal realm, promoting fertility and harmony. The Witches appear chthonic in appearance and arrive at the same time as the faeries. The faerie is dressed in white with bells and a slightly pointed hat, but as we know from previous faerie encounter narratives the passage through the chthonic realm and the Underworld is a necessary step in reaching Faerie. Although the martino wears white and has bells he still comes from the mountains outside the town, and rather than representing light versus the darkness of the Witches and the deer people he instead seems to be about fusion and the creative uniting of opposites—a true dweller in the twilight realm. After the deer man and woman return to the woods the Witches stay, drumming and playing flutes and bagpipes for the people. Their place as the emissaries of wild nature and as guardians of the chthonic gateways to the paradisical realm of Faerie are affirmed and enacted here.[11]

In Wales we see another such seasonal drama between a Summer King and a Winter King. The Summer King looks much like the faerie of the mountains in Italy, dressed in white with bells. Whereas the Winter King has a blacked out face and is reminiscent of the faerie rade of the Wild Hunt, the dark elves, and many black-faced male figures from the Witch Trial records. This ritual combat was semi-playful in Wales, involving the king of summer throwing handfuls of flowers at the Winter King.[12] There is no sense of the faerie courts or two kings being deeply opposed to each other in any good versus evil sense.

All faeries, whether of summer or winter courts, could be either good or bad from a human perspective, depending on the proper ritual actions, keeping of taboos and offerings linking them with mankind. This is only logical as both inclement weather and drought with terrible heat can ruin a crop. There are times when the darkness must be vanquished, other times when the dead need to be appeased and fed. There are times when the faeries of sum-

11 For more information on man-deer rites please see: Natalie Mikhailova's, "The Cult of the Deer and 'Shamans' in Deer Hunting Society," *Archeologica Baltica* 7 (2005).

12 Marie Trevelyan, *Folklore and Folktales of Wales,* (London: Forgotten Books) 19.

mer must be offered to for fertility, but there are also times when those spirits can become a force of disorder, disease and chaos in their own right. When not properly engaged with through the purifying lens of correct ritual interaction improper relations begin, and it is improper relations—improper governing of the liminal thresholds between human and faerie that result in human misfortune—according to the mindset of the Faerie Faith.

The calusari had a warrior-like, sacrificial take on being mediators which involved a very complex and strict understanding of right relations, but all of the faerie rituals above contain an element of mediation where medicine is extracted, converted and transmuted from faerie poisons through ritual. Illness and revelation are always right beside each other, ready to be transformed from one state to another and always interpenetrating one another, just as the world of humans and the world of faeries. In this we can see echoed the Faerie Faith as described by Kirk, and its emphasis on cycles and transformation of one thing ceaselessly becoming another.

MEMORIES OF OLD GODS

Before city-states had agreed upon pantheons of Gods, divinity lived wild in the forest. This is remembered in the European-wide traditions of sacred groves. Irish stories tell of the banishment of the Tuatha de Danann to the realm beneath the land and water which is perhaps a memory of the original "fall" story, upon which Christian ideas of a fall from heaven into an Underworld were later grafted to create the fallen angel hypothesis. Angels fell from the sky but the Tuatha de Danann came from the sky in a cloud of mist and later fell from the surface to below the Earth and water, out of human sight, submerged into the subconscious. Yet it is doubtful if this meant total banishment in the past, as we are also told the druids worshipped in open air oak groves with trees being the perfect symbol uniting the heavens with the ground below.

The word "God," even "a God" as opposed to "the God," is tainted with the brush of hierarchical, nationalist fantasy. If we aren't careful in how we frame it can take us a little distance from the great and powerful teacher spirits that shamanist and animistic societies worldwide turn to as their familiars and helpers. When you call something a God, a little of the thinking we associate with the God in monotheism, is evoked by accident alongside it. Yet, when it comes to the Queens and sometimes Kings, Princes and Princesses of the realm of Faerie most people acknowledge that we are probably dealing with entities that would have once been local Gods. Or in some cases even more widely-spread Gods.

The Tuatha De Danann are mostly thought to have been Gods who were later remembered later as the Sidhe, but only the names of their leaders are known in anything like a pantheon. Powerful faerie men and women like Dagda, Morrigan, Lugh, Brigid, Aengus, Boann, and

Ogma come to mind as Gods, and yet there is a certain archaic uncertainty about the godhood of Celtic spirits. The same lack of certainty about divine status can be said for the figures of the Mabinogion such as Llew, Gwydion, Arianrhod, Blodeuwedd, Manawydan, Gwynn ap Nudd and Rhiannon, who many argue are legendary heroes or faerie women (in Rhiannon's case most clearly so, and in that of Blodeuwedd whose maidens are turned to swans and is made out of nine flowers). But could this lack of clarity about who is a hero figure and who a God perhaps be a mark of an old way of thinking? The Brythonic Polytheist community is quick to point out with great scholarly vigour that not all the figures in the Mabinogion should be thought of as Gods, but does this mean they aren't powerful spirits? What weight do we place on this word God? And does it have any final meaning in the context of sorcery?

We have already touched on the widespread presence of Faerie Queens and princes like Sibylla and Robin Goodfellow but let's examine a few other examples of faerie figures that are also likely Gods. A general pattern seems to be that the Kings, Queens, Princes, Princesses and aristocracy of the Faerie Courts are the ones that we would most likely identify as divine. But when we use this feudal language, the clear product of a bygone human era, we should be wary of assuming it means the same kind of thing it does in human society.

Gwynn ap Nudd is a wonderful example of the winter demon style of hob man, as is Arawn who is also a Wild Hunt leader. His face is blackened out with soot, he wears furs and is accompanied by demonic-seeming black dogs with red eyes. Sometimes he even comes bearing chains clanking and is intimately associated with the Wild Hunt, whose connection with Goetic demonic depiction we have previously noted. Gwynn ap Nudd is often called "King of Goblins" and so his role as King of the Winter Court of Faerie seems indisputable. Given that he appears in the Mabinogion being at all the places where the dead are slain from end to end of the land each time blood is spilt and men die it seems fair to accept that Gwynn is a God of the Underworld, death and the Wild Hunt, a psychopomp of sorts. But he is also very clearly a King of Faerie. If he was once considered a "God," then he was one who arose as a Faerie King. And perhaps, from a sorcerous perspective the designation of "powerful spirit" is more important than whether society as a whole generally reckoned them a deity.

Rhiannon is just as clearly a Faerie Queen as Gwynn is a king. She is even first spotted on a special mound, likely an old Neolithic burial mound like many faerie beings before her. Similar to True Thomas's Faerie Queen she appears on a hill riding a white horse. Like Mari of Basque folklore she wears a gold gown, you could almost imagine her owning a gold comb to brush out her golden hair. She is a woman of Annwn, clearly a faerie otherworld where the hounds are all faerie dogs with pink eyes and white fur. She gets further away the faster you ride, a typical "faerie inversion" example of a back-to-front world, much like weeping instead of laughing and laughing in the place of weeping. But there is more to this motif of Rhiannon's; one has the feeling that Pwyll is being given a lesson in right relations with Faerie. He is being told firmly that all of his spurring his horse, all of his striving to capture and dominate and show off will mean nothing to her, he simply needs to learn how to humble himself a little and ask for what he wants.

Rhiannon is a high-ranking faerie woman who some might call a Goddess, but the changeling narrative that underpins her story, and that of the Mabinogion as a whole, is perhaps the most interesting part of the medieval tales from the perspective of the Faerie Faith. To begin with both Mabon and Pryderi are stolen away from their mothers before they are a few nights old, in the case of Pryderi an otherworldly hand comes through a wall like it's simply a permeable membrane and snatches him, replacing him with a foal. Mabon is simply stolen and is later found imprisoned in Annwn, requiring the traditional harrowing journey to reach the land of Faerie.

In Rhiannon's changeling story the previously powerful Faerie Queen is blamed for the loss of the child, who may in fact be stolen from Faerie into the human world—for an inversion on the normal theme. The foal replacing links him and Rhiannon with Witchcraft, because in Wales the horse is the creature that acts as go-between between the faerie world and the human, with horse heads being played by Witches and their skulls burned on ritual fires.[1] Rhiannon's punishment of "becoming the horse" and carrying people on her back may refer to a ritual position where she must serve as a threshold keeper who takes people back and forth between the worlds.

Each year on May Day the faeries take one of Teyrnon's foals and don't replace it with anything. But this year he manages to catch the goblin or troll-like hand in the process, and thus has the foal replaced with a faerie boy.

1 *Ibid*, 135.

WITCHES' HORSE, DEVIL'S GOAT AND FAERIE COW

The link between horses, or some other kind of mount, in Witchcraft is as undeniable as it is with shamanic traditions such as those of Siberia. Witches ride things, whether it is hag-riding people (both some kinds of faeries and Witches), stabled horses (again this activity is also done by elves), or brooms, which function as a symbolic horse. The Witches of Wales play to the spirits of the dead on a horse's skull and sacrifice a skull into the fire, they also drink the Devil's health out of a horse's hoof. During the initiation of the Horseman's Word the proceedings happened in a stable, and one was to shake the hoof of the Devil through a hole in the wall, a practice that brings to mind the troll arm reaching through into Teyrnon's stable. Cain is also connected with horsemanship. A divinatory king-making ritual of the Druids is said to have involved a prophetic sleep whilst sewn inside the skin of a sacrificial mare.

Faeries also have associations with horses and are suspected of "elf riding" them and "elf knotting" their hair. Both faeries and Witches, as two sides of the same liminal creature, are adept at climbing inside something with a skin, whether it be horse or drum, and riding it. The skin between, the membrane, like the wall to Teyrnon's stable and the wall of the stable through which one shakes hands with the Devil, allows for things to pass across between the worlds, and the drum beat is a kind of knocking on the wall asking to be let in.

As a way of thinking this may go back as far as the painted walls of Paleolithic caves whose animals were often painted to look like they were emerging from the wall, and whose hand prints suddenly come to mean something much deeper when you consider the idea of someone or something on the other side of the wall trying to reach out for you. Humans are brought into the realm of faerie through a harrowing process when they cross this membrane, and the story of the Green Children suggests the same applies for faerie beings when things happen in the opposite direction. The line between riding, revering, and sacrificing the horse, and whether horses are attractive or off-putting to faeries, has been just as mixed and ambiguous as our response to faeries themselves.

If the act of riding contains mixed messages of reverence, sexuality and dominance all at once, what does this tell us about Witches who hag-ride people? It's always been clear that hag-riding is linked to the succubus traditions where the line is very fine between sexuality and vampirism. So who, or what is the horse that both Witchcraft and the Faerie Faith are so interested in riding?

At the beginning of *The Golden Toad* it is suggested by Andrew Chumbley, past Magister of the Traditional Witchcraft sodality Cultus Sabbati, that the name of the horse one acquires power to whisper is in fact "man."[1] As Chumbley also says in salute of the mysteries:

> *"Here's to the horse with the star on its head*
> *and the chestnut tail and mane,*
> *a star on his head and a patch on his foot*
> *and his master's name was Cain."*[2]

It is highly interesting that it's not only to Cain these honours are due but his mount. This equine twin, who he must be symbolically slain in the form of the toad and risen again, carries echoes of ancient horse sacrifice. It is perhaps these echoes that resound in the Welsh practice of burning the horse's head on the ritual fire and the interring of horse heads under dwellings as a kind of sacrifice for the foundations[3]. But horses were also engaged with sacrificially in ancient times during the king-making rite, where the same horse in Ireland was slain

1 Andrew Chumbley, *One: The Grimoire of the Golden Toad*, (San Francisco: Xoanon, 2000), 23.
2 *Ibid*, 24.
3 M.S Brown, "Buried Horse Skulls in a Welsh House," *Folklore 77* (1966), 65-66.

and the king bathed in its broth.[4] There is also something potentially sexual about Rhiannon's association with being mounted.

It is fascinating to note that Rosaleen Norton's Goat Fold tradition, details about which were recorded by Doreen Valiente in *The Rebirth of Witchcraft*, allegedly used the identifying words: "I have been in the cauldron and they told me I am of the green shoots of Pryderi." I take this as a likely reference to the Cauldron of Rebirth, out of which one emerged alive if thrown in dead, but in a faerie condition of muteness. Clearly this cauldron is being evoked as having initiatory meaning, the sacrifice and cooking of the self to achieve the mute (faerie-like) state of initiation, which also disallows the divulging of secrets. The mention of green shoots is evocative of faerie and my above reading of Pryderi as a changeling. He is also of the tribe of Annwn, and was possibly believed by some traditions to be one of those ancestor changeling figures like the mother of Myddfai line. So being of the "green shoots of Pryderi" could have more than one potential meaning.

There is something primitive and perfect about the image of the faerie, so tied up with sacred animal forms. Like the Donas de Fuera the Basque laminak unites all of these features of both light and animality. And one of those features is a hidden animal part. Goose feet, cow tails, swan or other types of wings, the feet of horses or goats, are all prominent faerie features. In Wales dancing Witches show their faerie origins by leaving animals tracks where they've been, horse prints for female Witches, goat prints for male ones.[5]

But this association of horses with the female is not absolute in faerie lore, as the poucca/puca/buca who we have previously linked to Robin Goodfellow is known to be able to turn into a horse. An important spirit familiar of both British and Irish traditional craft is

4 A tale first told by Giraldus Cambrensis, or Gerald of Wales.
5 Trevalyn, 136.

very much part horse as often as he is goat. Horses have feminine connotations but they also simply belong to "those who can cross over." Horses are not the only kind of Sabbat mount. Goats are ridden to Sabbat and the *samodivile* of Rumania are known for riding deer tethered with snakes!

Although dogs and wolves are almost always associated with the Host of the Underworld there is intense ambiguity about the horse. Being ridden by bright Faerie Queens like Thomas the Rhymer's mate, Rhiannon and the host of the Sidhe, commonly white horses with bells at their bridle, they are also ridden by the Underworld company of the Wild Hunt and have deep death associations.

The Mari Lwyd of Wales, covered in ribbons and brought out on a pole during the depth of winter with a snapping bottom jaw, is a great example of a winter spirit with a horse's skull for a head. The horse's head also frightens away some kinds of faeries but encourages the dead when played as a drum in the Witch Sabbat. We may conclude the horse's head is an ultimately ambivalent symbol of power and the ability to cross over like many of the faeries themselves is both dark and light, death and birth, male and female.

The Rusalia and their horse attributes are however a strong example of the horse being worked with by men, as is the close relationship between men and horses in the Society of the Horseman's Word. The vexed question of the horse's skull and faeries is a little bit like the relationship of the faeries with bread. As a cultivated, human food not found in the wild, bread is sometimes used to ward *against* the faeries, and at the same time, when it's baked just right (neither cooked too well nor raw as the faerie wife insists in Wales) it and the aroma it creates is used as an offering to faerie. *The same thing that under one circumstance can ward them away can also feed them.* This is a concept that returns to us again and again whenever we discuss traditional ways of maintaining right relations with the faeries.

The Viking *niding pole* or *scorn-post* were poles about nine feet long upon which curses were carved in runes. A horse's skull was fixed to the top of the pole, and it was stuck into the ground with the skull facing towards the house of the accursed person. The pole channeled the destructive forces of Hel, Goddess of the Underworld. It was said to work by frightening away the good elves that kept the land alive. [6]

And yet horse's heads have also traditionally been used to protect homes and barns from malicious faeries, from storms and to protect enclosed gardens. And of course the horseshoe is equally protective. As Eva Pocs puts it:

> *"The masked figures of the Calusari [can be placed] among the wolf, horse etc, masked representatives of the dead returning home at the time of the winter solstice. On the other hand, the oppositions of the dead and the fertility bringing goddesses is not exclusive: fairies are in one of the aspects themselves the returning dead; while the winter demons and especiall St Theodore's horses also have a fertility-bringing role."*[7]

In Wales goats were created by the Devil and like in many other places, such as the Basque province with Mari's black goat, the connection with Witchcraft is explicit. This link between "devils" and faeries at a folkloric level is quite important. It shows how despite the attempt to turn Underworld-associated faeries into devils, the two remain linked together in mutual ambiguity without one narrative ever having fully triumphed. The layers of myth jostle uncomfortably with each other, but this uncertainty itself is part of our cultural heritage.

Goats are in Wales held in peculiar esteem for their supposed occult intellectual powers. They are believed to be on very good terms with the Tylwyth Teg, and possessed of more knowledge than other animals. It is one of the peculiarities of the Tylwyth Teg that ev-

6 For more information on nithing poles and associated curse practices please see: Nigel Pennick, *Rune Magic: The History and Practice of Ancient Runic Traditions*, (London: Thorsons, 1999).

7 Pocs, *Fairies and Witches*, 51-52.

ery Friday night they comb the goats' beards to make them neat for Sunday. Their association with the mountain faeries called *gwyllion*, which I have spoken of above as being of the harsher sort of character, is related in the legend of Cadwaladr's goat:

"Cadwaladr owned a very handsome goat, named Jenny, of which he was extremely fond; and which seemed equally fond of him; but one day, as if the very diawi possessed her, she ran away into the hills, with Cadwaladr tearing after her, half mad with anger and affright. At last his Welsh blood got so hot, as the goat eluded him again and again, that he flung a stone at her, which knocked her over a precipice, and she fell bleating to her doom. Cadwaladr made his way to the foot of the crag; the goat was dying, but not dead, and licked his hand—which so affected the poor man that he burst into tears, and sitting on the ground took the goat's head on his arm. The moon rose, and still he sat there. Presently he found that the goat had become transformed to a beautiful young woman, whose brown eyes, as her head lay on his arm, looked into his in a very disturbing way. 'Ah, Cadwaladr,' said she, 'have I at last found you?'

Now Cadwaladr had a wife at home, and was much discomfited by this singular circumstance; but when the goat—yn awr maiden—arose, and putting her black slipper on the end of a moonbeam, held out her hand to him, he put his hand in hers and went with her. As for the hand, though it looked so fair, it felt just like a hoof. They were soon on the top of the highest mountain in Wales, and surrounded by a vapoury company of goats with shadowy horns. These raised a most unearthly bleating about his ears. One, which seemed to be the king, had a voice that sounded above the din as the castle bells of Carmarthen used to do long ago above all the other bells in the town.

This one rushed at Cadwaladr and butting him in the stomach sent him toppling over a crag as he had sent his poor nannygoat.

When he came to himself, after his fall, the morning sun was shining on him and the birds were singing over his head. But he saw no more of either his goat or the fairy she had turned into, from that time to his death."[8]

It is clear from this that the gwyllion in particular were probably part-animal faeries. The part-animal form is the most important signal of the archaic race of faerie. The gwyllion mountain faerie, able to wear the goat skin, seemed to be approaching Cadwallon in the faerie lover guise, sometimes called the fetch mate. But the Faerie King of the Gwyllion seems to have rejected him as a suitor, probably because of the violence he did to "Jenny."

The goat, like the horse, is also a stead animal in many Witchcraft traditions. The Lady Mari herself, known as mother of sorginak and laminak alike, rides on a black goat sometimes known as Akerbeltz, the "field of the He Goat." Of course this association with goats and the Devil became widespread via demonology. But it could not be said to be a foreign feature. The goat, with its cunning and recalcitrance, is a symbol of Robin Goodfellow who was depicted with the goat horns in the most famous image of him, and also in his Poucca form. Even the *Malleus Maleficarum* describes incubi as being called by Pagans "satyrs," and says "by satyrs here devils is meant."[9]

Sometimes faeries were part animal, and the animal parts they had were those most connected to the deities who were their Kings and Queens. The horse and cow are both sacred to the Queen of Faeries, drinking from a cow or horse's hoof, as Witches did in Wales would have been symbolic of receiving the liquid straight from the "hand" of the Queen of Faeries herself. The horse is the death side, crossing over to the land of the dead, the cow is the be-

8 Wirt Sikes, *British Goblins: Welsh Folk-lore, Fairy Mythology, Legends and Traditions,* (London: Low, Marston, Searle & Rivington, 1880), 48.

9 Heinrich Kramer & Jacob Sprenger, *Malleus Maleficarum,* (New York: Cosimo Classics, 2007), 24.

nevolent fertility Goddess part. Laminak often had cow tails, but when faeries have horse parts they are usually hostile vampires.

It seems in places where the faerie's nature is more complex, more multifaceted and hybrid are also the areas who distinguish less between Witches and faeries. This seems to further support the idea of a time when the distinction between this world and the Other was less, to a time when the distinctions between light and dark, human and animal were not as stark as they became later. Those who see the world in terms of black and white and place Witch and faerie magician at the poles of those two realities obsess themselves with the thorny and the wide and sunny path, missing the Crooked serpentine path in the middle.

The faerie is ever of the mid-country, neither human nor angel, neither plant nor animal, living in a world with neither sun nor moon, always on the edge of dawn, with one foot on either side of the hedge, riding the barriers—just like the Witch.

SERPENTS AND THE FAE

I have previously identified the part-animal faerie as an archaic feature, but "animal" does not always imply mammalian. Even some of the most ethereal and Upperworldly-seeming faeries who seem to be made of nothing but gossamer and starlight, whom one might associate with the Summer Court, have swan skins, wings of birds, appear to erupt with songbirds from the mouth, possess the wings of butterflies, moths or dragonflies, or reptile qualities, snake tails, or insect-like facial features. Here we will discuss some of these hybrid forms as they relate to the reptilian kingdom and also in the process touch on that of birds.

Faeries of all kinds from the most malignant goblin to the most luminous member of the Shining Court live close to the creative inferno of Nature's heart, a whirlpool of force at once black and shining, made of a cold fire, a most destructive creativity, and this swirling paradox is reflected in their forms. They wear the faces nature wears, the archetypes of creation. At times they seem an outbreath of that creative energy, at other times its architects. It is said that one can wield power to the extent that one can be changed by it, and They are the ultimate changed, or changeling, beings. There is greenish-white tree sap like milk in their veins, according to the Irish concept of faerie blood.

Erupting leaves inside their heads and hawthorn wood where their bones would be. Rather than asking ourselves: does the life of a faerie start with a spirit tree? The seer's eyes gaze upon the tree and see the expression of faerie elegance and precision. As we breathe out, the green world breathes in, and we are locked in creative synergy with them via our breath. Yet there is no plant world without the insects that fertilise their flowers, and the birds that spread their seeds. The faerie body often reflects these creative intersections between plant (thinking of the hollow backs of the Hidden Folk, so like an ancient tree trunk) insect, bird or snake.

The relationship between bird parts and serpent parts are described by Francisco Vaz Da Silva who states *"that the alternation between predator and prey constitutes an image of endless death and regeneration involving the unity of fighting halves."*[1] Similar circular relations exist between plants and insects, who also represent a continuum of influence. The insect penetrates and titillates the flower to win its pollen; the flower encompasses the bee and gives its essence to it. Both are interpenetrated by each other. The serpent swallows the bird's egg and excretes another egg full of serpents, which when they are small are often eaten by birds.

The ability of the snake to shed its skin inevitably links it with skin-turning, and in many cultures both Witches and faeries themselves are described as taking serpent form. One of the Ukrainian names for Witches is "snakes." South Russians thought they had tails, a sign of their once having been snakes. The Faerie Queen, Witch-teaching figure of Sibylla is also described as having a serpent's tail in some places, and of putting initiates through sexual and physical ordeals involving snakes before they can win instruction and initiation inside her mountain. In the Basque province Sugaar, a great serpent God, is the father of the laminak faeries. In Wales serpent spirits were closely associated with *geni loci* particularly places with buried treasure.

Serpents were known to live below and guard each house in Wales. They had a king and queen serpent of each area and they wore diadems on their foreheads.[2] These seem like very ancient, titanic life forces within the Earth, spirits of place, no doubt dat-

1 Francisco Vaz De Silva, *Extraordinary Children: Werewolves and Witches in Portuguese Folk Tradition,* (Budapest: Central European University Press, 2007), 264-265.

2 Trevelyn, 110.

ing back to an early period of our history. Serpents guard homes, springs and wells, as well as "buried treasure" in the land. Often they are associated with the lines of power linking one holy site full of virtue, which in some cases might be the real "treasure" to be found at those places.

Of course the saints were fond of killing dragons, which in Britain were usually a winged serpent. But if we look carefully at Eva Poc's research into dragon spirits of storms we see that there were times even in non-Christian traditions where you might indeed want to battle a dragon.[3] Two popular reasons for dragon slaying, which have strongly sacrificial undertones were either to end a drought or turn aside a violent storm. Sacred as these titanic forces may be they can still be dangerous to human life, and so there have probably always been specialist magical practitioners who defended against them, even before the saintly connotation of subduing indigenous religious forces.

So it appears that images of St George or St Michael spearing dragons are not as foreign to European Faerie Faiths as it might seem. Francisco Vaz da Silva in the fascinating *Extraordinary Children, Werewolves, and Witches in Portuguese Folk Tradition* points out that the connection between slayer and slain may actually be far more intimate even than this:

> *"One implication is that the slaying of the old dragon is homologous to the snake's casting of the old skin. But then, the dragon slayer is himself like the young snake—which Vladimir Propp rightly sensed as he stated, 'he who was born from the dragon will kill the dragon'."*[4]

Within such a context the dragon-slaying images found among the saints can well be reinterpreted as images of renewal, fertilization of the land by the fiery lightning bolts of the heavens, skin-casting, as well as battling for the crops.

3 Pocs, *Fairies and Witches*, 53-61.

4 Vaz De Silva, 290-91.

What then is the relationship between the serpent and the dragon? Are they the same thing? Welsh folklore tells us that the origin of dragons was in snakes that had drunk the milk of a woman, and through having also eaten of the bread consecrated for the Holy Communion, became transformed into winged serpents or dragons.[5] A story redolent of the witch-teat suckling of familiar spirits. Could this story of transformation point towards what the Witch's familiar spirit stands to gain in return for its work and it's suckling? What and whom are these dragons and serpent spirits?

Eva Pocs describes numerous instances of ecstatic sorcerers battling dragons and winged serpents who are usually storm-bringers. They may be attacked to drive back a storm or instead to pierce them with a spear, in a clear echoing of fertility-bringing sympathetic magic, to let the water out, just as the blood of the dragon flows, with the intention of ending a drought. Although connected closely with faeries Eva Pocs describes the dragon or serpent as an older more archaic part of the spirit world. This fits well with both Romani Gypsy lore which positions the "serpent people" as residing in the lower parts of the Underworld and being among some of the oldest of the spirits.

It may seem that in discussing dragons we are getting further away from the central topic of this book—the relationship between Witchcraft and the Faerie Faith. But this could not be further from the truth. In fact, buried in the dragon lore of other European countries we are able to unearth links in the chain that help us better understand the relationship between faeries and the particular fallen angels known as the Watchers.

The following, quoted at length from Radomir Ristic due to its extreme relevance, explicitly links the figure of the dragon to both Serbian faeries and Witches:

5 Trevelyn, 111.

"According to Serbian tradition, many heroes originate from marriage between human and fairy, which gave them supernatural powers and ability to excel in battle. Those are the so-called dragon-men. Fairies have great sexual appetite, so they often seduce beautiful men that they meet in the woods and mountains. Those men must keep their relations with the fairies secret... Other types of dragons can also take human form, and they could go and visit women by night. There is a myth that says they are great lovers and that women can hardly resist them. Children from those relationships are always human-dragons and by virtue of that, great heroes also. According to tradition, Witches often had such relationships with them. Among both women and men, exhaustion and paleness were signs of such a relationship; maintaining relations with dragons is extremely tiring because it is very hard to 'follow' the life rhythm of a creature with supernatural characteristics. If a drought occurs, it is usually said that a dragon has taken up that residence with a nearby Witch and his presence brought it about. Then house of that Witch must be found, and the dragon must be expelled in the way that we described earlier, when we talked about vrzino kolo (the witch's dance). Some people connect these dragons to fallen angels, from the Book of Enoch, who occupied caves and trees after their fall. Because of that, their offspring are dragon-men." [6]

Ristic speaks elsewhere of how the "witch myths" of his country say that dragon men have fallen in meteor showers.

"Some of those dragons have fallen in rivers Danube, Timok and Pek and other in forests and mountains. Those who had fallen in rivers have continued to live in them under the water. They look like male mermaids, they have their middle long, big circle eyes, wide nose and long canine tooths. Those who had fallen in forests inhabited big trees, mainly old beeches with holes. How they look like is hard to say

6 Radomir Ristic, *Balkan Traditional Witchcraft,* (Los Angeles: Pendraig Publishing, 2009), 99.

because some witches claim that they are just big lights and other that they are anthropomorphic serpents with wings and that they become big light only when they start to fly. Those who have fallen in mountains inhabited caves and they look like previous dragons. As we can conclude, all of them are same dragons but after they fall in matter they take different shapes depending of their new habitation."

Is this a glimpse at the earlier source myth that "angels" were later grafted onto? Here we have a fall from the sky in the form of meteor showers and a faerie being whose physical characteristics, especially the presence of eagle wings, could easily fit with that of an angel. Ristic discusses these "dragon men" who have a faerie for a parent or have fed on the milk of a faerie woman as a babe:

"The third group consists of human-dragons, and this is the most interesting one. Usually those are people whose astral body is not really human, and when they leave their body, it is possible to see their actual appearance. Descriptions of these dragons are different. They could be big winged snakes, big eagles, or men of huge proportions, with extremely hairy bodies, long hair, and beard. It is possible to determine if a person belongs to this type of dragons by testing their strength. As a rule, they have superhuman strength and powers. It is said that many folk heroes were dragons; this is evidenced in various folk stories and songs."[7]

The link to great heroes and superhuman strength brings to mind immediately the faerie parentage of various Celtic heroes, including the changeling origin story for Pryderi who later grew into a warrior figure. The mystical parentage of Cú Chulainn, fathered by mysterious spirit work by the God Lugh is also associated with a synchronistic birth between a boy child and a foal, just as Pryderi's is. And Cú Chulainn, like Ristic's dragon-men heroes, was also famed for his improbable-sounding strength.

7 Ibid, 98.

These are not the only ways in which dragons can be linked to the later angelic layers of Craft mythos. In Wales the "flying serpent" style of dragon is described in quite some detail, with the same kind of eye-witness detail faerie sightings are treated with in testimonials from the same era. An aged inhabitant of Penllyne gave the following description:

> *"They were coiled when in repose, and 'looked as though they were covered in jewels of all sorts. Some of them had crests sparkling with all the colours of the rainbow'. When disturbed they glided swiftly, 'sparkling all over' to their hiding places. When angry, they, 'flew over people's heads with outspread wings bright and sometimes with eyes too, like the feathers in a peacocks' tail.' "*[8]

This connection with eyes in the wings and elsewhere is mentioned again where "eyes in the back of the head as well as the front" are ascribed. This connection between multiple eyes, such as one would see in a peacock tail, links the Welsh "flying serpent" very closely to early depictions of angels. As Ezekiel 10-12 puts it: "Both the cherubim and the wheels were covered with eyes. The cherubim had eyes all over their bodies, including their hands, their backs, and their wings." Of course the mention of flying beings with wings reminiscent of peacocks feathers brings to mind the Yazidi deity Melek Taus (Kurdish: Tawŭsê Melek), translated in English as "Peacock Angel," who is often acknowledged in Traditional Craft circles as a manifestation of Azazel or other similarly Luciferic Witch God.

If dragons or winged serpents were the original "angels" upon which Christian terminology was simply grafted onto over time, and faeries were believed to be fallen angels, what is the link between these two types of spirit being? Certainly there are plenty of traditions linking dragons to faeries. Ristic describes them as "male faeries," so it is certainly interesting, if they were the original model upon which

8 Trevelyn, 112.

the word "angel" was later grafted, that Catholic Christianity managed to provide a gloss for these male spirits as positive beings.

Along with having "fallen" into mountains and rivers and guarding those places serpent spirits were also known to create magical stones. The Welsh said that serpents came together on Midsummers Eve to mysteriously blow into being the *Glain Neidr* ("serpents' stone"). Joining their heads together and hissing, they form a bubble around the head of one. They blow it down until it comes off at the tail and hardens like glass.

Pliny also wrote of this tradition among the ancient Gauls. They said that snakes in great numbers intertwined themselves to create an egg from the foam of their saliva, and tossed it upward with their hisses. It bestowed victory if you found one, which is another interesting connection between serpents and warrior practices. Another Welsh tradition held that this snake-congress took place on May Eve. The serpent-stones were round, pastel-colored pebbles believed to confer second-sight and healing, especially of the eyes. The Welsh had many tales about the healing powers of snakes[9] so it appears serpent stones and their makers were as multifaceted as faeries, providing martial prowess with one hand and dispensing healing manna with the other.

From all this we can divine the following: the serpent or dragon people live both in the ground and fly through the air, just like angels and "fallen angels," some of them are probably the ancient form of the Watchers, those who illuminated the witchblood with their cunning fire. Faeries and Witches (the same creature on two different sides of the hedge, both with one foot on each side, a twilight, liminal creature, both) are the children of them, or are sometimes manifestations of them in human/faerie form. Baltic tradition suggests that "dragon" is but the name given to a pow-

9 Trevelyn, 170-171.

erful male faerie, or in later language, a kind of warrior angel, much like St Michael.

To bring these two threads together we need only refer to Welsh folklore. Romani lore and many other British depictions of serpents as spirits place them as a vitalist force, a titanic layer of power in the Underworld, where as Ristic's Bulgarian sources make dragons into something much like the Watchers. But Welsh lore tells us serpents and dragons are not quite the same thing. A dragon is a winged serpent, and a serpent only becomes a dragon from suckling the milk of a woman or eating a communion wafer. We could take this further and say that dragon-men start off as serpents, titanic beings of great power which become more humanized, possibly even gentler, after serving as familiars and suckling at the teat of a Witch.

What then are we to make of faeries that present themselves with reptile or insect parts that are not entirely of the "serpent" or "dragon" nature, but are merely part serpent? As the form are of faeries always suggestive of their true nature we can tell a great deal. Such creatures would be more alien to us in their nature than one that presents as part mammal, because in Faerie things look like what they are.

It is no accident then, that when modern day people see beings they find so unlike themselves they consider they must be from the stars, they experience them with insect-like eyes or reptile faces. Just as the dragons come down in meteor showers, these "aliens" are experienced as coming from the stars.

People riding the waves of powerful entheogens who don't believe in aliens see similar spirits guarding the gateways to experience with those plants. Many crop circles have been openly faked, but it is interesting to note that ones less easy to explain exhibit plaiting in the wheat. I myself have witnessed this kind of braided grain in the remains of a crop circle in Wiltshire. The way the wheat is both braided in some spots and then knitted together so tightly it almost suggests tangling in others, is the same pattern found in elf locks in the manes of horses in people's hair and sometimes in the grass. Both Graham Hancock[10] and Patrick Harpur[11] have unpacked the numerous similarities and crossovers in abduction narratives between alien cases and the older "faerie abduction" cases far too thoroughly for me to rehearse their findings here. But it is worth asking ourselves about the continuous references in both the faerie and alien abduction narratives to reproduction and "hybrids."

Does this perhaps tap in more to a need felt by faeries for our particular species of human vitality? Or does it point instead to another somewhat deeper image of our interdependence upon each other—an expression of the mutual feeding and nourishment so eloquently expressed by the way plants breathe in what we breathe out and exhale what we then breathe in? When they talk about improving their stocks with strong human babies do they perhaps mean the element of soul? That mysterious "shadow" cast by mankind that allows for the growth of a heart, the part which faeries were traditionally believed to lack?

10 Graham Hancock, *Supernatural: Meetings with the Ancient Teachers of Mankind*, (New York: Disinformation Books, 2006).
11 Patrick Harpur, *The Philosopher's Secret Fire: A History of the Imagination*, (London: Penguin Books, 2002).

FAERIES AND THE GRIMOIRE TRADITION

If we are to understand the presence and place of faeries in the grimoire tradition and amid the circles that such volumes were circulated we can do worse than to give a close read to what Cornelius Agrippa had to say about them in his Three Books of Occult Philosophy:

"There is moreover as hath been above said, a certain kind of spirits not so noxious, but most neer to men, so that they are even affected with humane passions, and many of these delight in mans society, and willingly dwell with them: Some of them dote upon women, some upon children, some are delighted in the company of divers domestick and wild animals, some inhabit Woods and Parks, some dwell about fountains and meadows. So the Fairies, and hobgoblins inhabit Champian fields; the Naiades fountains: the Potamides Rivers; the Nymphs marshes, and ponds: the Oreades mountains; the Humedes Meadows; the Dryades and Hamadryades the Woods, which also Satyrs and Sylvani inhabit, the same also take delight in trees and brakes, as do the Naptæ, and Agaptæ in flowers; the Dodonæ in Acorns; the Paleæ and Feniliæ in fodder and the Country. He therefore that will call upon them, may easily doe it in the places where their abode is, by alluring them with sweet fumes, with pleasant sounds, and by such instruments as are made of the guts of certain animals and peculiar wood, adding songs, verses, inchantments suitable [enchantments suitable] to it, and that which is especially to be observed in this, the singleness of the wit, innocency of the mind, a firm credulity, and constant silence; wherefore they do often meet children, women, and poor and mean men. They are afraid of and flie from men of a constant, bold, and undaunted mind, being no way offensive to good and pure men, but to wicked and impure, noxious. of this kind are hobgoblins, familiars, and ghosts of dead men. Hence Plotinus saith, that the souls of men are sometimes

made spirits: and of men well deserving are made familiars which the Greeks call Eudemons, i.e. blessed spirits: but of ill deserving men, hags, and hobgoblins, which the Greeks call Cacodemons, i.e. Evil spirits; But they may be called ghosts when it is uncertain whether they have deserved well or ill."[1]

Agrippa calls faeries "more like human beings" than angels or demons and associates them with common people but nonetheless suggests his learned readers make contact with them. In Folger 26 Oberion and a variant of Queen Mab are listed with demons such as Lucifer with no real essential differences between them noted. The faerie presence in the grimoires from the seventeenth century onwards is extensive. Both in Dan Harms' essay in *The Faerie Queens*[2] and elsewhere in a variety of David Rankine's works is the extent of this material well explored.

Rankine states in his essay for *Hands of Apostasy* that the presence of faerie material is clear evidence of Witchcraft having an influence on the grimoire tradition, rather than influence flowing solely in the opposite direction. It is almost as though Witchcraft, increasingly a persecuted behavior by the seventeenth century, was partially absorbed into the more acceptable form of grimoire invocations, a hiding place in plain sight. What is also important to us, given the topic of the current work, is that Rankine links the invocation of faerie with Witchcraft in no uncertain terms. Despite the strong demonology influence on the image of Witchcraft, magicians invoke angels and demons, but Witches, it appears, invoke faeries.

Or at least until faeries found their way into grimoires, after that the waters appear muddier. We hear the astrologer William Lilly speaking of how frequently those who invoke the Faerie Queen fail to endure the sight of her.

1 Agrippa, 567.

2 Sorita d'Este and David Rankine, *The Faerie Queens: A Collection of Essays Exploring the Myths, Magic and Mythology of Faerie Queens,* (Glastonbury: Avalonia Books, 2013).

> *"Since I have related of the Faerie Queens, I shall acquaint you, that it is not for everyone, or every person, that these angelical creatures will appear unto, though some may say the call, over and over again, or indeed is it given to many people to endure their glorious aspects; even very many have failed, when they are ready to manifest themselves…"*

The author goes on to explain how a man of otherwise "undaunted spirits" had invoked the Faerie Queen in a wood, only to be left trembling with his hair erect on his head at the sight of her.[3]

There are several interesting things about this testimonial. One, which is perhaps most obvious is that "many people" were invoking her at this period which provides us with extra proof of this faerie conjuring craze that appears to have emerged in the seventeenth century. It is also interesting that Lilly describes her as "angelical." One can't be altogether sure whether this indicates he subscribes to the typical folk narrative of faeries as fallen angels or whether he is simply describing her appearance as "angel-like." Perhaps most importantly we see from this testimonial that the manifestation of a faerie was still greeted in the seventeenth century by appropriate levels of awe and terror, leaving many an intrepid conjurer partly incapacitated.

As David Rankine says in his "Pentacles of Wood" essay: *"The link between witches and faeries was an emphatic one,"* but why the ingress of faeries into grimoire magic at the height of Witchcraft persecution? There can be two initial explanations. One is that it was a natural outgrowth of the printing press, which led to the "book of secrets" additions in the margins where Witchcraft charms were often added to grimoires. And that over time, with the increased availability of printing, this material made its way out of the margins and into the main body of the grimoires. The other explanation, which I find more compelling, is that there was more interaction between Cunning Folk, Witches and grimoire

3 Purkiss, 159.

magicians than previously thought[4] and that absorbing the material learned from Witches and Cunning Folk into a ceremonial format, replete with references to God and Jesus "rescued" the practices from the taint of Witchcraft. Perhaps the very thought that Witchcraft was to be associated with demons, and Cunning Craft with Christian mages was partially created by this "rescuing," and without it we would know far less about early modern interactions with faeries.

What we can tell very clearly from the grimoire traditions that include conjurations of faerie beings like Obreon (Oberon), Mab and Sibylla is that their close links to folklore didn't spring out of the ground whole in the seventeenth century. Before the grimoires picked them up someone else was nourishing and developing these traditions and conjuring these spirits, and those people would probably have been accused of Witchcraft for it. We can infer this from how frequently the Faerie Queen is substituted for the Devil in Witchcraft confessions of the period and how often the familiars of Witches were faerie. If we lift off the ceremonial magic framework from the conjurations of faeries from this period we are still left with a surprisingly large amount of information, which I will explore more carefully in the grimoire section of this book.

The very fact that the Witchcraft persecution mindset linked beings like the Queen of Faeries with the Devil and often considered them interchangeable in the confessions also must have helped for faeries to slip into the realm of the grimoire, to appear with demons without anything to distinguish them as different. This throws a spanner into the works of the popular idea of dividing magical practitioners into Witches who work with devils, demons and sometimes faeries and Cunning Folk who work with Christianized material.

Another important aspect of the migration of faeries into the grimoires is that it allowed for these spirits to travel over quite some

4 For more on the topic of how literate and illiterate traditions were not as cleanly separated as once thought see the introduction to David Rankine's edition of *The Grimoire of Arthur Gauntlet: A 17th Century London Cunning-man's Book of Charms, Conjurations, and Prayers,* (Glastonbury: Avalonia Books, 2011).

distance. The documented history of Sibylla for instance begins in the Greek *Hygromanteia* where one is instructed on how to set a rich table for her in return for her answering the magician's questions, and extends as far as the extreme North of Britain where Reginald Scot records workings to invoke the faerie Sibylla. Obreon (Oberyn etc.) is also found both in Britain and on the continent. This ability of faerie lore and charms to travel via grimoires began to change the very nature of the highly localized Witchcraft legacy, allowing people to conjure faeries from other regions.

Many people argue that Witches were just Cunning Folk that fell out of favour with the population and that they worked alone, with the Coven being a modern invention. But as Rankine astutely points out, the grimoire tradition that we see evolving into an outlet for native faerie magic contained operations intended for small groups. Lilly's account of the conjuration of the Faerie Queen that we quoted above concludes on the note of the man's "companions" laughing at his awe-struck and incapacitated state after the Queen's manifestation, suggesting he had at least two other people with him. It is intriguing to conjecture that whilst the grimoires were absorbing and sanitizing faerie sorcery, helping to remove the taint of Witchcraft, they also passed influence in the opposite direction. We know this because we frequently find seals or sigils copied from grimoires in Cunning Folk charms, but it may have gone further than that. Although most historical cunning practitioners do indeed seem to have worked alone or with one other protégé at the very most, the very grimoires that discuss the conjuration of faeries provide a template for a working group, with multiple offices or jobs, such as Magister and Seer, indicated by separate circles they were to stand in. That what we now think of as Traditional Witchcraft owes something to this heritage seems almost indisputable.

A PLACE AND A STATE OF BEING

Human accounts of Faerie differ wildly from a fantastical place, through to somewhere much like our world except with pleasures which you never grow tired of, and wine and food which never cloys or loses it piquancy with familiarity. We hear about this quality of faerie has in places as diverse as faerie abduction narratives and literary sources like Spencer's "The Faerie Queene." Anyone with a great interest in Faerie has probably read sentences mentioning wine or music that you never tire of in different contexts a few dozen times. Most of us will think little more about the meaning. But let us stop for a moment to consider the true implications of such an idea or experience. An imaginative exercise is necessary to clear the dross of familiarity that makes us falsely assume we've already truly considered it.

It is often said that the state of "being faerie" is much like the state of a human child. In some ways this could be said to be true but in others it could not be further from the truth, this is why changeling children are deemed so strange! Anyone who has spent time around a young human child will tell you that being in a state where nothing ever bores them and they could gaze at the fine detail in a flower for half an hour is about as far from standard child-like behaviour as it's possible to get. Human children are little balls of needs and wants continuously hunting for the next sensory gratification. Faeries are immersed in the all, in a way that precludes true hunger for novelty. The exquisite complexities of creation are the true nutriment. So whilst you could say that the faerie and the child have in common their openness and their sensuality, even their innocence, this part of faerie experiences is quite different.

For instance it would take quite a young child to find the game of the Cornish Corrigans fun: which simply involves chanting Sunday, Monday, Tuesday, Wednesday over and over again whilst dancing in the same circle for hours. But if you imagine that the part of our brain that begins to shut down to things that are no longer novel, the part that protects us from being overwhelmed by simple sounds and smells in our environment—that system filtration doesn't exist in the faerie consciousness. If you imagine those words you're chanting will always be as fascinating and strange (because they pin down time) than they were the first time you heard them. Imagine that your beloved will always feel to you as they did when love was new. Imagine how little work you'd ever get done in this world if everything was always that fresh...

It would be wholly possible to sit for ages fascinated by foreign words used to order time—for what is time to one who can never get bored? You would perhaps need to suffer from a touch of synesthesia to understand what might make Sunday, Monday, Tuesday, Wednesday innocuous but make Thursday a total poisonous, damp smoke-smell of a word that the faeries will punish you for uttering. In fact, human individuals once marked out by their society as "faerie" are probably referred to as savants in our era.

Most of the faerie peculiarities make sense if you think about them from the perspective of what is famously lacking in their realm. One needs to have known true suffering to experience gratitude, therefore saying thank you wouldn't make a lot of sense. Money only has value in relation to lack, which is a state that makes no sense at all. In a world without lack offering to give someone an object in return for something they've done for you is simply insulting.

With this in mind we should consider the Agrippa quote above about the sort of people who can hear and see the faeries. Innocent, childlike, guileless people are said to be so favoured. Which returns us full circle to where we began, at the very beginning of this book, where we spoke of how our world looks down on childish or innocent behavior, the very things that make people able to interact with the Good People. Our minds have become iron-bound, difficult to access.

It seems that on top of a certain guileless quality in the faerie state, there is an absorption in the present moment that can seem childlike in its focus with trivial things—but only to those who can't see the layers of meaning the faerie perceives when looking at reality. Here the humans that could best comprehend the faerie state of being would, as I've said, be those with synesthesia. In synesthesia, involuntary associations arise between patients' senses, causing information input to overlap, giving them colours that taste, and smells that sound. Monday might be blue, Tuesday tastes like ginger, the word Wednesday feels like velvet, but Thursday might smell like cranberries.

There are simple ways we can tell that faeries think in this manner. We know from the folk stories they experience time differently, because time passes peculiarly in Faerie and they live much longer than a human. So it is most likely they would experience the passage of time differently than us. And they are persistently depicted as coming from a world where everything is originally smaller than in our world, which suggests a world of fine detail. Think of how beautiful sand grains are when you gaze at them under a microscope and you will be getting closer to perceiving the unimaginable beauty of Elphame. Think about when you look at detail under a glass and suddenly all this intricate detail is visible that you couldn't see before, you realize how beautiful creation is and how intricate and ultimately artistic is nature! But then the pall creeps in, you get used to it, you've seen sand under a microscope before, it's already old... But what if it *could not get old.* What if you were in a state where nothing ever gets old? There is a constant sharpness in your perception of beauty in such a state, one that makes me think of Andrew Chumbley's quote from *Azoetia "tire not of pleasure, but seek thee the ever-virgin joys that live beneath Medusine veils."* Here he seems to be poetically suggesting the faerie state as desirable for those of the Art who know how to brave the obvious perils of Medusine veils.

Like the synesthesia sufferer the faerie might, for instance, become engrossed in stimuli the ordinary person isn't even aware of. These very qualities if they emerge in people today, which we might infer to be similar to the behavior of faeries, are denigrated in our culture because they remind us of drug users and layabout artistic types. In a materialistic culture the ultimate sign of low value is to produce something of a finer substance that cannot be grasped in one's hands and coarsely consumed. It is viewed by most as a self-indulgence.

It is bad in our world, like the faerie, to be absorbed in the moment, in the exquisite detail in things and to lose awareness of time. The world will punish you in numerous ways if you break this rule. It is bad to be so filled up on beauty that no one can buy or sell you anything, because capitalism requires you to be always empty and hungry. Rather than is this thing beautiful, we ask how will it make money? It is negative to not get quickly tired of one thing because how then will you buy new things? It is always important to remember that the things you consider gauche, puerile or naïve didn't get to be seen that way on their own, they required some social positioning. And thus we have come to a place where we have made our communal mindset almost impenetrable to faeries. We have made it dense like iron, with all our hard-nosed thoughts about what forms of productivity matter and about how the truth may only be known through one channel and that is the coarsely physical plain alone, the subtle aspects of physical experience we've been taught to listen to even less.

As you begin to open up the imaginative world of the fae, the place of wonder that the world becomes when you start to see all the little things expands. People with synesthesia see connections between their senses but the faerie state of being is more than that alone. It's about seeing an extra dimension in things, via the small details. Think of the nonsense that faeries like to sing: "Sili ffrit, sili ffrit" like the lake faerie of Wales as they spin, or "Monday, Tuesday, Wednesday" like the Corrigans as they dance. When you slow everything down and pay attention to minute details, when time falls away, when one sense begins to bleed into another, nonsense morphs into crystal-clear sense because each of the individual sounds of the words are actually music rather than semantics. When words become musical sounds, normal common sense becomes unintelligible.

In these ways we can describe being "in Faerie" as also being a state as well as a place. When our forebears said some living human "was a faerie" it is likely this was the state of being that they meant. Lady Wilde's descriptions of Faerie Doctors suggest that Irish society indulged their eccentricities and the fact they sought out the "gentle places" and liked to be alone. It was accepted that they lived in a different state of being not so very long ago, our ancestors were able to find a place for that even in their worlds where subsistence came a lot harder than it does to most of us in the West today. If people who lived from one harvest to another could accept the idea of human beings walking around among them in a different state of being, sittng for hours in gentle places and contributing something entirely insubstantial (faerie doctor healing, poetry or music is not insubstantial but it's source is) to their community, it is amazing how negative our comparatively comfortable culture is about such people. You would think we were the ones on the verge of starving if everyone didn't pull their weight in one single model of conformity!

When you think about Faerie as a state of being that the initiated human is able to acquire, then there is power entering it (temporarily so as to remain a functional person). We reveal the goal of Witchcraft to be able to become as the faerie is whilst still being human. Faerie Sight isn't just the ability to see faeries, it's to *see as the faeries see.*

CONCLUSION

We find ourselves after a long journey following the fragile trail of a source mythos, unraveling its mysteries slowly as we went. Like all stories these traces of myth form over the void. The mind of the sorcerer knows how to follow the way a story has gone even when the path seems impenetrable. Signs and signals abound on the Crooked Path. Along this way we find ourselves with angels who were perhaps once dragons, who fell not from Heaven for a wrongdoing, into Hell and Earth and all the elements in between, but from un-creation and oneness into creation and multiplicity, incarnation and mess. We find ourselves inside a story that contains what Chumbley once called "homespun Gnosticism."

In Celtic terms the "pre-fallen" state would be the era when the Tuatha de Danann ruled and had not yet been sent into exile, the source perhaps of a persistent melancholy that seems to be part of the Irish story of itself. Or does the draconian fall of the Watchers, simply remind us that the seeds of conscious life came from the stars? Some will want to see it that way. And the faeries, like ourselves, are the children of the stars, they on one side of the curtain of twilight, we on the other, with a thicker and thicker mist between us as the world ages plough onward.

And yet... Would it be too bold to suggest that one senses a shy stirring?

Witchcraft is forever the flame that can part that mist. Witches by their liminal nature shared with faeries, keep the door open a crack on that stellar reality that hides behind all things.

This amorphous ambivalence, of being one who potentially both kills and cures, of being both a possible poison and a possible medicine to one's community, is one that faeries share with Witches. In fact, without the narrative of faerie it is impossible to fully imagine Witchcraft. When the Witch Isobel Gowdie wished to fly she needed only make the faerie cry "horse and haddock" and her elf darts provided to her by elf boys. Whether in Scotland with Gowdie or as far-flung as Romania the Witch was a physical representative of the highly unpredictable and morally ambiguous world of faerie.

Even the diabolized faeries, called winter demons or succubi, were partly just another maligned part of the indigenous psyche over-emphasized to the point of pathology. In response an ultra-nice, super white and shiny faerie had to be created to counter that swing towards darkness and to separate faeries out from Witches, and that "fairy" has been progressively trivialized ever since. Here has occurred a great and terrible lesion in our relationship with Faerie, because when you remove something's darkness you also remove its depth.

In such a way the original integrity of the faerie worldview was shattered and fragmented. Thus the fall occurred not so much to the faeries, but in how we saw them. They went underground and below the lakes from our perspective. But really it is our eyes that fell, not them. We fell further from them. Yet we must not make the assumption that this does not affect them also, that we can only guess at by casting our mind into one of the most alien forms of consciousness imaginable.

It is perhaps not the Saint Days and other references to Christian folk customs, including angels, demons, holy wells and miracles that we need to send packing if we are to return to the true roots of the Faerie Faith, of which Witchcraft of both the left and the right hand are expressions in this world. It is the way spirits who thrive at different seasons or in different landscapes have been shackled to notions of a strict good and evil.

Long before the division into new shapes and forms and mutations, and still remembered dimly in some out-of-the-way areas, the archaic faerie was a creature of light, music, a hidden animal part, star-fire, perhaps an empty back, who combined beauty with deformity, Earth with air, darkness with light, in differing combinations and quantities. The ultimate twilight, liminal creature this pre-fallen angel of Earth was the very image and reflection of the true Witch—working with both the left hand and the right, cursing and healing, ridden by the beast and yet blazing with the cunning fire of the heavens. The difference between them and the Gods was a very hazy one indeed, the longer you looked at them. If they were missing anything, perhaps, it was the element of humanity that was broken off from them, as well as them from us.

It is here in our journey after we have come to know this faerie figure that we see how the archaic faery and Witches are almost the same thing, crossing over with each other just as easily as the sorginak and laminak in the Basque country. The only thing that makes us different to each other is our own addiction, or perhaps cursed eyes that see a fallen world where man and spirit walk separately. Not every person suffers from this curse, and not everyone you think you meet on the street is a person. Not every spirit you meet is only a spirit. Some ghosts are still among the living from the perspective at least of medicine.

Of course there were mora or mare creatures, trolls and goblins that might have possessed a shadowy, ancestral power even long before they were demonized, but death is no more evil and inappropriate than life or birth. Both forces are required to maintain health and balance in a community. There are certainly goblin forces that belong to the twisted roots, thorns and poison gardens of this world and yet many poisons when used in the right quantities have been the traditional allies of Witches, and there is something of the goblin art that rides in the mandragora and belladonna plants that enter our skin through unguents. There are also some faeries that shine very brightly and appear very beautiful to human eyes, yet in the early times no one ever said they were good.

There is in every twisted goblin a hidden, darkly green glimmer of cunning fire, a hidden light within the darkness. Things burn through that lighten to honey gold, special elixirs that brew in the hearts of the goblin folk and other ice-bright but cold magic lives in the fingers of troll-men. In the empty back where the heart should be, of every shining one is a cool awareness that can only be described as alien and terrible.

As Fiona Macleod eloquently put it: *"How beautiful they are, the lordly ones. Who dwell in the hills, in the hollow hills. They have faces like flowers and their breath is wind that stirs amid the grasses, filled with white clover. Their limbs are whiter than shafts of moonlight. They are more fleet than the march wind. They laugh and are glad and are terrible. When their lances shake every green reed quivers."*

PART II

A POETIC EXPLORATION OF FAERIE

Beneath the brooding arms of the Olive I met it who was God, by horns and smile I knew it, and O' how we played. We had our fingers in everything and ran about with only the sky to robe us and the earth to dance on. A shrine of fallen branches and the horse's bones we moulded, and when the moon appeared in the sky we would lie together. Upon our altar, God showed me all his tricks and sorceries.

—Andrew Chumbley, Penumbrae

It was a bursting point. There was even a pop. A sudden give and a release following. It wasn't like being strangled. The dead man had thought it would be like being snuffed out into darkness. But it wasn't even hell. He wasn't really expecting Hell like his fearful brain had while it was still fully functioning. His body hadn't believed in it during the last gasping. Only the next dry breath through the airway is God when you're at the end of a rope. The only hell Elijah knew was the sense of weightless air beneath his kicking heel.

Then the sudden reflex of pain in the head that burst into unexpected pleasure, of the spasming, sin-spangled kind... Images of baby mandrakes danced before his eyes, images of revelation, before the slow fading out. In those moments he recalled the name for the wicked little plants, "dead man's ejaculate," the product of angel lust. So that would be his one kin left to remember him in the world of man? Witch plants... Then it occurred to him that he was *thinking*. Still. Even after the light went out.

It seemed then that the light had actually *come on* so much brighter than ever before...

That was when They came. He hadn't had time to wonder whether Hell or Heaven would follow next. Because ahead of any invitation to either of those places came the men that walk the edge of dawn, the fearful ones who stood betwixt and between, straddling the abyss that Elijah's heel had just kicked out against. They came with the rustle of snakeskin hatbands, the rattle of toad bones and horses that moved like shadows but for the macabre little bells on their bridles. All the sounds that should have been quiet suddenly inexplicably loud, and all the ones that should have been loud becoming soft as tiny mice feet.

To Elijah the riders looked like men, outlaw men from a former era, back before the North was harrowed, but they did not act like men. Not any men that Elijah had ever seen. They stood and stared for so very long. Not doing anything, not showing any emotion, or even blinking. Just looking at him. Whilst he was aware of being looked at Elijah wasn't aware of having any limbs or form.

"Do you think he is a good man?" one asked the others in his toneless voice.

"Do good men hang unclaimed at the crossroads as food for crows?"

"Amongst humans? Doubtlessly," replied another. But no one laughed at his wit. Elijah was not sure it was a joke, and yet it was sharp, the comment, as pain is sharp. "I believe he is the one we are looking for."

"Then here you must stay," said another of them, addressing Elijah directly. "Until next an innocent man swings on the gallows tree. Here you must stay and cry your message out to each comer, whether they heed you or not. You must tell them 'go away, keep walking, pass by'."

They say the words in their grimoires, "fear God but do not fear him"—the gatekeeper of the way. The necromancers will tell each other this while sweating palms grip a fragile candle and tend it's flame lest the dry mouth of the crypt swallow them.

But you must *make them* fear you. This you must do to any human necromancer that tries to pierce the veil to the land of Faerie. Do this to test his mettle and his worthiness and he shall be thrice tested. But if the green necromancers of the ashen faces arise from the other way… Then be as you are now, a tongueless, eyeless, thing. Before you fear a human trying to pierce the veil of faerie, first fear the faerie man who comes seeking contact with humans. It takes but one to reveal themselves bodily and the whole earth quakes with change. Thus are you clear in your role?"

Suddenly it was as if the rider of the Host had seized him up, and with some blade of fire cut open orifices in his face so that Elijah could once again breathe, speak, hunger and see. Awareness rushed in through Elijah's face. At least, this is some approximation to the experience. In truth he gained his deep-senses, his death-gnosis.

Gazing upon the faerie man with these new senses seemed to be gazing on the face of the Master Artisan himself for a moment. The being had wounded him, and at the same instant given him light with his crafter's blade, shaping him anew. Whether faerie men, as they claimed or demons, they had already done more to demonstrate truth and power to Elijah than any church of the earthly God ever had. Humans had left him to swing in the wind as carrion-food, but They had claimed him and given him breathless light and dizzy refractions of being.

"Yes, sir, quite clear. When another innocent man swings here and I am free to go? What of me then?" he asked.

The pale-faced unblinking one came forward and leaned close.

"There are three roads Elijah. The wide one, well-travelled, it leads to what is below where all the echoes resolve in the gut of the Old Dame. The narrow, thorny one too dissolves, into the light above, but the winding, mysterious way between leads to Faerie. You will simply choose your road at that time. To be as the dead are, as the saints are, or as we are. But sadly for now you must play Judas, we will spread your blood when the time comes and free you to move on."

"But I didn't kill anyone," Elijah murmurs. "Let alone our Saviour Jesus."

"We speak a different name here, dead man. We know divinity as truly as you, yet our world lies somewhat in reverse. For humans it matters little who actually does a deed. They have made their sacrifice of you, to us. Hanged you up on the edge of town for claiming. Tied a red ribbon around your neck and sent you into the wastes to pull the faerie off them! We could have taken your skin and worn it, ridden the winds dressed in your face, yet we saw the ribbon tied around your neck and you released into our wilderness and thus we chose you."

"You told me what would befall mankind if a green necromancer wandered through the door you give me power over. But what of human necromancers who wish to penetrate into the Faerie realm?" Elijah asked. And he had good reason for asking, as he knew something about how he'd come to be here that they did not.

"They must be tested on their merits. First they are tested for courage and if they get deeper they are tested again."

"Upon what are they tested?"

The man of the Host did not reply. His eyes had neither the light of life nor the clouds of death; he was attractive by mortal standards, yet he had not any blood in him for there was seemingly no emotion.

"Can they hold water and their eyes turn pearl? Or will they run when they should walk and walk when they should run? The Lady Sibylla guards her own gate with those who pass the first trial. You will never get closer to her by spurring your horse."

"Who is she?" Elijah was not very well-versed in the aristocrats and important ladies of his time, and he was not sure whether it was to mortal maid or faerie dame that the warrior referred.

"Our sworn Mistress," said another of the Host, taking out his blade, which held its own inner, mysterious light, and kissing it in her name. "For whom we ride along the edge of dawn, at the crest of storms, and penetrate even into the darkest abyss of hell or space, carrying lightning of the dragon's breathing, bearing a sword that penetrates the waters of the Underwood with the star-fire."

Elijah couldn't quite imagine such experiences and yet the words enchanted him. The species of magical force that crackled in the air around these creatures set him on edge at the same time.

"I believe I should tell you," Elijah said, from loyalty inspired by their glamour rather than logic. "A devil-man came among us prisoners, only nights before I was to die. He said he caught the smell of innocence upon me and came sniffing. He was a conjurer from the West, seeking the promise of a man due to swing that he'd rise from his tomb to serve the master's bidding after death."

"Why did you say yes if you misliked the devil-man?" asked the warrior.

"Because he offered a purse to my widow and a good half of me didn't believe what he meant to do would come to pass. I thought it was mere shadow-puppetry and dreams."

"Well is this real enough for you? Your 'devil-man' will be back if you made a verbal bond with him. One who holds your soul in oath has you in bondage, yet let him not know of that. Let him feel the fear of all you can be... These are the faces you can wear." The faerie-man produced a series of skins that hung loosely at his belt and offered them to Elijah. "When you wear them you will have eyes and ears just like any other man or woman. You are constrained to appear as a nine year old girl child, a pale hound or a horned devil? Which would you choose?"

"I would appear as the girl child."

For the first time Elijah thought he saw the faerie rider smile, as if he was pleased with the choice he'd made. But until he had donned the face and skin of the child Elijah had no idea of what he had chosen or why.

The night the devil-man came was a churning, dirty, foggy night, crawling full of owls. His feet came along the hooks and crooks of the road with a dragging sound where his lame leg came along. Devil Jack, they called him, even churchmen were afraid of him and his slightly turned in ankle, they rumored was really a split-foot.

He had a few souls in his sack and some imps who lived in roots that were said to be goblins. The goblins came awake at night, their button eyes opening in the dark, when Jack would go down to the crossroads and spit and draw shapes in the dirt. Those goblin roots could be sent out to torment the chaste girls in their beds, and the chaste boys also, leaving them in women's underwear when they woke. Such were the tales they told of Old Devil Man Jack. None but him, and maybe one other, knew the truth of it all.

Elijah heard the muttering first and he bruised his way through into their voices. He vaguely felt it through the eyes of the child's skin, the way he had reappeared swinging at the crossroads, resolving back into his last memory of being in the flesh. The creak-creak of the rope on the gallows wood gave off a sound like the harsh cawing of ravens, as his corpse danced gently on the breeze. Unlike when he was alive where Elijah couldn't have spoken a word with this rope around his neck now he merely swung his head in the direction of his tormentor.

"What do you want with me, Witch?"

"I summon and constraint you spirit-"

Tom felt the contortion pulling his bones tight and then it was under his skin. His body was full of serpents, a sack of snakes about to burst at the seams, hissing and turning in all direction. Finally the feeling gave and he hopped down nimbly from the gallows. He could sense and drink like sweet water the dread of the necromancer, who gazed upon the death-pale girl of nine who had climbed out as a shadow through his raven-pecked eye sockets, and yet landed on the ground a normal size for a girl child.

"You know very well I already signed the contract. What would you have me do?" Elijah asked in the sweet voice of the little girl with blonde plaits he wore. The man's dark eyes reflected a thousand fen-land desires that Tom, hitherto now, had never even begun to dream about. But he tasted them vicariously through this man with whom he'd made the sinister bond. This was what the hob men paid him for his work, Elijah realized, these new senses that were opening in him. He was learning and suckling like the bee at the pollen of every new sensation and feeling. Every moment of this experience was making him more complex, his knowledge of the worlds richer, more varied and multi-textured.

"I'd have you for a goblin-man."

Elijah laughed with the little girl voice and advanced on the man, letting the deathly pallor of the girl's seemingly mortal sickness become stronger and stranger in his face. The men of the Faerie Host had bade him put the fear of God into these mortals who dared trespass. If this man could be shaken from his goal then he must be. Elijah knew his work. He was to test where this man stood on the line between desire and necessity.

Only the man who had found Fate's tracks in the sand, the three-pronged bird-foot track, the evidence of her tell, could pass this gate. The Old Woman's poker face was the best there was, so you had to be smart and there wouldn't be many who were smart enough. Desires among humans were as plentiful as flies on a three-day-old corpse in summer time, but when a man found his necessity… Ah… there he stood. It was a power that could frustrate even a faerie monarch.

"For what work do you want me, human sorcerer? And what would you be willing to give to obtain your ultimate goal?"

The devil-man laughed. It was not a pretty sound. All the monsters of the human mind seemed to live latent in those dark eyes. It was not clear who would affright whom between the two of them, or who was in fact the monster and who the seeker after monsters.

"My business is my own, servitor. And as to what I'd be prepared to do to get what I want—" He came in close to Elijah then, leaning down a little to accommodate for Tom's child form, to whisper in his ear. "*Anything*. And I'm not afraid of your little girl skin, dead man."

"Then you should fear the magic of the Hedge-men who made me."

The devil-man withdrew and stood up straight. "All sane men fear the magic of the Hedge-men who ride with the Host," the conjurer conceded. "But it's been a very, very, very long time since I've felt sane."

The devil-man had his dog pull the mandragora then and it was Elijah's corpse upon the gallows who made the strangled scream as the roots gave and blistered the air with shrieks. Elijah whose crossroad's curse fell across the back of the black dog instead of Old Jack the devil man. For now, Elijah was borne away with sack-cloth across his nose and mouth—an eyeless thing at the mercy of a Witch.

His hands were scarred around the knuckles, dirty, stained at the fingers with elderberry and lilac dyes, which stuck in the calluses; they looked like the hands of a man older than his years. People called him "old" Jack sometimes, even though he wasn't old or young, just shy of his fortieth winter as he was. They had started out calling him "that old devil" and just added his name to it over time.

As scarred and wind-burned and not altogether clean as most of his skin was, his hand was steady, his back was strong and his eye was keen, and that made him young enough for his own liking. As he sprinkled the powder that reeked of burned feathers and dried spiders his gaze was steady and intense upon the mandragora goblin he conjured. Muttering under his breath he'd been slipping by dark degrees into the territory of the gloaming. The edge-space just outside of where the light reaches.

If anyone had asked him how he did his witching he'd not have been able to give words to this intensified knowing that led him to feel as if he had eyes in every pore. But his blood and bones could have written full grimoires on the subject, his guts would have produced a parchment. He used to jest that his left ball could have taught the Craft as well as he. Indeed that was where he first felt the subtle creeping up of some of his spirits.

Jack was familiar with this territory. When his eyes rolled back into his head and you could only see the whites he saw more than when they faced forward. He knew the words by heart so it was easy to mutter them, even in this entranced state.

"I charge thee spirit, that thou shalt not go out of the root; nor yet to alter thy shape at this time, except I command thee otherwise; but to come unto me at all places, and in all hours, when and wheresoever I shall call thee, by the virtue of our Lord Jesus Christ, and to show me true visions, and also to go and to fetch me the faerie Sibylla, that I may talk with her in all kind of talk, as I shall call her by any. I conjure thee spirit by the great wisdom and divinity of his godhead, my will to fulfill, as is aforesaid. Fiat, fiat, fiat. Amen."

A seething followed, as if the ground beneath the mandrake root were yawning and heaving, preparing to vomit. The spirit would attempt to scare him again. Jack had seen his own death. He'd harrowed Hell and walked through rivers of blood up to the knee for three days and three nights to reach the Kingdom of Elphame. He wasn't one to expect an audience with the faerie Sibylla for nothing. The Host would test him and test him well.

It started as a skin crawling, up-with-the-hairs draft, and became a high-pitched marrow-withering shriek that only Jack could hear. He threw his hands over his ears but he kept his eyes calmly open and still. When the shade had finished its theatrics Jack took the bound mandragora into another chamber where he'd inscribed a chalk circle on the floor for himself and another for the faerie Sibylla.

He took out a round crystal stone and into it he pressed the virtues of the mandrake root and the heat of the spirit it carried within.

"I conjure thee Elijah into this crystal stone, by God the father, by God the son Jesus Christ, and by God the Holy-ghost, three persons and one God, and by their virtues. I conjure thee spirit, that thou do go in peace, and also to come again to me quickly, and to bring with thee into that circle appointed, Sibylla faerie, that I may talk with her and so charge thee declare unto her. I conjure thee spirit Elijah, by the blood of the lamb which redeemed all the world; by the virtue thereof I charge thee thou spirit in the crystal stone, that thou do declare unto her this message."

Jack struck the crystal ball lightly with his hazel rod. The three beats resounded loudly in the still chamber. Even the cat was put out, got up, arched his back and turned three times before resettling. A deep silence had come up like something stalking you, there was no sound but Jack could still tell it was there. With that loud-buzzing silence and the gentle incline of the candle flame Jack began to feel the vertigo of Their coming. He was a necromancer almost before he was a man, so Jack felt no fear of the dead. But this screaming faerie stillness was full of unquiet potentials and the longer it went on the more it wore away at him. His palms began to sweat with tension.

It was visceral at first. The sensation that snakes were crawling on him, either on his skin or under it. He hated the feeling and how he couldn't control it or confine it. At first the feeling was everywhere but now the snakes that infested his skin were circling in on his spine. From experience he knew you just had to surrender to it. He'd provided a place for his body to safely slump down in the circle for when he shed his own skin.

As always happened in any serious magical working Jack saw his sister's face smiling blithely the day before the travelling people came to town, back when everything was still all right. Her face was like a demon, sent there to throw him off his objective. He held his course. It was a test and he knew that well enough. They were trying to see if he'd be budged off course. He wouldn't let the goblin-man see him rattled, even when the images that followed were so disturbing. Something in him let go and his resistance was a light scattering of dust across the abyss as he passed over it.

Jack was suddenly drawn forward as if he was very small and shooting out through his own forehead, or perhaps that he were simply an eye capable of throwing itself great distances. His spirit rushed through a booming silence of sentient dark that buzzed and crackled like touching the skin of God. The darkness yielded to a forest path, rutted and crooked which emptied at last in to a haunted grotto. Jack gazed in wonder at the vision that lay before him. Inside the grotto, partly veiled by greenery was the waterfall of frothing milk. The air itself smelled of warm milk and honey.

Up came a girl's shape from the white opaque foam... Up out of a honey textured substance that coated her for only a moment, before sluicing off her skin as if it were made of silk and couldn't hold stickiness.

"Greetings sorcerer," she murmured, her voice as melodious and sweet as the ringing of mellow-toned bells. Her hair was long, blonde and tangled into elf-locks all the way to the back of her legs, but her face was too strange to be beautiful, ageless yet too defined for one so young. Her eyes looked blind and unfocused, as if fixed on something far away. In all the girl could not have been more than ten years of age, showing only just the barest beginning of puberty. She made Jack think of the form Elijah had worn when he'd first captured the goblin man. This wasn't what he'd been expecting, not at all. *When they said 'faerie virgin' there was no jest in it.*

"Are you the faerie Sibylla?" he demanded.

Fire seemed to ripple behind her death-cold eyes for a moment and she lifted the pure white skirts of her one thin garment. Jack's glanced uncomfortably away from the revelation of the nudity of one so young. But even from the corner of his eye it was possible to see that below her skirts was nothing but the writhing and hissing of serpents, which seemed to emerge from where loins should have been. She laughed coldly as she dropped her petticoat back down. Jack supposed that the half-snake lamia body confirmed her identity as well or better than words.

"What do you want of me? You who serve the Winter Court wailing ones and ride with the Hunt of Phantoms?" She twiddled one of her elflocks lazily as she spoke.

"It is true that my work and nature lies elsewhere," the necromancer answered her. Beguiled as he was by the strange heady scent that filled the air, seeming to come from the nectar like substance that clung to Sibylla, he did not let his guard down. The substance was faintly radiant and entirely entrancing to gaze at for too long. If you gazed for too long you found yourself dissolving into a glamour that faintly whispered to you that all you had ever desired in life lay on the other side of your submission. "But I come today to ask you an important boon, for it touches upon one of your... daughters."

"My daughter? Human, you have seen what I have under my skirts and yet you can't bend your mammal brain to see that I have no faerie daughters?"

"Well a girl of your people... Agnes the faerie girl who stumbled into the Wolf-pit."

There was no discernable emotion in the creature's elongated eyes. They were very beautiful eyes but they either contained no emotion at all, or else such complex nuanced ones that it would be impossible to guess them. It was discomforting, especially as the kind of knowledge her gaze belied was utterly inappropriate on one who looked so young. And yet was she so young? Her height and lack of much of any breasts had led him to imagine so, but as a woman of faerie he found himself now not at all certain that she was a child at all. "She is a Faerie Doctor now, is what I heard. I need you..." Jack could hear the all-too-human quaver in his voice for a moment. "I need you to locate her for me."

"Spin your dagger on the hard floor and I will stop the blade in her direction."

"No," Jack said firmly. "If I'd wanted the advice of a cheap conjure man I'd have got it from myself. I want her actual location."

It seemed that perhaps the elf-girl smiled, ever so slightly. Or perhaps she only narrowed her funereal eyes like a cat watching the antics of a lizard, judging whether it had taken in enough sun-shine to run quickly for its life or not.

"Come," Sibylla beckoned slowly, almost meditative was the gesture. "If you want real answers, you are going to have to come inside my mountain."

The sound of hissing had become very loud then, the frothing of the river of milk and the hissing of serpents combined with a strange hum that came from the faerie girl's body itself. Jack didn't need to deliberate.

◆

The green cap that covered her hair told of many battles fought and many victories won against the demons of illnesses. Each struggle was remembered with a feather, ribbon, or a small saint medallion, allowing her hat and its owner to accumulate their Virtue. Agnes preferred to keep all of her hair braided and covered, to only let it down, like releasing a beast, when it was time to exert influence over someone.

As she spun the delicate strands of her dead brother's hair into the fine silk she was working, her foot pedaled with meditative regularity. Making the green silk girdle to wear about her at all times, would remind her always of her connection to Faerie, and to her brother who'd placed his foot on the land of man and had everything inside him turn to dust. Shortly after his body had followed suit. Ivy grew on his grave now, the world of faerie taking back its own, Agnes had thought as she'd watched it grow, sometimes for many hours at a time. She'd taken tiny slivers from the green insides of the ivy to use in her healing salves. The power in her brother's fae body informed all her healing work.

It was an irritant to Agnes at first when her door was knocked upon. Her foot paused on the pedal and the luminous threads she saw coming together in her mind fell away like a broken web. With a sigh she got to her feet, brushed down her apron and moved the cat out of her way with her foot. This was how it was in the world of man, there was no respect for the elegant complexities of simple things. No sooner had you become immersed in the detail of such a work as some human came bumbling in to spoil it.

Agnes paused after opening the door. The tinker woman was not what she had expected to find on her doorstep. They both stood still, regarding each other like predators from foreign packs with their hackles up. Realising both their predicaments Agnes quickly ushered her and the little boy who accompanied her over the threshold. As she did a tiny white mouse appeared in her peripheral vision. Ever since the day in his death chamber her brother had gone into one of the mice inside the walls. It followed her everywhere. As if her privilege in living when he had died were one she must ever be reminded of whenever she did her work. The white rodent didn't speak but it gestured ominously to the child of the tinker woman.

Agnes looked at the boy. He was an extraordinarily pretty child, with hair like spun gold and dramatic, stormy sea-green eyes. The way his parents kept his hair, in lustrous locks down to his shoulders, it had been initially difficult to tell if he was a boy or a girl until she saw the latent strength in his proud jaw and brow.

"My name is Eliza," the woman said, in her strangely accented way. Agnes was trying to pick whether the accent was from Shropshire or fully Welsh. The woman was travelling folk at any rate, so clearly there was to be some admixture expected. She had but glanced into Eliza's pale-sky eyes when her elf-sight caught the vision of the spectral winding sheet, as the woman's future shroud snaked around her still living body, well past the knee. It enveloped her as though in the maw of some rising white serpent.

"You must already know I'm Agnes," she said, shaking off the sensation the prescience left her with. How she hated it when this happened just as she met new people and made her appear confused or simple. If they only knew what I see and have to pretend I don't, she thought, they would wonder why I behave as level and steady as I do. "Are you here on a... matter of delicacy?" she inquired as she led them into the front room. "For if it's an unwanted... well I'm a Faerie Doctor I don't fetch out the unwant-"

The tinker woman stopped and turned to her quite suddenly, her pale eyes that had seemed so soft burned hot and proud suddenly. She didn't allow her facial expression to give away her emotions but her eyes told their own story to eyes that could see. And her still lips told a story to ears that could hear. *Privileged bitch. You assume because I am what I am that I could be here for no other purpose.* Agnes smiled subtly to herself. She liked the woman's spirit.

"I am not looking for those kind of services, mum. I am here for my sister's son, Robin," she said, gesturing at the boy, who had taken himself over to the shutters and now sat dreamily in a ray of morning sun, the light dancing off his dark gold hair.

"What seems to be the matter with him?" Agnes enquired.

"Well haven't you heard?" Eliza said, stepping forward and whispering urgently to her as if they were both in grave danger. "He's *Him.* That's what's the matter with him. He's Robin Goodfellow!"

"Follow me."

◆

As soon as the faerie Sybilla spoke her form began to melt back into the greenery of the wall behind her. Jack realized it was no longer a wall at all, but a doorway into the green. Stepping into the virid maw of creeping things of root and sucker, he felt the crawling sensation over his body that the green world was swallowing him whole. It gave off numerous little sparks of electricity, as if he was stepping into some kind of conscious field that zapped and stung and whispered shifting thoughts and snippets of impressions.

When he emerged on the other side Jack felt one of his boots sink almost to the knee into something warm and viscous. When he looked down he observed that it was blood he was walking through. Immediately he felt violated. He wished he could wash it off. For some reason it recalled vividly to his mind each life he'd taken. As he was now forced to wade through the blood and gore if he wished to follow where Sibylla had gone, there was no quick way through. The more his thoughts turned to the past the heavier his step seemed, and the denser the sanguine stew at his leg as if he was wading through the thickness of his own guilt.

How quick the faerie glamour of honey and pulsating light gives way to the blood and tears of millions and the thousands of sticky pods all pupating faerie larvae inside human hearts. How quickly the horror and the beauty. How stiff the price of entry. So thought Old Devil Jack without words. If there had been a poetry of the limbic system, an art of heart-knowings, Jack would have been a renowned bard across the land. As it was he was reckoned by most a simple man, but underneath some simple things black fen-swamps of secrets go down and down into the dusky brake.

That was when the serpents rose from the ruddy slime. Shortly after the swallowing and the liquid came the digesting palpitations of the snake bodies. Jack had an unpleasant sensation they were the same snakes he'd seen emerging from under the dress of the faerie girl. As though they could detach and come for you. They writhed their way down from the walls, there were no walls anymore as they came down. As the panic set in he knew they were watching, the cool faerie eyes, but he was now sure they were looking at him from everywhere at once.

He tried to stay granite firm knowing they were there, but as the serpents went about his legs and rose on his body he began to struggle. Jack had no great talent for submission, even when it came to submission to the inevitable. In the belly of the holy beast there were only two outcomes: submission with grace, or submission without grace. Jack chose submission without grace.

They went over his face despite his struggles, drawing him tight so he could barely breathe. The more he fought it the tighter the snakes held him. He was wrapped and rhythmically pressed, especially around his head, and it gave him the disconcerting sense that he had progressed backwards into a mere babe in the birth canal. When they began to hiss as one, Jack was alarmed to feel the hissing coming as a vibration from his own backbone, which seemed to be a shared single spine with the undulating serpents.

There was something sensual and ecstatic about it. Jack let himself dissolve into the undulations as he felt the sphere-like pressure rise around their collective form. His mind seemed to merge with those of these other reptiles. It made perfect sense all of a suddenly that he who spoke to toad and fenny-snake, lizard and viper when he conjured should be able to think like a snake. Yet he was riding the dragon-fire of it, part of him remained the Eye Outside, part of him was ever observer to his own annihilation.

His forehead wore the diadem of Lucifer, after the serpent stone was birthed from his own brow. And when the other serpents withdrew from the congress they bit into his left hand, removing the upper joint on his little finger as if in exchange. They replaced the bone with a carved wooden peg. None of it felt like suffering, but all things, even the biting and shoving were now dripping with a lush sensuality of immense detail.

It was only when his eyes were thus purified by ordeal and realization that the faerie girl Sibylla came forward again. This time she appeared a few years older to him, and was starting to verge on an age group that Jack found it acceptable to look at as a woman. The thought of course was pointless, for upon this being her apparent age meant little. She smiled and there was the cunning of serpent in her eyes, pale damask pink rose petals and honey upon her lips that attracted the attention of bees—which would sometimes land on her face or mouth. This adornment of insects didn't seem to worry her in the slightest.

Jack knew without words that she was holy, she was virgin, child, nymph, lamia, whore, prophet, teacher... The perfume of her presence made his throat sting with thirst. He realized he had wandered through an arid desert till this moment where now he fell to his knees before a dark green, clear at the surface, oasis. Beneath that surface, which mirrored him back at himself, she was full of honey, secrets, crystal lakes, and at the centre—the seething alchemist's flame of her sex full of snakes.

"I will tell you where to find her," the faerie girl said. "But you must promise me something, in return." Although she now looked about thirteen she continued to twiddle childishly with her white-blonde elflock while the bees came and covered the pinkness of her lips as if she were a flower.

"Anything, my lady Sibylla," he muttered, going down on one knee before her and taking out the knife in his belt to lay at her feet. He couldn't remember where he'd learned to do that, but it seemed the right response to her presence.

"I want you to find the child Robin Goodfellow."

"Is not Robin Goodfellow a faerie boy? A hob-man?"

"In as much as your Agnes is a faerie woman, yes."

"How shall I find him? The stories that speak of him say he ran away from home."

"Where is the true home of the Travelling Man? Find Agnes and you shall find the child. Just remember what Puck is at all times, Devil Jack. And do not let your guard down."

◆

"The boy with the faerie father..." Agnes murmured, looking steadily at the child. That explained everything. It explained why she didn't want to stop looking at him, why he felt like home, why her gaze followed the boy like a hungry plant follows the Sun. He was as fae as her own children, and as the little one quickening like a green shoot in her womb. *You will find your friends on the heath one day, little green shoot… Mother Mary be watching over him and my little girl.* Nobody was safe, after all, if Robin Goodfellow was in the house. Even being who she was Agnes was well aware of this.

"Well we always knew my sister was carrying a dragon-man as soon as we knew she was with child, for his father came down upon us with a meteor shower as his sign and the boy came forth during a lightning storm. The sign from the sky was right before the night at the Sabbat where the dragon lay with my sister. We knew it was possible it would happen... Sometimes the Good People take the mother in exchange when they give such as he to this world. After she died giving birth to the wee lamb, Mother Mary rest her soul, I never worried too much about what they said, I just loved him as my own. He was all I had left of my sweet sister. The boy was an orphan, was all I thought of the matter and needs love like any child. But then the troubles began…"

"What kind of troubles?" Agnes asked, not looking at Eliza at all because her eyes never left the boy. Without realizing she was doing it her hands went protectively to her belly, as if to shield the child within from some unknown influence he may yet have on her pregnancy.

"I'll show you," Eliza whispered ominously. "Puck? Come on out now, Puck," she said, as though calling to a child or a small puppy.

Agnes watched with growing unease as a second-skin slithered out of the boy and stood beside him, identical but for the smirk. It was a faerie boy of some extra-powerful kind, the type these travelers called "dragon men" and nothing about that fact concerned Agnes. What made her squirm in her seat was her uncertainty of whether she was the only one who could see him. Most knew the story about how she was found, some even believed she'd stumbled out through a faerie door and couldn't get back in again. Others just said she was a deluded and confused orphan looking for an interesting story to get people to help her. In some ways she preferred they believed what they wanted to. She didn't like to confirm if she didn't have to how often she saw the world called "other," walking and weaving, right beside and on top of our own. Sometimes it meant seeing terrible things, that others have the bliss to be ignorant of.

"Do you… Do you… See that?" she asked cautiously.

Eliza nodded. "Of course," she waved away the idea of not being able to perceive the spirit. "Robin has always been light-shadowed and fae, but these days his dark shadow gets about and does its own thing without his knowledge—sometimes to the distress of modest milkmaids. I rather wish there was a way we could sew his shadow back onto him, at least for the time being, while he's too young to control it."

Agnes smiled faintly and looked back to the placid, dreamy gaze of the physical child, who looked to all spiritual purposes to be a copy made of wood, with pretty wooden eyes. A mere faerie stock sitting there, disturbing in the way life-sized puppets are. A child too well-behaved to be real.

"We call that one Puck, and that one Hob," the tinker woman said, pointing at the twin-like children.

"Then which one is Robin?" she asked.

Eliza sighed. "He's Robin when he's all in one place, that's what I'm here to see you about. How can we keep him in his body more? You might not see it today but sometimes fits of a sort come upon him before this blank state creeps up. He suffers during that part. Those with the Eyes, we see the Shadow slither out, but the normal folk? They just see an idiot child and they throw things at him and call him names. Once I had my back turned while I was working and he was beaten terribly by cruel people who don't understand."

Agnes watched Puck crawl underneath some furniture, pursuing Agnes' cat in a predatory manner. "That is probably not so wise of them."

"Indeed," Eliza agreed, a weary tone in her voice. "Hob will forgive them only for Puck to put an elf dart in their eye and say now he forgives them, and then we have to leave the village again. Things are hard enough for travelling folk. We are but humble horsemen and smiths, our lives are precarious at best. All I ask of you, as a faerie woman, and as a mother," Eliza said, taking a brief glance at Agnes' still flat stomach. "Please help our Robin."

◆

Ahh… wolves, they had been plentiful in the land when Jack was a boy. All the pit traps and the price fetched by the pelt or head meant they were a rare sight these days in England. The animal that came to stand by Sibylla's side was powerful and icy, like he'd been carved out of fire so hot it felt cold. There was an arctic purity in the beast that Jack had never noticed before, he was nothing like a dog. A dog was not half of what this being was, his nature contorted around pleasing the whims of man in return for easy living. No, this animal had not surrendered its will. In fact, he was certain, suddenly, that he was looking at a man in wolf skin, or perhaps a godlike being superior to both. A hob man perhaps. It was something in the eyes and the crackle the beast left in the air around every bristle of grey fur that made Jack feel this sense of reverence.

That was what made it so hard to watch when the faerie girl struck, slaying the wolf with one efficient blow to the neck with a silver blade. Reaching down Sibylla came to her feet holding the wolf's skin, which had simply slipped away from the bones of the beast like a bloody cloak, lined in viscera. He gazed in horror at the red bones where the wolf had been standing.

"I dress you in the skins of the outlaw, the wolf's head, the outlying one so that you will move among them unnoticed. I gift you,

Devil Jack, the nose and ears of the wolf tracking blood in the snow." She said this as she laid the wolf skin over him and the blood on the raw flayed flesh ran down his face, as blood caked him up to the knee also. Jack had the distinct feeling he was being knighted, and so he stayed down on one knee. "You shall find your way always by the heat of your hunger, may the Moon ever be your mistress, the night your teacher, and the dark hot love of the Sun at Midnight become your true north." Some of the wolf's blood ran into his mouth and he felt the strange fore-echo of a growing hunger, as though the essence of the wolf had run inside his bloodstream and began howling in his guts. He knew the beast already. It had been in him for a long time, wandering the lonely cave corridors in his marrow, pacing and waiting. Sometimes it didn't look like a wolf, sometimes it was a terrible wolfman with other parts. But it was there, waiting. The animal scratched to get out. It scratched to break down the fences and burn the strongholds of the feudal lords. He would howl at the sky while the black smoke of destruction spiraled up and up.

Jack fell onto his hands and knees growling and salivating. He couldn't keep his own spittle in his mouth as the fur shuddered into being all over him, as he twitched and undulated with primal sensation. Some part of him, something closer to the newer part of him, the forebrain, told him he mustn't let the beast come. Because if the beast came he'd tear a hole in everything false and feast on the hot blood of the wicked. There wouldn't be any going back to a comfortable life. Did Agnes really mean that much to him that he should burn the world down for her?

"That's right," he heard Sibylla's voice say, as she stroked his head. It disoriented Jack to feel her fingers in his fur and the strange placement of his sensitive ears. "Let it happen, Jack. Your human pride won't let you see the God this creature is, but you'll know when you're in it. You'll know the cold inferno of the wolf's fierce kill rush, you'll know the excruciation of his keen scent. You'll know a hunger as big as the world. But you've darkness enough inside you to hold all that, don't you, Sin Eater?"

He meant to open his mouth to speak but a sound like ghouls in torment came out instead and bruised with its chill, bestial keenness.

◆

"Hob? Would it be all right if I asked you a couple of questions, child?" Agnes asked, trying to be tender with the poor tinker orphan. There were few that could be said to have been born to a more wretched situation in life, she thought. Expression was not thought to be her strong point, many accusing her of a blank demeanor. But Agnes liked to think her deeds if not her facial expressions conveyed her compassion for mankind. She hoped the faerie boy could sense it without the elaborate pantomime of human affect.

The child ignored Agnes' words but for a gentle smile that seemed to suggest the sweetest of natures. Meanwhile his shadow stared at her with something between a glare and a leer from the corner of the room, having been unable to catch the cat. Whilst the eyes of the physical boy seemed vague and far away, the spectral boy's eyes were bright and feral full of a manic energy that looked barely containable. It occurred to Agnes that she was probably taking the wrong tact. It was to the shadow itself that she must speak. He was the one in charge here, the elder being whose eyes told long, ancient stories full of stone, clay, fat, ochre and the hot blood of the kill spilling out onto a frosty tundra. Yes, she could all but smell it on him, the deep past.

"Why don't you talk then, Puck?" she challenged. You could almost see his ears prick up as she threw down the gauntlet. The dizzy power in the room made her think of the feeling around some possessed folk where she'd been called to pull the black faerie off them. But Puck was something different again to anything she'd ever been called in to do before.

He slithered up close, crouching then scampering forward quickly, pausing and coming closer again. His movements seemed insidious to Agnes. Once he was beside her on the bench he came up close near her ear to whisper to her.

"I'm faerie like you now," he murmured, like nobody knew. "We're the creeping thing. Up into your garden. Oh yes. We are many-eyed in the hedgerow about the speed that ivy grows on your brother's mold. Oh yes. Moving. We never blink or forget or hold enough inside us to stop the wind playing music fingering on our inside ribs through our hollow backs. We live so long and we feel no pain. We burn so hot there will be frostbite! Oh no. Do not look back after you walk away from us, yes? Our death-lily fingers are making the hissing through the grasses as we follow behind you."

Agnes just nodded, though Eliza looked at her in a way as to say "see what I mean?" From a faerie woman's perspective the Puck's introduction of itself was all she needed to know. It told life stories and more.

"Why do you torment this human child?" Agnes asked, more because she knew it was expected of her than not knowing the answer. The Puck laughed with seemingly genuine amusement.

"Torment this child?" It asked, jumping down from its position near Agnes to go and sit beside its human double. "He's me! He may as well get used to it! Mightn't he?" he asked, when no answer was forthcoming. Before Agnes could agree he seemed to leap on the boy. Immediately Hob's body lurched backward and the child began to cry, clawing at his own throat as the Puck rode him.

"Aunty, make it stop! Aunty, make it stop! Aunty, make it stop!" he sobbed over and over again, his little back buckling up on the bench where Eliza held him.

"See? This is what happens," she said. For a moment Agnes feared the Puck would lift the boy clean into the air. "Sometimes he's covered in bruises."

Agnes wasn't listening to Eliza any more, her eyes narrowed in on Puck like an aerial predator. If necessary she would call her familiars down on him. With a stamp of her foot that shook the contents of the cupboards and shelves Agnes brought silence.

"Calm yourself!" The white mouse appeared again, hovering just over Hob's head. "You will hurt the poor boy!"

"The poor boy *is* me," the child's human lips mouthed the words as the shadow slid back in.

◆

It was a longer and more crooked walk to the door of the Faerie Doctor than any path Jack had walked before. He sniffed the wind regularly, finding his way from each small piquancy the wind held, aerial memory wrapped in scent. As he found his way along forest paths and across heaths he started to whistle an old tune. It felt like some old Viking refrain, but he couldn't remember why he thought so. The past seemed very close and the mist came in early, as though the air needed something to hold the thickness of this feeling.

Knowing that after all this time he had come so close to his objective was terrifying. Was there anything truly more dreadful than getting what you charmed and prayed for? If there was Jack wasn't totally sure he knew what it was. What would he say to her? Would she think him mad for trying to find her after everything that had happened? *Surely there comes a time when a certain amount of water has passed under the bridge where it is either ridiculous or perfect to suddenly turn up on another person's doorstep?*

With his blackthorn walking stick and his slightly turned ankle he still made smart progress. The people he passed claimed to see the cloven shape his devil's hoof left in the dust behind him. When he passed them they didn't speak until his back was turned. No one knew why he travelled with his leather pack and his bow and his old black hat upon his head. It was best not to ask questions when it came to conjurers and necromancers, everyone knew that. The ones that knew he was a Sin Eater wouldn't even make eye contact. Jack was someone you went to see for business you told no other man and never spoke of again once you'd crossed his hand with silver. People spat over their left shoulder to avert his evil eye and walked on as though he'd never charmed, cursed or eaten their grandfather's sins for them.

Jack felt better once he was out of the town, out beyond the hedgerows and walking the lonely path beyond all gazes. He hoped he wouldn't be stopped by anyone or asked to explain what his business was.

A storm came upon him towards afternoon, when he'd walked since dawn and half the night before it. The teeth and claws of the blue-black hag were upon him, almost out of a clear sky, with points of stinging ice that seemed to want to separate flesh from bone. He closed his eyes and let be, as he had not with the serpents. Their coiling had gone inside him now, and their cooling brewed a rising heat in him that could burn out this cold if he but let it. A witch fire burned in him hot enough to steadily turn the water on his skin to steam. He had won the prize of the Underworld and now the light in the darkness throbbed under his skin.

Devil Jack walked on.

◆

Agnes' twisted insides just wanted the tinker woman and her possessed child to leave. *Really*, her stomach seemed to argue as it knotted, *we do not need to make their problems our problems. I have worked so hard to get the people of the village to think of me as a human being and not of faerie stock. I didn't ask to stumble into a pit of staked and gore-smeared wolves. I didn't know when I followed the sound of bells out into the land of the bright, harsh light that I wouldn't be able to go home again.* After all these years and all she'd been through that day she just wanted to be normal. She wanted the tinker woman with her ever-higher coiling shroud to walk out the door with her mystery child and never return. The boy was soon to be orphaned yet another time, and Agnes was in no position to help him, or her.

"Give me a week or two to put some questions to divination," Agnes said. "And then we'll talk again."

Agnes wasn't lying. She had always possessed a tongue that could not lie. It had been threatened and beaten out of her and yet even as an adult she would turn mental and social backflips to avoid saying a lie. No, Agnes did not lie to Eliza when she asked for two weeks grace in determining where to go with the case. What she didn't say was how close she saw the winding sheet coming about the woman's body. How fast the moisture of grief was already creeping up it like a rising stain, a blue-gray watermark of sadness. How pungent the early scent of disaster that clung around that family. Agnes could barely stand it already by the time she closed the door on them and bolted it shut. It had been for the best, she told herself. When the black dog slathers so close to any man's heel as that, there is naught you can do. *Naught you can do…*

Yet a wind came in under the door, bearing grit and leaf litter and sporting coldly with Agnes' ankles. The wind carried warning, fat with melancholy. For a moment Agnes thought about racing out through the front door and calling the tinkers back. She could simply say she felt a storm coming and offer them shelter. Perhaps her action would avert that other fate somehow, stop her from being at some place she was meant to be at a certain time…

With a sigh Agnes opened the door and went out into the wind and gathering rain. Shielding her eyes from the wet Agnes looked after them but did not see them. They had passed another figure on the road, and once Agnes saw the vague outline of the man she quite forgot the tinker woman and her child.

She squinted to see better. All she saw was a man in black with a stick, who seemed to walk out of the storm. There was a dark hat upon his head and ever such a slight limp in his step. For a moment she was too afraid to hope. Her heart felt like it caused a pain in her chest suddenly. With a certain determination she stepped forward to see better. When she saw him start to walk faster she smiled and her legs began to go toward him. There was no thought as to whether her husband's servants would see, or the tangled gossip vine and the consequences, only the magical seeming event of seeing him again.

When they reached each other they collided. There was the strangeness of her frail form dressed as she was in soft materials, coming into contact with his barrel chest, clad in hard leather. He smelled of the dark magic of the Outside, woodlands and old secrets.

"Hello, lass," he whispered in her hair.

The thread she had been spinning came all unraveled in her hands before she'd even spoken to him.

◆

Jack stood very still while she undid her dress with her back to him. There are some moments in life that you don't want to rush over, where you need to carve and etch the memory into your mind so it's the last thing you see upon your deathbed, and that's what Jack was doing in his silence when he appeared to be doing nothing so much as brooding on vengeance. Of course those thoughts always came up too, when he saw her scars.

To have known her since childhood as he had, for her to have blown open all his ideas about what was possible. To see the magic she was not only wasting on a rich cur of a man, but to know he abused her... But what could he do? It had been her who had sent him away. No amount of guessing that she'd done it for his own good so her husband wouldn't have him killed ever made him certain of it. Not until he'd seen her eyes when she saw him on the road.

He was fascinated by every line of her, but most of all he loved how, even though he imagined she must have all the same internal organs as himself, her back did seem to curve inward somehow, around her spine. The hollow back of the Hidden Folk was like an old tree that had been emptied out by the ransacking hands of time, opening a space in the wood out of which many voices whispered, as they did from the green tabernacle of her flesh.

"Before you see me..."

"All right." She would hear no impatience from him, not after the journey that had led to this moment. He submitted to her vision of the situation the same way he'd given over to the rainstorm that had battered his body and stung his skin.

"Why do you imagine our backs are hollow?" she asked it of him like it was a riddle. Like in the old stories they told about how you had to win a faerie bride by guessing her name or picking her from her identical sisters.

As usual Jack's thoughts ran in dark rivers that were far deeper than his tongue could give form to, yet he grappled in the dirt and bones down inside himself to find a shape to use for them. "I imagine," he muttered, and as he spoke she unhooked another few of the fastenings on her gown, as though keeping a beat with the sound, to some music only she could hear. "That back when the world was baby fresh God gone and ripped mankind out of the backs of faeries. That's where we were dug out from," he said, taking a step towards her and placing one calloused finger against the dip behind her sharp shoulder blade. "Neither of us have been whole ever since."

Perfectly timed to his last syllable her gown slid to the ground like sensuous punctuation. It wasn't until she turned that he realized she was pregnant. What a bittersweet thing it was to gaze upon her… "That's a good story, Jack. It makes poetic sense, which is always a kind of truth. You can fill me back up again, if you like."

As he moved into her space he still didn't appear in any hurry. Jack did love long and slow like saying the rosary or rocking his way into trance.

Nothing Jack did was ever done without dark, feverish attention. He lifted her head to him and pressed his forehead down over hers. They stood like that for a long time.

When his darkness and solidity had settled into her and her thin ethereal light into him, he became someone new. The fuzzy-edged creature that he was breathed but had no name, it was male and female both, faerie and hobgoblin, light and dark, it was as edgeless as the gloaming.

◆

Hob stopped still and gazed through the crowd, resisting his Aunt's attempt to pull him by the hand. He didn't even feel the pressure on his arm. How had nobody else seen the girl? The colour of her hair smelt like freshly-cut cucumbers and tasted like bee pollen.

This sort of thing happened to him all the time. The whole world cross-pollenated and mixed its metaphors inside his skull cauldron. Many sights had a taste and they all had a meaning that made perfect sense to him. The suffering of others tasted like iron and smelt like a mixture between strong alcohol and alarmed horse.

"Hob! Come on with you now, child!" He vaguely heard his long-suffering Aunt say. But he was staring at the girl with the blonde plaits who had become God. People and animals and trees all turned into God a lot around Hob. He knew deep down that Puck was just his moment to become God, but no one understood that, so you had to fight it down hard.

Hob never wanted to bring pain to anyone. The way pain tasted was hateful. And what was worse was how often they would kill or beat God in this world. You could be simply looking upon God's face for a time while others wanted to hurry and be fast about everything, and they would use sharp sticks to make God dance at the end of a collar and chain. Sometimes they would whip or pillory God. Only recently they had hanged God because he was guilty of being poor and trying to eat.

Hob had seen God in the eyes of Elijah as they'd led him up to the gallows that day. His heart had been hammering in time to the man's, as if Hob could hear it across the distance between them. Wet and crucial in his ears like explosions. It all became louder and louder until he was sure he could hear the silent as mice-feet sound of the shaking knees of the man facing death. How could they not see! Hob had begun to panic, he fought, he screamed and bucked in their grasp, only able to struggle and weep in the end, he kept eye contact with Elijah all the way till they put the bag over his head.

"I see you! I will go with you as far as I can! I see you!' he had screamed out so his words would penetrate into Elijah's stone-heavy fear and walk with him. People were laughing at Hob but he didn't care. Hob knew he was "touched" because he couldn't ignore God or flowers and he couldn't walk past other beings while they cried out in pain. He accepted that he was mad for this reason, because people said so. It was what everyone said so it had to be true. But what he couldn't accept was that a sensitive woman like his Aunt couldn't see what he was seeing.

"But look Aunt! She's God!" he said, pointing at the blonde-haired girl watching them from the battlements with the Sun behind her.

"Don't start this again, Robin!" she snapped. He could feel her stress and exhaustion and he was sorrowful to be the cause of it.

He fell to kissing her hand over and over again hoping to make recompense for who he was. "Sorry, sorry, sorry, sorry. So sorry. I will try to be normal. I don't want you to feel sad. But look with me, Aunt Eliza! It's something beautiful…"

Reluctance was clear in her eyes for a moment. But after a few breaths he felt the tension of resistance leave his Aunt's muscles. She smiled, her face softening. She bent down to him so he could smell the rose water that she always splashed on her face and hair. "I'll tell you a secret," she whispered to him. "I see God too. But don't tell anyone, I encouraged you! That's Agnes Barre's daughter, the faerie girl from Woolpit."

Shielding his eyes from the sun with one hand he looked up at her again but she was gone. It wasn't until he couldn't see her anymore that he started to hear the other voices. They were voices filled with scorn so he didn't bother to pay too much attention. People whispering or shouting things at him was part of the backdrop of any interaction he had with the world outside his family. His brother was inclined to seek to visit retribution upon them but he didn't care what they said. *Mooncalf, idiot, touched, fae, crazy, ditch-born tinker, scum, whoreson, witch-get, Hod's-kin, inbred, freak...* When he was younger he'd thought some of them might be other names of his, as he already had at least three.

His field of vision was interrupted by the presence of one of the iron-bound men who carried more objects to harm other people than they did anything else. "What are you looking at, idiot?" When Hob didn't respond by dropping his eyes as he was meant to the man cuffed him about the side of the head with the back of his mailed fist. The blow dizzied him and hitting the cobblestones took the air right out of his lungs. He lay gasping and he could hear his Aunt using all those words that smell like fear. "Please! Please! Please don't hurt him. He's just a little... he's just... different."

"Well the mooncalf was being defiant."

"I'm so sorry, Sir. We are both sorry." She was stepping between him and the man. Robin was sobbing hysterically and it wasn't because of the blow or the people who were laughing at him and jeering, it was because he could hear her begging and he came from a proud people. "Surely we can... Surely..."

"Make it up to me, eh? That's what you tinker whores are good for, isn't that right?"

Hob could hear his friends supporting him with jeers that tasted like a knife's edge against your tongue. Something flew up into his head then, something that had wings and the top of his head seemed to come open to let heat in. He was up on his feet flying at the man who tried to touch his Aunt's breasts screaming at him within seconds.

"Leave her alone don't you dare touch her!" He didn't care that he beat his fists against the cold iron of his armor, it didn't matter that it wasn't hurting the man a bit because it was all the resistance in his tiny body. The man casually hit him away, but for all its careless look the blow was far harder than last time and this new impact with the stone sounded wet with the slap of bloody flesh against stone. He heard his Aunt's cry of horror. The iron-clad man turned to Hob and spat on him. "And you stay down where you belong," he added to the further accolades of his companions.

"If you hurt him you'll live to regret it!" No sooner did the edge of defiance in his Aunt's voice cut through the air as brief silence fell. The iron-clad man hadn't been prepared for this, it was clear he hadn't come here expecting to do serious violence, not here in a public place where there might be consequences. He had just been out for some light bullying.

The man laughed in the way meant to encourage the jackals he travelled with to laugh. "What do you reckon, De Rue? Maybe we need to show this tinker bitch where *her* place is?"

In a kinder era he might have been reckoned a child too young to understand their insinuations, but he had not been so fortunate. And it didn't seem outside possibility, not from what he understood of what man does to man, that they might manage to rape her here in front of all these people and that no one would lift a hand to help her or even run for assistance.

Hob heard something go click just inside his left ear and all the sound dropped out of the scene for him. Everything slowed down and he found himself scanning the weapon belts and boots of the men who stood nearest, coolly considering how long it would take him to roll to one side, draw the blade from his boot and slit open one of the arteries in the iron-clad man's leg that was not fully protected by his chainmail.

"Don't worry," he heard Puck whisper next to his left ear. "I am also the blessing of all the curses and the cursed one with all the blessings. I can show you how to make the bullies pay."

Hob flinched away. He associated Puck with pain, but he was willing to reach into the centre of that searing fire living just behind his head for his Aunt. Before he could act on his plan to abandon himself to a total and terrifying possession, the girl who was God was suddenly beside him, pressing a soft piece of damp cool cloth to his wounded face. Her touch was the very softness of mercy itself and with her came other guards who were telling the iron-clad men to disperse.

Village women had folded in around Eliza to protect her as soon as they saw it was safe to do so. It made him weep to see it. They weren't heroes, Hob knew, they were nowhere when she stood alone among her tormentors like a lamb about to be hung up for slaughter, but they were human, decent, they were afraid but wished no harm for their sister. They wouldn't have stopped it, but they would have looked away from her rape… You had to forgive them and their pure but shabby, imperfect humanity, because they wanted to be kind, they just weren't brave enough…

But God was brave. God was defying them all to touch his face.

Hob smiled sadly at Her. "I see you," he whispered in Welsh. The little girl didn't understand him, but God always did. In his dreams he'd been one of God's angels once, so he knew this much.

◆

Agnes was annoyed when her maid said a tinker was at the door again. But she checked herself, knowing it was really guilt rather than irritation. She hadn't felt right ever since she'd sent that poor woman away. Rumour of the woman's murder had rocked the village and surrounding areas, which was unusual for the death of a travelling woman. Perhaps it was because the girl was young and pretty and her death particularly brutal. But most likely it was everybody knew about her charge Robin Goodfellow, and so she was almost famous by connection.

"Bring him in."

"Inside, Ma'am? You mean, inside the house?"

"Yes, Gudrun! I mean inside the house. I'd rather as few people saw me receiving a tinker as possible."

This wasn't the real reason. She almost expected to find her accuser on the doorstep, telling her that she could have done something for that poor wee tinker boy and she didn't because she thought her long unfulfilled love affair was more important.

But Agnes had to be careful, she knew, if her husband found out anything untoward was going on it could well cost Jack's life and possibly even her own. There had been some beatings in the past that had been a near enough thing for her. Any willingness to stand up for others had been long since knocked, bruise by bruise, out of her until she was too frozen with fear to stop him when he struck her little daughter… She had been showing simple compassion to a child, her eyes didn't see the difference between gentleman and tinker. Just as Agnes herself had always trouble perceiving the difference she was told was there.

No matter what they said, it still looked like all the people who came to see her for a cure bled the same shade of red. Yet her husband had whipped the girl sorely for her compassion towards the tinker boy. Agnes sighed. She supposed it was best the girl learned young how to obey and didn't get the kind of faerie devils in her that Agnes had sometimes.

She almost gasped when she saw the tinker was a young boy of no more than eleven. He was travelling alone and looked a scrappy little thing you'd imagine had been stealing bread and fighting in the street since he was old enough to walk on two legs. You could tell what he was from the beads, teeth and animal claws they worked into their clothing, their braids, the plaids they'd wrap around themselves for warmth, but other than that they looked just like normal folk with the same blood colour.

"What do you want, boy?"

He walked towards her and held out an item of fabric. It was a soft sort of fabric, such as a woman's nightclothes might be made of.

"I'm Blaith of the Twll Du blood-line," he said, his dark solemn eyes making bold contact with hers. "This is my murdered Aunt's nightdress, and this is the semen of the man who did it." Eliza gasped in shock at this blunt, adult statement. She didn't reach out for the object even though he seemed to insist she did so. "Would you use it to find him for me?"

Agnes frowned. She hardly needed to use the man's body fluids to find him. He was her husband's second cousin, she knew his name and location already. But what could you do? Nobody would accuse someone like him. "What for?"

The boy's dark eyes narrowed slightly and seemed to flash with viciousness. "That's my folk's business. I hear you're good at locating lost objects."

"Well yes… lad. But objects, not so much people."

"Will you help me or not?"

She mistrusted the boy. He seemed cunning and older than his years. The kind of little thief you needed to watch in a market place. His eyes held a knowing that should never be in the eyes of a pre-pubescent child, it was eerie. She sensed something of Otherness on him that she didn't recognize or quite know how to respond to, but there it was. A solid knot of guilt rose from her stomach to her chest, accompanying the feeling. "Fine," she sighed, gingerly taking the stained gown from him. She took it with her to her chair where she liked to spin and sat down. It would take her a little while. As long as the boy didn't directly ask his name she wouldn't have to lie.

The tinker boy took a seat without being asked to. She found herself wondering if she was going to need to clean after he left, such was the feeling of wild nature that seemed to cling all over the child's person. Lower in her stomach than the guilt she felt a stab of longing to come from where he did, to wander off with them into the forest.

"I know what you are," he said conversationally, kicking his legs, which didn't quite touch the ground in the chair he was in. "We'd take you away with us, if you wanted to go."

She looked up at him sharply. "Silence, boy! I'm trying to concentrate."

He shrugged. Like all his people he treated abuse and rejection like it was just expected and seemed to shrug it off as if his skin were coated like duck feathers. "Suit yourself."

After she'd given it enough time to make it look realistic she began to flutter her eyelids and give the appearance of going into trance. "I see him living behind the walls of castle with mote and bailey. I see him riding in the lists... His coat of arms has...yellow on it." Almost as soon as she had begun to fake her performance she felt the beginnings of real knowing creep in on her. The white mouse was there. She knew it, though she didn't open her eyes. She could hear the mouse chattering truth. He always spoke the truth, so sometimes she had to fight him. "He's a hunter of witches," she murmured, frowning. The words didn't seem to make sense to her. "Not a religious man, but one who... one who craves women of power... He takes the blood above the breath but so much more... This isn't the first time he's killed someone like her." Suddenly she pitched the night-gown away from her onto the floor and jumped to her feet, frenziedly rubbing her hands on her apron to cleanse them.

Blaith was just looking at her, his dark eyes seeming to appraise her. He crossed his legs, thoughtfully, in a way that seemed far too elegant for a boy and too poised for a child. "I was beginning to think you were a fake." He looked at her for a few more seconds and then seeming to decide something, got to his feet. Reaching into his pocket he pulled out a silver coin and placed it on the table.

"Oh. No. Please. You need that more than I do."

The boy ignored her, left the coin where it lay, picked up the stained garment and showed himself out. Agnes watched him go from the open casement. She knew Jack was out there hunting for Robin Goodfellow, because some spirit had told him to, but it felt futile. The boy had been missing in the woods for two days, so he was clearly already dead. Perhaps the last of the wolves had taken him.

She shuddered at the thought of wolves. That's what the tinkers reminded her of, she realized. That too-bright sharpness in their keen eyes. Like the wolves she imagined them all bloodied on stakes.

But Jack could track a will-o-wisp if properly motivated and perhaps he would be the one to find the boy. It interested her that the boy's brother had not asked her to track Robin. Perhaps he knew something they did not. Nonetheless she strongly believed that if Jack couldn't find Robin Goodfellow, nobody could. She rubbed her hands unconsciously on her apron again. Her palms felt clammy and unclean.

◆

"You've earned your freedom," Elijah heard the voice of the devil-man say before the wind serpent breathed them out from his distended gullet. "Go, find your destiny. I release you."

The mandragora root that had held, shaped and defined him with its twisted, cunning form, came loose. I was a bit like dying again, with the pressure followed by release. As the sky disgorged the men who rode the dragon horses, snorting black smoke with eyes of starfire, Elijah felt a mild sense of relief. He had been soaking in the other people's story for too long. All he lusted for now was to hang limp and empty at the crossroads for a time. To be void, still, and interrupted by nothing but the circling of crows and the lament of the wind. To not know the sorrow of the tinker child, or the slow but inevitable self-betrayal of the faerie woman, nor the dark tangled passions of the conjuring man.

The story he'd been a part of was one of throat-thickening sorrow, bound tight with the black, tangled, gut-strings of Fate. It wasn't his place in his goblin child skin to ask questions. It wasn't his place in his dead man's face to make changes to outcomes. It wasn't his place in his girl child shape, so much like that of the faerie Sibylla, to try to make live what is doomed to die or track down that which does not want to be found. It was not his place when he was caught in the sorcerer's crystal, where he viewed the resplendent glass palaces of the fae and danced in their oceans of refracted light, to wonder what magic was worth if it couldn't save a single vagabond, orphan child. Did not Christ himself so often walk in the form of the dispossessed, the abject? Was not the child they had spat on potentially Christ? Had not Christ Himself been spat upon and reviled?

"You did as well as you could by my son, Elijah," Obreon, the leader of the Host said. His eyes appeared part serpent and part angel, dizzily dancing with refracted light as oil on water. His whole being seemed to inhale and exhale nothing but fire and white-hot gathering force. He was as much dragon-spirited as the animal between his knees. Elijah imagined they both ate nothing but lightning.

Elijah shook his head. "I didn't do enough. It was his voice crying out to me on the day I died... It was the only kind thing in my head while they strangled out the life from my neck."

"He is my offering to the world of man, but they do not understand my gift. You harrowed Jack just enough to test his resolve. I'm pleased with you."

"It isn't going to work out though! Jack will get there too late after they find him, the tinker camp will be gone by morning. No one will know where they went. Vanished like a faerie dance, gone at daybreak, into the wild woods... He will never know the little boy he passed on the road at Agnes' door was the Robin Goodfellow whom Dame Sibylla told him to find and look out for! And by then it will all be far too late. The fate threads aren't going to line up, they are a mess."

"You are still very human aren't you?" Obreon said softly, as though in a spirit of mild melancholy but maybe also of sympathy.

Elijah sighed. He still did things like that sometimes even though he didn't need to in this new world. "I could see how it would all line up differently if he'd just got to Agnes' house a bit quicker."

"There was the storm and his slightly turned ankle," the faerie man observed.

"Aye but it was possible, probable even that we could have stopped the whole thing if Jack arrived earlier. That whole terrible thing..."

"Yet it did not happen, that other happier fate. Do you know why it didn't happen? No mortal does, they only know which story had the most power. Ride beside me human and you would see eleven different fates spinning at once without getting dizzy. After a while you'd learn to understand why one story has more power than another and how that power is acquired. An awesome and terrifying power."

To Elijah's surprise he held his hand out to him then, as though he wished to hand him up into the saddle. He hadn't realized the faerie man had meant "ride with me" as a literal invitation.

"They say the Host steals the faces of the newly dead and shoots the living with elf darts from the storm-darkened sky?" He didn't know why he worded the statement as a question. It wasn't really a question because he thought he knew it was true.

"When your answers have been replaced with questions you will have become wiser. When you ask instead to what fateful *purpose,* and with what artful intent, might a being steal a human face, and for what reason throw darts at the living, then we will have proper conversations. Until then you may ride with me quietly."

"It seemed like the sorcerers had answers to those kind of questions," Elijah suggested timidly. "The ones I watched, like Jack and Agnes." Is that what he should do? Stay closer to the living? Throw himself into the maelstrom flicking out its first light in a woman's womb? Return to the red world? Or was this the better story? This fade into the half-light, this pulling out tide along the borders of time?

"Where you find faeries you always find Witches, and where you find Witches, faeries," was Obreon's only reply. "We are of a shared, mixed race with each other."

"I want to go with you, but why do you want to take someone like me?"

Obreon just smiled. It was an odd, calculated-looking gesture, which didn't set you at your ease or look natural on him. "Have you ever wondered what it feels like to gallop along the edge of the wind, Elijah?"

PART III

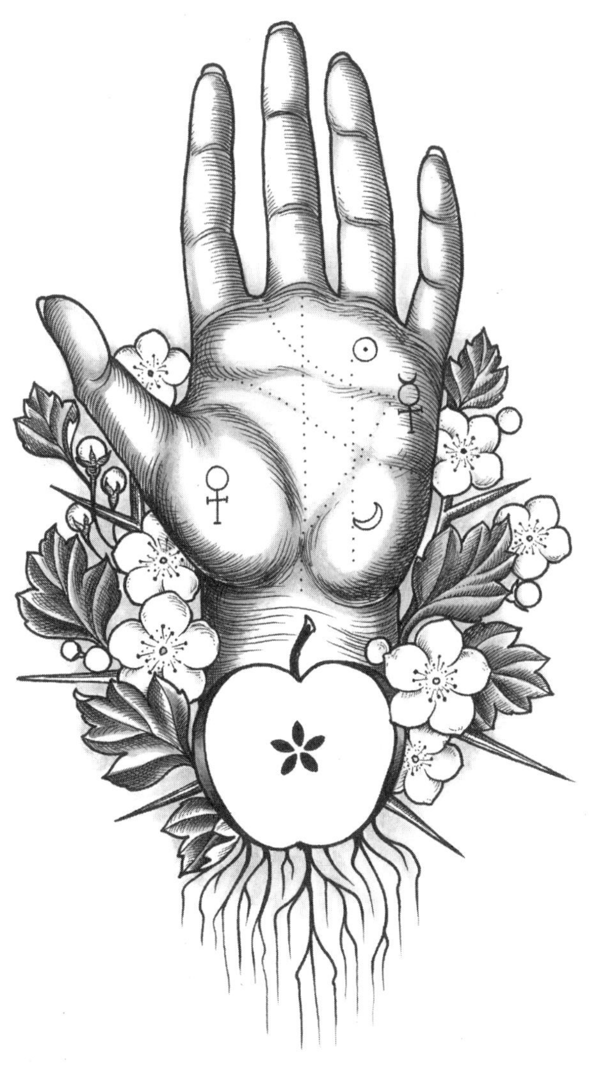

PART III: INTRODUCTION

A GRIMOIRE OF SIBYLLAN CRAFT

It began as research. I wrote of silences, of nights, I scribbled the indescribable. I tied down the vertigo.

–William James

Ritual is a form of poetry that uses sight, action, sound, smell, taste and sometimes naturally-occurring chemicals to stimulate the sensorium of man into a state of attention and defamiliarization—one that seeks to mimic the state of being known as "Faerie." When a ritual is at its most successful it slows time down or speeds it up, makes common objects appear with an aura of the mysterious, blurs our senses together so that tastes or smells hold a deeper significance than usual, and like any good art form, makes the unseen visible and inflicts story on chaos. It doesn't just bring the Otherworldly closer to us, it brings us closer to the Otherworld.

As Daniel Schulke showed us in "The Blasphemy of Things Unseen"[1] there is a sense of transgression around the revelation of what is hidden. The faeries as the hidden folk are a walking blasphemy. In ritual we seek to join them in behaving and experiencing reality in this transgressive way. These activities are transgressive for the same reasons our society places no value on poetry. There is no immediate material or pecuniary value acquired by the performance of ritual, at least not in any way that can be proved with current science.

The reason to perform a ritual written by someone else is the same as the reason to read a poem composed by someone else or listen to music you didn't yourself create. To those with the sensibility to appreciate beauty the value is self-evident. But the beauty of ritual is

1 Daniel Schulke, "The Blasphemy of Things Unseen," in *Hands of Apostasy*, 315-330.

not the cosmetically altered beauty of the facile modern age; it is the splendor of the sublime, the awe that is beauty and terror—and for there to be terror something must be effective. A ritual should excite all the extremes of aesthetic experience or it is unlikely to attract the attention of the spirits, and unlikely to lift the veil of familiarity from mankind's eyes long enough to reveal the numinous.

As you would expect with an art form so complex that it utilizes so many senses of man to create its impact, the composition of a ritual is multifaceted and must appeal to the intellect as well as the imagination. For this reason there is precise rationale as well as the standard of beauty applied to the rituals in this grimoire. Strategic recorded rituals in both grimoires and folk sources were unlikely to have been done in that way for the hell of it but because they worked.

David Rankine outlines the cross-fertilization between the grimoire tradition and Witchcraft that is so important for the movement we now call Traditional Witchcraft. Somewhere in the 19th century—as Andrew Chumbley, past Magister of Cultus Sabbati so rightly pointed out—some fraternities began to arise that took cunning craft and family traditions to a new level of sophistication, to the level of lodges. There is something about lodges that has proven very powerful on the early modern psyche. As though while we watched the old village ways of life slowly die under the marching heel of industrialization we concurrently began to find a way to patch up that lost group mind, that lost sense of tribalism which had hung on in the form of the country village. Family traditions were still effective, but the lodge became another way of magic protecting itself, finding, following and gathering those of the blood.

We cannot fully know in any intellectual way what the native sorcery of Britain or other parts of Europe was like before contact with Christianity or even Gnosticism. But we can sense as sorcerers rather than academics something of the scent of it, the spirit laying behind those more recent archeological deposits. We might sense the spirit of something evolving, a beast that consumes narratives and appropriates methods, a changing beast that over the centuries is busy becoming something. When we specifically focus on Witchcraft that "something" is by its nature something Other, something that flies in the face of the direction taken by the general herd of humanity.

When Witchcraft entered the grimoire tradition full of Wild Hunt demons, hazel wands, wood pentacles, necromancy with dead body parts and faerie familiars, Witches became part of the textual magic tradition, whether or not that tradition in return became part of us is another question. For this reason, whilst grimoire faerie invocations inspire these workings, they are a form of faerie magic inspired by ceremonial magic, it is debatable whether it continues to function in the same way as ceremonial magic.

CONSECRATION OF THE TOOLS OF ART

The tools of a grimoire encode its cosmology. If we rush over the process of understanding or collecting them we will miss something essential about the ritual itself and the nature of the spirit invoked by it. For those who do not respond well to the ceremonial-sounding nature of the word "invoked," we may also use "invited," as with faeries this is more to the point anyway. As the astrologer Lilly remarked above, *"It is not for everyone, or every person, that these angelical creatures will appear unto, though some may say the call, over and over again."*

When we open a grimoire, it is common for we time-starved moderns to reckon how long it will take to acquire those things as we decide whether to engage with the practice. The idea of saying the call over and over again, perhaps starting the rite all over again on a different night and waiting for when They are "ready to manifest themselves," as Lilly also put it, would be the work of a rare practitioner in this day and age. Many will engage with bargaining about whether a lesser equivalent of the objects listed will do instead. Some might begin wondering how long it will take to get to the goal if they absolutely must have a wand of year-old hazel wood in particular.

But this is to think in opposition to the mindset of Faerie, which is the one we must adopt if we wish to see into their world. To have the sight of the faeries, we must think like a spirit that exists outside of time. Therefore if we want to facilitate the likelihood they will appear we need to sideline our usual human mindset about such things into timeless absorption in the Now. I cannot stress this enough. The objects themselves pale in importance by comparison to the state of mind and the process of their acquisition. Everything I have ever needed for a rite I set my heart on appeared to me at the right time and I was able to afford it, not a moment before it was right that I perform it. This is in itself a way that Faerie has of letting you know it is already aware of your preparation.

There is no preparation phase for these rituals, with the ritual consisting only of what is performed inside circles on the ground, but instead the ritual begins from the moment of reading of it. Unless we can learn to think like a spirit how will we ever conjure one or be able to interact with it? So before you ask yourself the question of "how will I obtain x, y and z" cease to consider the conjuration as a means to an ends, remind yourself you are engaged in an artform, something you are hoping to make pleasing to the fae, enough that they will want to join in. From the first reading the working has begun. It will continue to unfold both in waking and in dreams, up until the climax of the ritual reached during the performance.

To think like a spirit is to have fully conceived of the ritual at an imaginal level long before it is walked through, to have performed it first in the temple of consciousness, in the halls of memory, and known every ingredient and tool long before you ever find their physical manifestations.

To better appreciate the tools as spirits we must analyse the parts of a conjuration where they are used, to see what purpose they serve, so that we may know them in relation to the working as a whole. The components of a ritual serve to do the following things:

- To stimulate the sense of beauty or visceral, potent novelty, creating a state of attentiveness and defamiliarisation, so what was previously unseen begins to become visible—simple actions take on deeper or doubled meanings
- To prepare your spirit—through the use of coded symbols relating to a secret narrative—to receive and resonate with the power of the tradition the spirit is attached to

- To gain the attention and participation of the spirit
- To give the spirit substance and form and in some way gift it with power in the form of sacrifice
- To protect yourself from the spirit and/or in some circumstances to have power over it

How do the tools resonate with each of these potential goals? Some of the major tools considered.

HAZEL WAND: The wand offers the promise of command over the spirit but it does so from the starting point of wisdom. Via using the hazel the narrative we are attached to is one of imbibing a nut of wisdom. But it takes some time for a nut to grow into a tree and thus the wand speaks of wisdom got slowly over time. It is in fact wisdom (according to the poem of ritual where one thing means or points to another), not a piece of wood that allows us to gain power in the spirit world. Like the hazel wand that must be of one year's growth the ritual requires wisdom—wisdom of one year's growth, which has been bathed in fire. This wisdom symbol could be said to serve the operator in terms of gaining the attention and interest of the spirits.

CRYSTAL BALL: The crystal ball is well known but it is more than a skrying tool. In Ireland and Wales it was often used for making a kind of healing water and in Reginald Scot's Scottish material it is also used to catch and hold spirits. Like the hazel wand this practice of making healing water is Celtic in its history. The ball as it is used in these rituals is a vessel for spirits, not just a mirror to see them in. It could be said that in these rituals the crystal ball helps to enchant or englamour the spirit with its light properties and forms the first point of contact which the spirit becomes aware of in our world. It also helps to provide a subtle medium (reflected light) which is malleable to the spirit's influence and allows for faerie images to appear to the operator.

SNAKESKIN: Snakeskin suggests skin-changing. This tells us the spirit Luridan is some kind of poucca or shapeshifting skin-changer, which would make sense for a spirit that went from inspiring Welsh poets to being thought of as a brownie in Scotland. The snakeskin used to invoke him tips us off to his nature, it also links to numerous British magical traditions found in folklore regarding powdered snakeskin or the ash of the skin. Snakes guard treasure and wells and are a primordial power living below things. Luridan is a bogey or poucca, a type of faerie being sometimes called a hobgoblin, known for changing its skin but also likely to be an Underworldly creature. The snakeskin serves to create the glamour of the ritual, to defamiliarise and create receptiveness in the operator through atmosphere, but also to prepare the spirit with the symbols relevant to particular traditions or currents.

PINE AND HUMAN BLOOD: Pine or turpentine is reckoned to be of the realm of Mars as is the iron in human blood. This tool is a sacrifice to the martial spirit Balkin. It serves the ritual as a whole as a sacrifice of power that allows for the enfleshing of the spirit in the form of smoke. Because it is of like nature as the spirit conjured it also acts as both attraction and mild inducement.

FRANKINCENSE: This offering to Sibylla indicates she is a spirit of light, associating her with Christ and celestial powers. Like the pine resin and blood mentioned above it serves the rite as a sacrifice allowing ideation to take on form, as an attraction but also in Sibylla's case as a form of cleansing influence on the environment which makes the way easier for her to tread.

A STONE CAIRN: An effigy or artwork of a mountain. The presence of stone and fire together are important in this ritual as they conjure the presence of the Terrible Mountain, which is a homeland for both Luridan and Balkin. The fact it can be drawn gives away that drawings and words can replace things where they must, but the presence of stone will link you to the spiritual home of these beings more powerfully, as both Luridan and Balkin seem to have elements of the "spirit of place" about them. This object serves the rite as a form of attraction and compulsion for the spirit but also creates the artistic power of the rite in terms of effect upon the conjurer. The very business of building the cairn can be taken as a slow and purposeful form of meditation.

A WEAPON: A Witch of an underground traditional lineage here in Australia once showed me their blade and its edge. "It's the spirit of the awareness," he told me, showing me the knife. "And it's kept sharp for a reason." Like the hazel wand it is not just the blessed knife or sword that protects the magician from the spirit but the keen edge of awareness. Our safety in the Otherworld relates to whether we've kept our edge sharp and keen, honed and polished. There is a mystery in keeping an object that reflects this.

The fact that we understand the poetry behind the object does not negate the power of having the tool itself, it merely shows us that tool's spirit and story, which can be accessed even when it isn't in our hands. The tool is very much for the protection of the operator, but it will mean nothing unless one understands what has been said of the blade above.

CHALK FOR DRAWING CIRCLES: What is the circle drawn by chalk? Whiteness. In Wales the word white (wen but also sometimes gwyn) was a synonym for holy. Whereas red is incarnation and flesh, white is the death state, the pallor and chill of snow on the cheeks of the deceased, bloodless white...

Outside the circle is the world of spirit—or is it? Often the spirit itself is placed in another circle. A second circle is used for Sibylla, never a triangle for Sibylla. If you harken back to what has been said regarding the synesthesia-like experience of the world common to the faerie state, triangles mean sharp-edged manifestation whereas circles mean the fuzzy edges of Faerie. Just like how Monday, Tuesday and Wednesday are suitiable to say in a faerie song but Thursday emphatically is not!

When we circle something in whiteness we mark it out as holy. The Witch is not inside a hedge created by a circle that circles the spirit world OUT, a Witch is inside a whitening of ground that is circled IN as holy.

So is the faerie, but we are in different circles, at least at first, but there is a place where the two circles touch. The grimoires that tell of conjuration of the virgin faerie Sibylla and elsewhere of seven faerie sisters for the purposes of intercourse clearly do not include keeping the faerie realm in a different circle to yourself. They merely begin that way. Both holy, both whitened with chalk, like a corpse turned into an artwork of death, but beginning separately only to end as one, just as two circles can be drawn overlapping at their edges to form the *vesica piscis*.

These shapes serve the artwork as a whole in terms of protection at times, but also prepare the spirit via the use of symbols key to a particular known pathway between their world and ours.

GRAVE DUST FROM A FRESH DEATH: You don't see grave dust enter the grimoires until the seventeenth century,[1] which indicates it probably came to them from folk traditions often associated with Witchcraft, just as the faerie practices did. Further evidence this tool came into the grimoires via folk magic at least, if not explicitly Witchcraft, can be found in the use of grave dust whilst it's still in the ground. In Welsh folk medicine people were often buried in grave dirt so that it could take away their rheumatism, and in the much further past letters for dead people were sent to the below with the dead or thrown onto funeral pyres.[2]

Folk wisdom tells us that where a grave is, a doorway to the Unseen opens. By taking something linked to a place of unraveling you are allowing other things to be unraveled along with it, like your rheumatism. If you use grave dirt of one newly dead in ritual you use it to undo the space between this world and the next, opening a door. The presence of grave dirt in this ritual provides a tangible assistance to the spirit in regards to manifestation, though it cannot exactly be classed as a sacrifice.

1 Rankine, "Pentacles of Wood," 46-63.

2 Phillip Freeman, *The Philosopher and the Druids* (New York: Simon and Schuster, 2008), 162.

CONJURATION OF THE DEATH WALK

Although this working forms a preliminary rite for the other conjurations, I have chosen to treat it separately to highlight its significance. In the version copied by Arthur Gauntlet the death walk is described under the heading "how to have the spirit of a dead man." One should probably read that sentence more than one way and ponder both possible meanings. It does no harm at all to make this a habit when reading or hearing anything to do with the realm of faerie, as much is unexpected or topsy-turvy.

We have discussed above how those who are taken away to Faerie usually experience some kind of dark harrowing—forty days walking through blood in True Thomas's case—before the eyes of Faerie Sight are opened and the faerie land reveals its features. So too in this grimoire, which attempts to recreate the sense of a journey into the realm of Faerie, we will encounter the dead and the dark guardian powers first.

Those who interact with faeries and ghosts outside the auspices of the protective circle are explicitly Witches. The circle, as used in both ceremonial and folk magic, has layers upon layers of meaning in it. But when it is placed between the conjurer and the spirit as a form of protection it becomes the Hedge. The barrier, veil or membrane between the world of the living and the uncanny realm of faeries, ghosts and Gods living outside, otherside, otherwise.

Although I don't mean to suggest Witches *never* used or use circles, spirit congress related in the trial records suggest circles were very rare, save for a couple examples such as Alice Kyteler and Ann Bodenham.

The famous astrologer Lilly mentioned before in relation to the conjuration of the Faerie Queen that when it comes to conjuring faeries "some people" don't even use a circle. Was this because faeries were deemed safe to work with, whereas the shades of the dead, angels and demons were not? Not exactly. The most famous conjuration of the Faerie King Oberon explicitly says "whom no man should be conjuring unless in fear of his life."

I will suggest here what was different was not the spirits being dealt with but the practitioner who dealt with them. The ceremonial magician could deal with demons but walk away unscathed and unsullied due to the use of magic circles and prayers to Jehovah and his angels to dominate and subdue them on the magician's behalf. The powers of the old world had been drawn into a framework that by its inherent nature relied on faith in God, circle barriers and forced compliance.

As a philosophy it could be accepted within church-dominated culture because it drew the wild powers of the heathen world into a demon/angel binary and then subjugated all via the power of God's Word. As a form of meta-sorcery it made perfect sense.

But something a little strange and other entered this tradition when faerie magic began to permeate it, we find fuzzy circle barriers (as we discussed in relation to the logistical confusion around the Rite of Sibylla and the suggestion of intercourse) no circles at all cropping up.

We have explored earlier this idea that faerie taboos were broken safely at times by those who were faerie-touched or light-shadowed, and that the powers of the dead can't hurt those who have already died. The Witch gives all that is between her two hands, is marked with otherness, lets the Devil suck her blood, her imps drink her milk. He has sexual congress with faerie women and breeds half-breed inhuman children with them. He goes out past the village boundaries and becomes possessed by faeries dancing frenetically. He too is marked by the Devil and may suckle imps, stepping outside normally-gendered body experiences to do so. The usual boundaries, even between strict male and female binaries are eroded by the Witch's uncanniness. The Witch cannot be hurt by this uncanniness because they themselves are of it, just as one who, through the ingesting of poisons, has made them immune to them.

Whether in circle or outside one the Witch always carries what is outside the circle inside herself. There is no pure space unhaunted once the Witch's unhallowed step has crossed there with the dust of the crossroads still upon it. Thus in this ritual we find ourselves on a meditative walk to a fresh grave to acquire the spirit of a dead man. I have counseled the reader earlier to remember the two ways in which this statement can be taken — for such is the way of thinking redolent of faerie cunning.

We are here to obtain the spirit, more properly the still intact second skin or shadow, of a newly dead man. He will become our go-between with the spirit world. But we are also here to affirm that we ourselves possess the spirit of a dead man, to identify with and walk home aligned with the dead. Only in this way, the initiated state, can we safely interact with Lady Sibylla. This ritual could be interpreted as initiatory but preferably it would simply reaffirm a pre-existing initiation, as this grimoire as a whole is not suitable for working by a compete beginner.

If you read the original Reginald Scot material the current working is inspired by—also in *The Grimore of Arthur Gauntlet*—you will find in this ritual great injunctions about the horrors and nastiness the dead man will put you through as you seek to obtain his skin for the use of faerie manifestation. This visionary component of the rite is the dismemberment and alignment with the dead aspect of the working. Going into the dark and encountering the terrifying visions of the dead relates to the descent to the Underworld in faerie encounter narratives we have explored previously.[1]

Fast and pray while you search. Obtain for the working a crystal ball, a hazel wand and a candle of virgin wax. The work begins from

1 Rankine, *Arthur Gauntlet*, 235.

the commencement of this fast. A fast means avoiding all activities strongly invigorating of the red powers of the body, such as sexual intercourse, the doing of violence or the eating of red meat. Try to spend some time in the green world amid quietude.

The sorcerer will hold a hazel wand, the companion a candle and crystal ball. If only one operant is present place the candle down at the head of the grave and hold the crystal ball yourself.

It might be wise to come to the grave the night before to ascertain the general ambiance of the place and whether or not the dead person feels like a good candidate for the work. Any new burial will feel like a disruption in the air to those with adequate senses for attempting the operation, but it shouldn't feel intensely menacing. If you feel sick to the stomach or break out in a cold sweat it is best to divine the location of a more suitable burial site, as this may be the dead's way of communicating to you that they want none of your ritual.

Remember also that the dead person you choose will carry the qualities not only of the person they were in life, but will have become somewhat of a locale of the numinous. They will become the first dead, representative of the first ancestor, the source, or to put it another way, the collectivity of the dead. Keeping this in mind will assure the correctly respectful attitude with which to make your approach.

When a suitable site has been found and the ritual begun say unto the dead:

> *Arise, arise, like Lazarus arise oh spirit N! Come unto me in this crystal stone and show me true visions.*

Place the candle down at the head of the deceased and light it, as you do you must visualize their awareness coming on in the dark, as if their eyes had come open under the loam and gave off ghost light. Pour a circle of some offering of strong spirits around the candle. Lie down on the grave with your arms crossed in coffin pose holding the crystal at your own chest between your crossed hands. If this is impossible because of piled-up earth on the new burial lie down beside it or straddle it like a lover and hold out the crystal.

> *Arise spirit come forth over the dark seas and the blood seas, the frozen north and oceans where seals howl, come on a black cruk shell, come in the form of a black angel, a white hound, man or woman, child or horned beast, come as a white angel or green. I would have you as a goblin-man to live within a mandrake root and go forth for me, receiving offerings.*

Say this or words to this effect. It is best to memorise the main symbols and key images rather than a word-for-word dictation.

During this time as the dead man passes through you, you will be harrowed with unpleasant feelings and images as the dead man appears to try to trick you from your objective, but stay strong as you feel him arise, draw his power into the crystal instead of yourself. Conjure the crystal to become as a fetish of fascination to the spirit, moving it in circles with your hands so it catches the candle light.

> *Therefore in the name of our Master, and by his birth, descent, resurrection and ascension, and by all that appertains unto his passion, and by the Virtue placed in all Witches I conjure you spirit N. that you appear visibly in this crystal stone. I conjure you N by Cain's Mark, which ensanguines my brow. If in his name you answer up this call candles shall be lit for you seven nights running to the glory of your soul if you will answer.*

Tap the crystal with your wand in time to the rhythm of your spoken word whilst saying the final invocation. The crystal should feel warmer, colder or heavier when the spirit is inside it.

> *In Nomine Mater, Patris, & Spiritus Sancti, Fiat, Fiat, Fiat.*

Do not look back upon leaving the place, but take the crystal to your home and set it up in a chalk circle, all without speaking.

THE CONJURATION OF LURIDAN

Both magicians and academics have tended to treat the concept of conjuring a "mere boggart" or hobgoblin using ceremonial means with scorn. Though on the surface the subject of hilarity is the appearance of the creature, his countenance is no more unusual than many demons in grimoires. The Otherwise as we experience it isn't only dark and terrifying but strange, ugly, freakish, absurd, surreal or even ridiculous by turns. It isn't always elegant or stately; such an expectation attempts to limit the limitless, and is a very human, very iron-clad way of seeing things. Such rigid ideas about power as emerge from the social machinations of primates should not allow us to underestimate the power of a spirit that appears small in stature.

If you reach back into Luridan's story his dwarfish appearance has layers of resonance we will miss entirely if we fall prey to power-structured mockery. One of the primary symbols of Luridan is his mountain. In his story, recorded by Reginald Scot, Luridan explains that he previously hailed from the North of Wales where he instructed the bards in poetry. In other words he held a position much like that of a Muse. This should put us on notice if nothing else does. If it seems ridiculous to consider the idea of a bringer of Awen becoming a boggart we probably have missed a few things about the organic mess, blossoming and decay of the world of Nature. It is not surprising we would miss the lessons the Earth is trying to teach us each day, as we are immersed in an anti-Nature story of massive power and violence. A story that tells us that which is of the sky is always inherently more noble and worthy than that which is of the ground and below it. Those who observe the secrets of life's creativity will know that both forces are required to brew the Awen which Welsh inspirer of bards would have needed access to.

It is therefore illuminating to note that Northern Wales, the Scottish highlands and the icy realm of the "terrible mountain" are all mountainous locations, as though Luridan is primarily a spirit of cold, mountain and rock. In this light the description of him as being like a dwarf has mythological importance that should not be derided simply because of modern fantasy genre associations. The mythology, after all, came along before the fantasy!

His stead the chameleon is not only powerfully surreal and unsettling to all our usual expectations, as you would expect with a strong eruption from the Otherwise, but is a potent symbol of shape changing. Which of course answers our questions about the wide number of powers Luridan claims access too.

During the invocation of Luridan we hear of the four horseman that must be invoked before him: Athanaton, Orgon, Boralim and Glauron, by name. These powerful spirit men of the Host wouldn't be required in attendance of Luridan if his power as a boggart were not at least as respected as theirs. It seems likely in fact that he is a foremost spirit amongst his kind.

It is intriguing, especially considering Luridan's report of hailing from Wales, to note these same spirits are mentioned in the Welsh folktale *John Gethin and the Candle*.[1] Which is interesting because Scot's material was collected in Scotland, so literate transmission and redistribution into oral tradition is likely. Or elsewise the practice of calling these four members of the Host from the four quarters of a directionally-aligned circle was very widespread. When looking at the text of *John Gethin and the Candle* we can see that some specifics for the performance of a similar rite can be found here.

Once again the story involves ascending a particular mountain to talk to the spirit there. Just like the Luridan ritual in Scot the Welsh

1 A retelling of this can be found in *The Welsh Fairy Book* by W. Jenkyn Thomas (Mineola: Dover, 2013).

folktale describes the drawing of two circles next to each other, like unto a "figure eight." In the story the appearance of the Welsh magician is described in some detail.

> *"He put on a robe of black covered with talismanic characters, girded himself with snake-skins tied together, and placed on his head a cap of sheepskin with a high crown bearing a plume of pigeons' feathers. In his hand he had a whip, the thong of which was made of the skin of an eel and the handle of bone. With this he traced two circles on the sward touching each other like the figure 8. After that he took a great black book and lit a candle and stepped into one of the circles."*

Also like Scot's account is the girdle of snake skins which you will see in the ritual instructions below.

What we can tell from the John Gethin account is that calling to these four horsemen, drawing the two circles and wearing the girdle of snakeskin are rites that have some association with mountains and spirits of place. In the folktale's case they are associated with a treasure-bearing mountain.

So by invoking Luridan we are moving from having acquired a familiar from among the human dead to a land spirit whose nature is intimately tied to mountainous locations (much like the goat-changing gwyllian we've discussed above) but is capable of moving around so long as he might reside in a local mountain or cairn. He is also a master of shape-changing with a background in the bardic arts.

When things begin to turn bad during the conjuring in John Gethin's story—after the Devil shows up—he invokes the names of "Athanaton, Boralim, Orgon and Glauron" who seem to act as saviours.

These four spirits who appear briefly in the ritual below are members of The Host who make the way safe to encounter Luridan. Below is a brief poetic description of the Four Horsemen, based on my own conjurations of them, to allow us to build a connection with these spirits.

The Horseman of the East: Athanaton—He comes forth wearing a silver headdress with the horns of the mountain goat worked into it, a sheepskin about him and riding on a white horse. He is a strong, somewhat austere man whose clothes and hair are windblown in appearance, with blue eyes, an aquiline nose and high-cheek bones.

The Horseman of the West: Orgon—He has a boar's tusk through his nose and greenish camouflage on his skin, he wears copper and bronze bracelets, his skin is tattooed heavily even on his face, and his horse has also been stained virid. He carries poison-darts.

The Horseman of the South: Boralim—His face and whole body is ruddy and smeared with ochre and blood, there is gold at his neck in a torc-like item, and he wears a headdress made of a lion's mane. His horse is red. He is heavily armed.

The Horseman of the North: Glauron—He wears the hide of a highland bull stained dark with soot, his face blackened out, and a bull's horn bugle is at his hip. His stead is as black as midnight and bridled with iron chains.

Their appearances should be meditated on, as should the hook-nosed twisted visage of Luridan as he appears riding his giant chameleon. Their images are key to their inner nature and will help should they choose to make themselves known to you on the night.

Here follows the particulars of the rite, which is to be performed in a solitary valley in the moonlight, in two touching or overlapping circles. The magician is wearing a girdle of snake skin and has upon them a hazel wand and the crystal ball in which we previously invited the spirit of the dead man.

Build a cairn of stones outside the circle, to represent the Terrible Mountain of Luridan. Construct it facing the direction your nearest mountain faces to you. In this way you are poetically connecting your local mountain with that of the spirits, the place of ice and fire where this court originates, and making a connection through an intermediary with spirits of place.

On the stones of the cairn write the following names in charcoal or natural chalk:

+++ *Glauron, Opotok, Balkin, Urthin, Swaknar, Nalah* +++

After the Mountain is constructed, it must be consecrated with the following words, written upon the stones in chalk:

Ofron, Anephexaton, Baron Barathron, Nah halge tour Hecla

Hecla is the name of the Terrible Mountain.

Which done, he or she must begin to Invocate the Spirit in the following manner, visualizing the appearance of the horsemen each time they are mentioned.

> *O ye Powers of the East,* **Athanaton***; of the West,* **Orgon***; of the South,* **Boralim***; of the North,* **Glauron;** *I charge and call you by the dreadful Names here mentioned, and the Consecration of this terrible Mountain, to present yourselves one of every sort before this Circle. Go forth Dead Man and charge Four Horseman black, red, green and white to open the ways of the crossroads to us.*

Tap the crystal ball three times with your hazel wand. When you say "go forth," insert the proper name of the dead man.

After this has with fervency been thrice repeated with the tap on the ball at each repetition, the practitioner will hear a tumult of swords, trumpets, horses and fighting sounds as though battle is approaching. If this does not occur at least to some extent begin the verbal conjuration again.

If the invocation has succeeded naked boggarts of Luridan's kind will surround the circle speaking continuously in what might be ancient Irish.

The Witch must ask them, if they know one **Luridan** a familiar; who is servant unto **Balkin**, and if they seem affirmative charge them to bring the said **Luridan**. If all goes according to plan the familiar spirit Luridan appears as a small dark man with hooked nose and crooked countenance, riding upon a chameleon. The magician must request a verbal pact of Luridan's good will and service, this will be given in return for some of the sorcerer's own blood which she or he will offer as long as Luridan agrees to assist with making contact with the other beings in this grimoire, and to serve the sorcerer as a familiar for one year to allow for the completion of the work herein, appearing whenever they should say:

Luridan, Luridan, Luridan

If the operator has come this far they have passed through the valley of the shadows and emerged with a familiar from among the human dead, who has been slowly nurtured into one of the goblin-dead with offerings that tempted him into the root. He or she has then obtained for themselves the learned companionship of the boggart and warrior-poet Luridan. Reginald Scot's original material gives us amazingly deep insight into the purpose and powers of these spirits of which Balkin is the head. We learn that the "terrible mountain" is Mount Hekla, Iceland's most active volcano. When Scot speaks of Luridan he tells us a great deal about the purpose of the company that Balkin presides over. We see here that they're a warrior-like order of spirits associated with the cold wind.

"He is a Spirit... in the order of ***Glauron****, and is said to procreate as mortals do; He is often sent by his Master upon errands to Lapland, Finland, and Strick-finia; as also to the most Northern parts of Russia, bordering on the Northern frozen Ocean: His office when called by magicians is to demolish strong holds of Enemies, destroying every night what they build the day before; to extinguish fires, and make their Gunshot that it hath no power to be enkindled; for his nature is to be at enmity with fire: and under his Master with many Legions he wageth continual warrs with the fiery Spirits that inhabit the Mountain Hecla in Ise-land, where they endeav-*

our to extinguish these fiery flames, and the inhabiting Spirits defend the flames from his Master and his Legions."

Mount Hekla is Iceland's most active volcano. During the Middle Ages, the inhabitants called it the *Gateway to Hell.*

In this contest they do often totally extirpate and destroy one another, killing and crushing when they meet in mighty and violent Troops in the Air upon the Sea; and at such a time many of the fiery Spirits are destroyed, when the Enemy hath brought them off the Mountain to fight upon the water; on the contrary, when the battle is on the Mountain it self, the Spirits of the Air are often worsted, and then great mournings and doleful noises are heard both in Iseland and Russia, and Norway for many days after.

It is interesting to note that whilst Luridan and Balkin seems to have an association with mountains it may in fact be the underneath of mountains that is their home, as when they fight "upon" the mountain the spirits of fire claim supremacy, whilst when they fight over the frigid oceans they often drown the fire of these flying (dragon?) beings of heat.

Not only does this story of spirit combat put us in mind of the Benandanti and Taltos battles, but it makes a clear point of how there is no constant good and bad in such a competition in Nature. For here where you would expect that the spirits of fire might be on the side of supposed "good' angels, and the cold spirits of the icy Northern winds might be demons, we see that in the presence of a volcano the spirits of the cold are friends to mankind indeed!

TO HAVE CONFERENCE WITH FAERIES

Here we will begin to pass through the world of shadow and out into the realm where the faerie food is offered, just before the Path to Elphame. This rite is a rite of preparation for work with some of the more difficult-to-conjure faerie beings.

Whether you are a member of a Romanian or Bulgarian Faerie Cult, a Sicilian faerie Witch, or a British faerie magician you all have in common the practice of laying out what I sometimes refer to as a "white meal." It was done in the sick room in Sicily to entice the faeries to heal the ill person and it was mentioned more than once in the grimoires. *The Grimoire of Arthur Gauntlet* gives the best account of how to lay one. He calls it "the faerie throne."[1]

Things you are using for your work such as the hazel wand and crystal ball can also be kept on the faerie throne.

On the night of the New or Full Moon you must be last up in the household and lay a bowl of clean water near the hearth, after having made the hearth clean asking the blessings of the faeries in a silent way and never looking back over your shoulder. You must be first up in the household and the only one to see the water or the spell will be broken. There should be a kind of film formed on the surface if the charm has worked. Draw it off into a small vessel of silver or tin and retain it. If it has not occurred try again.

After, prepare the space by sweeping, cleaning and suffumagating with aromatic odors. Then select a small table which is also clean, cover it in a fresh white cloth and lay out the following: a bowl of ale, a bowl of fresh water drawn from a running

1 You can also find a version of this in David Rankine's *The Book of Treasure Spirits.*

source, a dainty joint of meat, a small bowl of cream and sprinkle all with rose water.

Sit down not staring directly at the throne but able to see it out of the corner of your eye. Anoint your eyes with the film from the water and wait in silence and total stillness, trying to hardly blink. If faeries should come into the room to use the table you may nod your head but not look directly at them or address them.

THE CONJURATION OF ROBIN GOODFELLOW *(also known as Robin the Devil)*

There are few other faerie figures that have become as intertwined with Witchcraft as that of Robin. As early as the thirteenth century the connection between Robin and the Devil was well in place, as revealed during the trial of Alice Kyteler, but the attribution of him as the son of Obreon may have come at a later date.

Like both Obreon and Sibylla, Robin Goodfellow is believed to reward the virtuous, but unlike the other two he is better known for mercilessly punishing the wicked as well. If Obreon has two hands, one for giving physick and the other for using his bow, one of those is solar and one lunar. Robin's sinister hand is much stronger.

He can be a causer of sheer mayhem, because, like all spirits close to the heart of the spirit of Witchcraft, he is allied with wild nature. For this reason it is best to evoke him primarily when you are certain you have the right of a situation and want injustice swept aside, the high brought low, the tables radically turned.

Robin Goodfellow likes to create long-term relationships with the people he helps and often takes you into his company by putting a mark on you. He can provide the path to initiation via spirit congress to those who want it, in much the same way that Sibylla does with interested men. If throwing the chips up into the air or creating a pact with the Devil are among your aims gather together the following things:

- A broom
- A taper
- A bowl of milk and bread

- Nine peacock feathers
- A small urn or bottle

Betake yourself to a crossroads, a stile, or the edge of a wild forest in the depths of night with need burning in your heart.

Robin Goodfellow works best for the poor and dispossessed, but your need only be real to get his attention. When you reach the space sweep the ground inward and collect up the dust and collect it into the urn.

Draw the Robin Goodfellow (see opposite page) magical square on the ground and light your taper. Stand within the square and place the milk bowl just outside it upon a mat made of the peacock feathers. Begin to repeat the names of your faerie allies:

By Milia, Achillia, Sibylla, Obreon, and the affection you bear to your Sire and Sisters, I call upon you Robin Goodfellow, Puck, Robin the Devil, come as a flame, as black horse or goat but settle as the man-angel-beast with cloven foot and eyes legion in your terrible wings! In the name of the Faerie Queen Mycob and all your sister faeries, for the sake of the faerie women you love, allow me to enter your abode.

Robin give me my purpose!

Robin Goodfellow! Robin Goodfellow! Robin Goodfellow!

Images will appear before you as Puck tests you and seems to try to trick you from your objective. Hold fast and remember your purpose. This is just the effect of his nature upon the very atmosphere and upon all living things, it does not necessarily mean he wishes you harm.

When the images settle and you sense the unstable quality in the air following the appearance of this spirit, you may begin to perceive you are being watched. If your hair is long flick it over and display the back of your neck to him with your head forward, this is particularly powerful if your hair is long enough to braid and can be undone for him. If your hair is short simply bend forward and display the back of your neck.

Tell him with your words what troubles you and how you would like help fixing it. But stand back up before you address him because Robin likes you to speak to him as an equal.

Remember that he will read from your heart as much as your words.

When the rite is complete sweep away the square and pour the milk upon the ground where Robin did appear. Feed the urn with alcohol drops, sexual fluids, honey, sweet perfumes of frankincense and myrrh mingled with woodland scents, and kind words.

Robin particularly cares for the plight of downtrodden women and vulnerable children, and he loathes oppressors and hypocrites. If he finds you dishonest in your suit to him there will be quite literal hell to pay. It's important to remember he is a trickster and things will not always get done the way you envisaged them when you asked him for a boon. When working with this spirit things often appear to get much worse before suddenly getting better or showing you the way out of your troubles, almost like a test of faith. Once he has shown you the path he will expect you to show strength and ingenuity in finding your way through the forest.

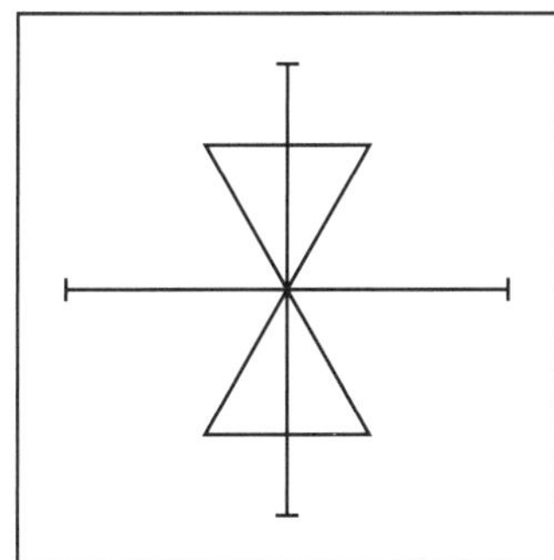

Robin Goodfellow
Magical Square

THE CONJURATION OF OBREON

Thanks to Shakespeare Oberon, also known as Obryon and Obreon, is a very well known Faerie King. Like Sibylla he is also very widespread both in Britain and France, which might have something to do with his popularity in the grimoires.

Obreon most likely drew his genesis from a dwarfish sorcerer named Alberich or "elf ruler," believed to be the otherworldly brother of Merowich the Merovingian, as early as the ninth century.

But as far as history is concerned Oberon makes his first appearance in a French song about a fairy cursed to dwarfish height. In the song Oberon has a magical cup, which has been compared to the Holy Grail, and is always full when the virtuous attempt to drink from it.

Oberon is a Faerie King associated with the woods. He wears a gown studded with precious stones that shine as bright as the Sun. His magical bow can kill any animal he takes aim at and when he blows his horn sickness and hunger are cured. This double nature, the hand that takes with the bow and the hand that cures sickness and provides with his horn, is echoed in his grimoire-identity where one of his hands is associated with the Moon and the other with the Sun.

In Britain it seems likely that Oberon was a name grafted over the top of a pre-existent Faerie King because there appears to be more than one appearance given to Obreon in the grimoires. One which might be amendable with his diminutive French persona appears as little more than a head with tiny limbs, whereas the other is a seemingly full-size knight in chainmail. We encounter descriptions and detail here in the grimoires about this Faerie King we don't necessarily acquire in folklore. As usual the two sources feed into each other in a natural cross-fertilisation.

The grimoires say:

"He appeareth like a king with a crown on his head, he is under the government of the (sun) and (moon), he teacheth a man knowledge in physick, and he showeth the nature of stones, herbs, and trees and of all metal. He is a great and mighty king, and he is king of the fairies..."

The association with healing or physick seems to carry through both from the French song to the later grimoires.

We are also lucky enough to have images from the time period of Oberyn. One source depicts him fairly straightforwardly as a faerie knight, like one of the men of the Host, in chainmail and helmet with the symbols for Sol and Luna inscribed into his right and left arm respectively. But a far more intriguing depiction of him exists which shows him as genie-like, or merely a head with serpentine tentacles making up his body. This makes him seem almost like a male lamia.

For this operation you will need this book, some fresh aniseed, rose water, a crystal ball or bowl of water.

At the beginning of the first crescent of the Moon take this book into the circle and open it to the following page with the plate of Obreon and the planetary seals of the Watchers Scorax (Luna), Carmelion (Sol), Kaberyon (Mars) and Seberyon (Mercury).

As each of these spirits is indicative of an aspect of Obreon's character and seem to have the power to lift him into manifestation, it's necessary we build a mental image of them as well as the Faerie King.

These spirits broadly fall into the category of "angels" rather than faeries, but Scorax and Carmelion in particular have their natures combined in the figure of Obreon.

SCORAX: A male-appearing being with wings and claws of iron and lunar patterns tattooed into his flesh in dark blue. His eyes are dark and there is a black line tattooed downward from his mouth.

CARMELION: A part-eagle man with the symbol of Sol tattooed into his chest. He is strongly muscular with eyes made of fire and his skin seems to regularly be shed like a snake, as though peeling away in response to his own inner warmth.

KABERYON: A dragon-like part man being, primarily dark red in colour even on his human-looking parts and capable of breathing fire. There is a flame-coloured jewel between his dark purple eyes and he carries an immense fiery sword.

SEBERYON: Whitish-silver cloaked man with a sword at his waist riding a white steed with eyes made of lightning. His boots and belt are made of snakeskin, the skins of dead men's faces sit at his saddle-bag and he carries a pale-coloured bow. His horse can run sideways along the edge of the wind.

After you have strongly visualised the Four Watchers establish a similarly strong image of Obreon:

OBREON: He appears riding an oversized white stag whose reigns are made of snakes. His chainmail is made of silver like light-spangled cobwebs knitted into armour. The symbols of Sol and Luna that belong to Scorax and Carmelian are tattooed into his right and left arm respectively. Jewels glitter on his sword hilt and he has a crown of silver made to look like hawthorn. Upon his back is a bow and at his waist a horn.

Prepare for this working by visualising him last of all. Pay special attention to thoroughly cleaning the feet with rose water and going into the circle barefoot. Also use an oil burner or other creator of vapour to heat rose water in the room you are to use. Find a quiet place to work and do your invocations facing toward the east.

Open the book to the first full image plate of Obreon (insert page number) and cense it. Place a crystal ball or clear bowl of water over the image of Obreon. Due to this rite the book itself in which these words are written is by necessity a talismanic object sacred to the Faerie King. Suffumigate the image with incense of myrrh, frankincense, dragon's blood and benzoin, one for each of the planetary Watchers we will be calling on. Next take some aniseed in your mouth and chew it before breathing on the crystal or clear bowl of water that has been placed over the top of the image of Obreon. Light your candle of virgin wax so it reflects in the water and illuminates the graven image of Obreon below.

Tap the crystal ball over the image of Obreon in the book as you speak saying:

Oh though Watcher Scorax of the side of Luna full of shadows and the pale light, he of the iron claws and wings. Carmelian griffin-hearted eagle-man of the Sun who strikes in the name of justice and carries in his gullet the Sun at midnight. Kaberyon thou dragon-winged man, with your sharp spiked spine bristling with Marsian wrath and bearing flaming sword. Seberyon great skin-changing warrior-angel of the realm of Mercury, knower of physic and remedy as well as bearer of the unseen arrow. We call upon you to draw forth and raise Lord Obreon into the crystal so that I may learn from him upon all the matters of the healing craft.

Anoint your eyelids with the faerie film that appears on the water bowl and gaze into the crystal or clear bowl of water.[1] Here Obreon will rise to commune with you. You may ask him questions or for boons, knowledge and skills relating to healing. He is particularly skilled in the curing of wounds and women's complaints, but he will only do the work for those he considers to possess the appropriate virtues. When you wish for him to depart anoint your eyes with rose water, chew more aniseed and breathe upon the crystal in offering to his spirit. It is always good to reciprocate any help he gives you with ongoing offerings of milk, fennel and rose water.

1 Some sources suggest an ointment involving the blood of a black cat, hen's fat and rose oil, but this does not seem particularly congenial to rub into one's eyes.

THE GRAND CONJURATION OF SIBYLLA

We have described the Italian manifestation of Sibylla above, where she was regarded as the Goddess of the Witches. In Ferrara people said that "wise Sibillia" presided over witch flights as *la signora del corso.* At the end of the feasts, she would touch all the bottles and baskets with her gold wand, and they would quickly refill with wine and bread. The Witches gathered the animals' bones into their skins; at the wand's touch, the animals recovered their flesh and returned to life. Spinning and sorcerous arts were said to be taught in the mountain of Sibillia. Serpents dwell in its underground grottos. Shape-shifting faeries come out of her cave to dance in the meadows. They too turn into snakes every Saturday until the pope says Mass on Sunday. So it is quite clear that Sibylla was originally a Faerie Queen, and that like other Faerie Queens such as Rhiannon, she was probably at one point considered a Goddess of Witches.

When a visitor went looking for Dame Sibylla inside the entrance to her mountain there was a chamber with seats cut into its rock walls. The cave ran deep into the mountain, with doors of metal leading to the inner labyrinth, followed by doors of crystal. A great wind would rise up from within the Earth along these passages. Finally the intrepid traveler would come to a narrow bridge over a torrent, and two dragons breathing fire. In some traditions when Sibylla would reveal herself she was found to have a goose's foot.

Her presence was not only continental though. In England we have Sib, appearing in a work about Robin Goodfellow. In the same work Sib says of the woman-fairies:

> *"To walk nightly as do the men-fairies we use not; but now and then we go together, and at good housewives' fires we warm*

our fairy children. If we find clean water and clean towels we leave them money, either in their basins, or in their shoes; but if we find no clean water in their houses, we wash our children in their pottage, milk, or beer, or whatever we find: for the sluts that have not such things fitting, we wash their faces and hands with a gilded child's clout, or else carry them to some river and duck them over head and ears. We often use to dwell in some great hill, and from thence we do lend money to any poor man or woman that hath need; but if they bring it not again at the day appointed, we do not only punish them with pinching, but also in their goods, so that they never thrive till they have paid us."

Here the "clean towels and clean water" is suggestive of the clean white linen cloth and fresh water that traditionally finds its way onto the faerie throne. The faerie Sib clearly has a Fate role in the bringing or withholding of abundance, deservingness seems to be a key in her apportioning, much like Obreon's cup that is always full for the virtuous.

When we encounter her in Scot's unintentional grimoire she is described as "gentle virgin," "fair," and "wearing white." She is associated with a crystal ball, as are many spirits. But it's particularly interesting to note that the final door into her mountain (much like how Sib mentions a mound) is made of crystal and censed in frankincense all of which associates her with the Shining Court. We shouldn't find this strange in relation to the goosefoot because such completeness harks back to the primordial faerie, godlike in their completion and resolution of contradiction. As discussed in previous chapters, it gives the indication she is very powerful. Whilst appearing with lots of white, light and images of beauty, even the Shining Ones are often hiding swan wings, empty backs, snake parts, insect wings or the foot of a white bird.

Sibylla also seems to often have sexual connotations in her mysteries. Not only is there an ordeal relating to serpent congress to be found inside the lore relating to the Sibylline Mountains, but grimoire material referring to her often suggests sex with this faerie. This focus on congress suggests that work with Sibylla is about sorcerous initiation inside the Sibyl's serpent mountain. For this reason I have marked this ritual out as a "grand conjuration," as I believe it's true aim is initiation into the realm of faerie sorcery. This is the deeper meaning behind the "faerie congress" as is seen inside the mountain of Sibylla on the continent.

For this rite you will need two chalk circles on the floor. You will also require frankincense, your crystal ball, a basket of assorted bones, some cream and honey for offerings, and a bell.

Draw two chalk circles upon the floor and set up the faerie throne within one. Place your crystal ball in the middle where the circles overlap.

Call the dead man to go fetch the faerie Sibylla.

> *I conjure thee spirit, that thou do go in peace, and also to come again to me quickly, and to bring with thee into that circle appointed the faerie Sibylla, that I may talk with her in those matters that shall be to her honour and glory; and so charge thee to declare unto her. I conjure thee spirit N. by power of Cain's blood in my veins; by the virtue thereof I charge thee with this mission.*

Of course, depending on the extent to which you lean towards dual-faith observance and incorporate Christian wording, you might complete the words in their original format, as can be found in the mouth of the conjurer Jack in Part Two.

When you sense the presence of the faerie Sibylla within the crystal stone push forward the basket of bones, offering that she revivify the animal by touching it with her wand. Begin to visualize this occurring. Before you, see a great metal door as you offer the bones. Take one of the bones and "knock" upon it, creating as strongly as you can with your own glamour the sound the bone would make in knocking.

Build the image carefully envisaging details in the metal. When you have built the vision strongly pass forward. On the other side you will see a stone door, build this image up and knock on it before opening the stone door and passing through. Each time you pass through one of the doors begin to make the images on the other side more ethereal, with the first one made of all stone and barren land, the second full of greenery and the third full of light and strange unnatural scenes. These visualisations will begin to yield to vision as you go along. It is helpful to wrap oneself in a cloak with a hood so as to properly block out light and limit oxygen supply in a safe manner.

When you have passed through the metal door begin to build an image of a crystal door, and as you do offer to Sibylla the bowl of cream and honey. Just as you did with the last, build the crystal door with intricate details, and perhaps patterns and artistry. Cense the crystal ball with frankincense. Keep visualizing the translucent crystal door refracting numerous colours. When you pass through allow the scene beyond to rise naturally before you, but it is common to feel the scene coming to life as if you no longer have to build it.

You will either visualize or be confronted by a bridge as thin as a hair.

It is more powerful to repeat the process until the image of the narrow bridge appears naturally without your conscious participation. When it does walk carefully across it. Folklore prepares you for dragons breathing fire, defending the lair of Sibylla and ordeals involving serpents. The snakes seem intent on something between eating or sexually devouring humans. But when submitted to with grace the serpent stone emerges from a ball of collective hissing, arising from the foreheads of the collective being you become with the snakes. That ball seems to birth the vision of Sibylla, or in some way it is the same thing. There are mysteries beyond here than cannot be fully spoken of.

Here be dragons.

When you meet Sibylla she may ask you what boon or skill you would like to have, choosing between healing, the Sight etc. You must never lie to her and when you leave her presence never look back over your shoulder. Always go back the same way you have come and never offer her money, do not sit when she stands and never thank her with the word thank you, but in offerings.

CONCLUSION

"Well, Mrs. Jasper, she said there was only one way to bring 'em. You must do it on a moonlight night just when the pollen was ripe on the catkins. I was always teasing and praying her to show me and at last one night she took me with her into the woods. I never shall forget it. She made me sit on the stump of an old tree in a little clearing where the moonlight came through, and she stood a few steps away with two small branches in her hands. I saw the gold dust flying from the catkins as she waved them gently, and sang a little song over and over in a funny low drawlin' husky voice — just as though she was coaxin' 'em :

"Come in the stillness,
Come in the night,
Come soon,
And bring delight.
Beckoning, beckoning, with
Left hand and right,
Come now,
Ah, come to-night!"

It almost drew me off my stump to hear her, and the dog came creeping to her feet. No, I didn't see anything — nothing but the gold dust fallin' from the catkins, and her fluttering hands. But she said she'd seen 'em, often, but they only came when she was alone, they didn't care about company. They'd come slidin' down a branch to her and laugh and disappear again. The dog, he couldn't bear them. He'd bristle up and growl and slink into the bushes. He knew they weren't canny..."

–I.M Stenning, from: "When We Were Children,"
SCM Vol. 26, No. 9 (1952)

SOUNDS OF INFINITY cover and book were designed and typeset by The Witches' Almanac art department in Providence, Rhode Island. The cover and section breakes are set in Lovelyn 50/60. The body text was set in Bodoni 11.5/16, with footnotes set in Calibri Light.

Issue 37 Spring 2018-2019
The Witches' Almanac
Ever a Keepsake
MAGIC
An Occult Primer
David Conway